THE DAILY STUDY BIBLE

(OLD TESTAMENT)

General Editor: John C. L. Gibson

ISAIAH

ISAIAH

Volume II

JOHN F. A. SAWYER

THE SAINT ANDREW PRESS
EDINBURGH

THE WESTMINSTER PRESS
PHILADELPHIA

Published by
The Saint Andrew Press
Edinburgh, Scotland
and
The Westminster Press®
Philadelphia, Pennsylvania

British Library Cataloguing in Publication Data

Sawyer, John F. A.
Isaiah II.
1. Bible. O.T. Isaiah II——Commentaries
I. Title
224'.107   BS1515.3

ISBN 0-7152-0528-5

Printed and bound in Great Britain
by Bell and Bain Ltd., Glasgow

ISBN (Great Britain) 0 7152 0528 5

Reprinted 1988, 1990

GENERAL PREFACE

This series of commentaries on the Old Testament, to which this second volume on *Isaiah* by Professor Sawyer belongs, has been planned as a companion series to the much-acclaimed New Testament series of the late Professor William Barclay. As with that series, each volume is arranged in successive headed portions suitable for daily study. The Biblical text followed is that of the Revised Standard Version or Common Bible. Eleven contributors share the work, each being responsible for from one to three volumes. The series is issued in the hope that it will do for the Old Testament what Professor Barclay's series succeeded so splendidly in doing for the New Testament—make it come alive for the Christian believer in the twentieth century.

Its two-fold aim is the same as his. Firstly, it is intended to introduce the reader to some of the more important results and fascinating insights of modern Old Testament scholarship. Most of the contributors are already established experts in the field with many publications to their credit. Some are younger scholars who have yet to make their names but who in my judgment as General Editor are now ready to be tested. I can assure those who use these commentaries that they are in the hands of competent teachers who know what is of real consequence in their subject and are able to present it in a form that will appeal to the general public.

The primary purpose of the series, however, is *not* an academic one. Professor Barclay summed it up for his New Testament series in the words of Richard of Chichester's prayer—to enable men and women "to know Jesus Christ more clearly, to love Him more dearly, and to follow Him more nearly." In the case of the Old Testament we have to be a little more circumspect than that. The Old Testament was completed long before the time of Our Lord, and it was (as it still is) the sole Bible of the Jews, God's first people, before it became part of the Christian Bible. We must take this fact seriously.

Yet in its strangely compelling way, sometimes dimly and sometimes directly, sometimes charmingly and sometimes embarrassingly, it holds up before us the things of Christ. It should not be forgotten that Jesus Himself was raised on this Book, that He based His whole ministry on what it says, and that He approached His death with its words on His lips. Christian men and women have in this ancient collection of Jewish writings a uniquely illuminating avenue not only into the will and purposes of God the Father, but into the mind and heart of Him who is named God's Son, who was Himself born a Jew but went on through the Cross and Resurrection to become the Saviour of the world. Read reverently and imaginatively the Old Testament can become a living and relevant force in their everyday lives.

It is the prayer of myself and my colleagues that this series may be used by its readers and blessed by God to that end.

New College   JOHN C. L. GIBSON
Edinburgh   General Editor

CONTENTS

CONTENTS

MATRI MEAE IN MEMORIAM

SOME USEFUL DATES FOR REFERENCE

765 B.C.   birth of Isaiah (?)

736 B.C.   death of Uzziah (=Azariah), king of Judah (787–736)

732 B.C.   Assyrian conquest of Syria (capital: Damascus)

727 B.C.   death of Tiglath-Pileser III (=Pul), king of Assyria (744–727)

725 B.C.   death of Ahaz (=Jehoahaz), king of Judah (736–725)

722 B.C.   Assyrians conquer Israel (=Ephraim; capital: Samaria)

712 B.C.   Assyrian campaign against Ashdod (Philistine city)

701 B.C.   Assyrian defeat of Egyptians at Eltekeh

701 B.C.   Assyrian conquest of Judah and siege of Jerusalem

695 B.C.   death of Isaiah (?)

622 B.C.   fall of Nineveh, capital of Assyrian Empire

609 B.C.   death of Josiah, king of Judah (640–609)

586 B.C.   Nebuchadnezzar, king of Babylon (605–562), conquers Jerusalem

560 B.C.   release of Jehoiachin, king of Judah (609–598), in Babylon

538 B.C.   Cyrus, king of Medes and Persians (550–530), conquers Babylon

515 B.C.   Second Temple at Jerusalem built

323 B.C.   death of Alexander the Great, king of Macedon (336–323)

167 B.C.   desecration of Temple by Antiochus IV, Seleucid king (175–163)

164 B.C.   rededication of Temple at Jerusalem by Judas Maccabaeus

145 B.C.   Jewish Temple founded at Leontopolis in Ptolemaic Egypt (?)

INTRODUCTION

The aim of this commentary is to present the meaning of the text of the Book of Isaiah as clearly as possible. The variety of material contained in the book is immense. In some places we can hear the actual voice of Isaiah himself addressing his contemporaries in eighth century B.C. Jerusalem. More often than not, we shall be reading "Isaianic" literature, that is to say, prophetic messages inspired by Isaiah, although composed a century or more after he died. But since we are concerned with the meaning of the book as a whole, this distinction between "Isaiah" and "Isaianic" is an academic one and for our purpose not of great import: our primary interest is in the rich and enormously influential "Isaianic" literature, all sixty-six chapters of it, not simply in what the great individual who started it off said.

Similarly, in some cases the precise historical circumstances referred to in the text can be quite convincingly reconstructed, as in the case of Sennacherib's invasion of Judah in 701 B.C. (chs. 36–37) or the rise of Cyrus, king of the Medes and Persians, in the middle of the sixth century B.C. (*eg* 45:1–7). But the text is seldom if ever concerned with history as such, and for that reason I have been concerned not so much with the question of what actually happened as with why the account is told in this way and not that way; not so much with whether the author is historically accurate as with what he is getting at.

To put this another way, reading the Book of Isaiah from cover to cover, one acquires a basic vocabulary of "Isaianic" terms such as faith, righteousness, salvation, Zion, the Holy One of Israel and the Lord of hosts. One also becomes familiar with graphic images such as the vineyard, and with prophetic formulae such as "Thus says the Lord..." and "Woe to...!" I have tried to concentrate on these, explaining the allusions and associations present in the original Hebrew and so letting the text speak for itself as much as possible. This has seemed to me preferable to spending time on historical matters which are important to the scholar but have not greatly concerned the millions of readers and listeners down the ages, in Jewish and Christian communities all over the world, for whom the Book of Isaiah has been a source of interest and inspiration.

Finally, we must remember that the book is an integral part of Biblical tradition, the first of the five prophetic books (Isaiah, Jeremiah, Ezekiel, Daniel and the "Twelve"), and must be read in that larger context too. In explaining difficult words and phrases, I have therefore paid particular attention to parallels in other Biblical texts, in the modest hope that readers of this commentary will become more sensitive to a wide range of Biblical words and phrases and ways of thinking, not only Isaianic ones.

THE DESTROYER

Isaiah 33:1–12

[1]Woe to you, destroyer,
   who yourself have not been destroyed;
you treacherous one,
   with whom none has dealt treacherously!
When you have ceased to destroy,
   you will be destroyed;
and when you have made an end of dealing treacherously,
   you will be dealt with treacherously.

[2]O Lord, be gracious to us; we wait for thee.
   Be our arm every morning,
   our salvation in the time of trouble.
[3]At the thunderous noise peoples flee,
   at the lifting up of thyself nations are scattered;
[4]and spoil is gathered as the caterpillar gathers;
   as locusts leap, men leap upon it.

[5]The Lord is exalted, for he dwells on high;
   he will fill Zion with justice and righteousness;
[6]and he will be the stability of your times,
   abundance of salvation, wisdom, and knowledge;
   the fear of the Lord is his treasure.

[7]Behold, the valiant ones cry without;
   the envoys of peace weep bitterly.
[8]The highways lie waste,
   the wayfaring man ceases.
 Covenants are broken,
   witnesses are despised,
   there is no regard for man.
[9]The land mourns and languishes;
   Lebanon is confounded and withers away;
 Sharon is like a desert;
   and Bashan and Carmel shake off their leaves.

3

10"Now I will arise," says the Lord,
    "now I will lift myself up;
    now I will be exalted.
11You conceive chaff, you bring forth stubble;
    your breath is a fire that will consume you.
12And the peoples will be as if burned to lime,
    like thorns cut down, that are burned in the fire."

Chapter 33 has a mysterious, dramatic quality about it which suggests comparison with some of the Psalms (*eg* 46, 82) and the Apocalyptic literature (*eg* Joel, Isa. 24). There is mystery about who is speaking in its various sections (33:1; 2–6; 7–9; 17–24), and about who the "destroyer" (v. 1), "the valiant ones" and "the envoys of peace" (v. 7) and other characters in the drama are. It also stands in splendid isolation: the vision of a new age in chapter 32 had a note of finality in it, and chapters 34–35 open the way to the "Babylonian chapters" (40–55). Like Job 28, this chapter at the mid-point of Isaiah has some of the elements of the chorus in a classical drama, summing up and commenting on the rest of the book in some of the most original and exciting imagery of the whole of Isaianic tradition. It is in many ways the hinge-chapter of the whole book.

In Hebrew, verse 1 suggests some kind of incantation. Its opening exclamation, "Woe!" (discussed in connection with the "Woe"-prophecies in ch. 5) and its four short sentences, full of alliterations (*eg shoded . . . shadud . . . boged . . . bagedu*) that cannot be adequately represented in English, point to some kind of ritual chanting.

In its present context, coming after 31:8–9, for example, and before chapters 36–37, the "destroyer" might naturally be interpreted as the Assyrians or their king. But the eerie parallel in 21:2, in the "oracle concerning the wilderness of the sea", may point beyond history to supernatural principalities and powers. There are hints that this might be so later in the chapter (vv. 7–8).

After the curse in verse 1, comes a prayer (vv. 2–9) beginning "O Lord, be gracious to us; we wait for thee", that is like some of the Psalms (*eg* 46; 51; 56; 86). Notice how "salvation" (*yeshu'ah*) is associated with "arm" here, illustrating how dynamic and concrete the word is as opposed to the rather more abstract English equivalent, "salvation".

"Morning" denotes the moment when darkness is put to flight (*eg* Job 38:12–15) and new hope dawns (*eg* Pss. 46:5—NEB—"at the break of day" for RSV's "right early"; 59:16). It is also a moment of prophetic inspiration (Isa. 50:4; Ezek. 12:8).

Verses 3–6 of Isaiah 33 are a confession of faith in God's power to overcome evil, corresponding to passages like Psalm 93:4:

> Mightier than the thunders of many waters,
> mightier than the waves of the sea,
> the Lord on high is mighty.

"Exalted" (v. 5) is a word suggesting a fortress on a rocky hill (*eg* Ps. 18:2). The "voice" (or sound) in verse 3 means the thunder accompanying a theophany, or appearance of God (Exod. 19; Amos 1:2; Isa. 17:12–13). With it God imposes his authority on the unruly, and establishes justice and salvation, together with stability, wisdom and fear of the Lord (11:1–3; Prov. 1:7; 9:10). "Salvation" in this verse is plural in Hebrew, *ie* "acts of divine intervention" (as in 26:18; RSV "deliverance"). These expressions come from the Royal psalms (*eg* 2; 18; 47; 110; 132) and prophecies (*eg* Isa. 11; 32), which are closely bound up with the fortunes of Zion.

The unruly elements which threaten Zion's stability, "peoples . . . nations", like the "destroyer" in verse 1, no doubt include the Assyrian army, but they are also symbols of much more than that, as many of the psalms make clear:

> The nations rage, the kingdoms totter;
> he utters his voice, the earth melts.

(Ps. 46:6)

Isaiah 17:12–14 is another illuminating example. The same applies to the "caterpillar" in Isaiah 33:4 (or "young locusts", NEB), and "locusts" in Joel 1:4. There are difficulties in the Hebrew here, but the force of the imagery is clear.

The next stanza (vv. 7–9) goes back to the crisis alluded to at the beginning (v. 2): "the land mourns and languishes" (v. 9). Again the scene envisaged could be one of enemy occupation (*eg*

1:7–8; 7:17–25; 36:1), but this still leaves unanswered the question of who "the valiant ones" are and what the "covenants" and "witnesses" in verses 7–8 refer to. "The valiant ones" is a traditional translation (RSV, NEB) of the enigmatic Hebrew word *er'elim*. Others, on the basis of "Ariel" in 29:1, suggest "Jerusalemites" or even "lion of God", an emblem of Judah which appears cryptically in another difficult passage (21:8) (see vol. I, p. 184). Jewish interpreters took the word to refer to "angels of death", which is a good parallel to "envoys of peace". The word translated "envoys" (RSV) or "those sent to sue for peace" (NEB) is the normal Hebrew term for "angels". Now if we accept the proposal that the word emended to read "witnesses" in 33:8 originally meant "protectors, watchers" (*ie* "guardian angels"), then the supernatural dimension in the passage is obvious. The struggle is not against flesh and blood, but among members of a heavenly host, "sons of God" (*eg* Gen. 6:2; Job 1:6; 2:1). This is perhaps a glimpse into the timeless realities more familiar to us from the Apocalyptic literature (*eg* Dan. 10–12; Rev. 17–20), but already underlying earlier texts like Isaiah 24. Psalm 82 is a text that, more than most, provides the link between these ways of thinking and the liturgy of ancient Israel; Isaiah 33 is another.

Lebanon, Sharon and Carmel elsewhere rejoice at the saving intervention of God (*eg* 35:1–4). But here we have a picture of the land before that victory, when the hosts of heaven are still under the sway of the "destroyer"; and the covenants with Noah (Gen. 9:8–17) and the patriarchs (Gen. 15; 17:1–8) are temporarily broken. Probably the covenant with nature, incidentally mentioned in Job 5, gives a further clue to what these verses are about:

> At destruction and famine you shall laugh,
>   and shall not fear the beasts of the earth.
> For you shall be in league with the stones of the field,
>   and the beasts of the field will be at peace with you.
>
> (Job 5:22–23)

The 'salvation oracle' (see commentary on 41:8–20) in verses 10–12 answers the prayer in verses 2ff. The defeat of the enemy (the "peoples" from v. 3) is conceived as a conflagration brought about by their own crimes: they are like chaff or stubble or thorns, burnt up in the fires they themselves have lit. "Your breath is a fire" (v. 11) suggests some fire-breathing monster (like Leviathan in Job 41:19–21) as well as, less literally, the destructive force of malicious talk (Ps. 123:3–4) or dangerous schemes (Isa. 50:11).

A PLACE OF BROAD WATERS AND STREAMS

Isaiah 33:13–24

13Hear, you who are far off, what I have done;
 and you who are near, acknowledge my might.
14The sinners in Zion are afraid;
 trembling has seized the godless:
"Who among us can dwell with the devouring fire?
 Who among us can dwell with everlasting burnings?"
15He who walks righteously and speaks uprightly,
 who despises the gain of oppressions,
who shakes his hands, lest they hold a bribe,
 who stops his ears from hearing of bloodshed,
 and shuts his eyes from looking upon evil,
16he will dwell on the heights;
 his place of defence will be the fortresses of rocks;
 his bread will be given him, his water will be sure.

17Your eyes will see the king in his beauty;
 they will behold a land that stretches afar.
18Your mind will muse on the terror:
 "Where is he who counted,
  where is he who weighed the tribute?
 Where is he who counted the towers?"
19You will see no more the insolent people,
 the people of an obscure speech which you cannot comprehend,
 stammering in a tongue which you cannot understand.
20Look upon Zion, the city of our appointed feasts!
 Your eyes will see Jerusalem,
a quiet habitation, an immovable tent,
 whose stakes will never be plucked up,
 nor will any of its cords be broken.

²¹But there the Lord in Majesty will be for us
   a place of broad rivers and streams,
  where no galley with oars can go,
   nor stately ship can pass.
²²For the Lord is our judge, the Lord is our ruler,
   the Lord is our king; he will save us.

²³Your tackle hangs loose;
   it cannot hold the mast firm in its place,
   or keep the sail spread out.

  Then prey and spoil in abundance will be divided;
   even the lame will take the prey.
²⁴And no inhabitant will say, "I am sick";
   the people who dwell there will be forgiven their iniquity.

Now the drama turns from God to man, from the heavenly court
to Jerusalem, from the King of Kings, "high and lifted up", to the
one "who walks righteously and speaks uprightly" (v. 15). It
begins with a dialogue reminiscent of Psalm 15 and of Psalm 24, in
which those who approach the Temple are challenged:

Who shall ascend the hill of the Lord?
  And who shall stand in his holy place?
He who has clean hands and a pure heart . . .

                         (Ps. 24:3–4)

The Isaianic version of this scene is very much more dramatic:
sinners and the godless are confronted by "devouring fire" and
"everlasting burnings" (v. 14) which recall the experience of
Isaiah described in chapter 6, as well as the intimations of Hell-
fire in 66:24. The reward of the righteous is more than entry into
the Temple ("he will dwell on the heights . . ." 33:16); and the
vision of glory in verses 17–24 goes beyond the "Who is the King
of glory?" of Psalm 24:8. The cultic background may have been
the same: but this account of it is far richer.

"Hear, you who are far off . . ." (v. 13) anticipates a recurring
theme in subsequent chapters (*eg* 34, 41, 49, 51). The term
"godless" is not common in Biblical Hebrew: we have met it
already in 9:17, and in 24:5 where it is translated as "polluted".

The questions in verse 14 seem more like the reactions of
people confronting the fire of divine holiness, as Isaiah himself

was in chapter 6, than of worshippers approaching the Temple: "Woe is me! For I am lost!" (6:5). Although in the form of questions, they almost amount to a confession that none of us can "dwell with the devouring fire".

The virtues enumerated in verse 15 consist of two positive and four negative ones. The positive consist of "righteousness" (*tsedek*) and 'honesty' ("speaks the truth", NEB). The negative ones are *not* exploiting the poor, *not* accepting bribes, *not* getting involved in the plotting of murders and *not* gloating over other people's sufferings. The last two require comment. The Sermon on the Mount contains similar teaching: "You have heard that it was said . . . , 'You shall not kill' . . . But I say to you that, [even if you think about killing, you are breaking the law]" (Matt. 5:21–22). "Looking upon evil" (33:15) could mean something similar, but it may be more idiomatic to take it to refer to gloating over some disaster (*eg* Pss. 22:17; 118:7; Ezek. 28:17; Mic. 7:10). Parallels with Psalm 101 could suggest that this liturgy here is derived from one originally intended to admit the king, as representative of the people, into the Temple.

The change of person in verses 17–23 ("Your eyes . . ." after "he will dwell . . .", v. 16) could signify a change of speaker, as though a priest in the Temple were addressing the newly admitted worshipper (the king?). In that case the passage is about the worshipper's vision of a new Jerusalem, "a quiet habitation, an immovable tent" (v. 20), and the king in verse 17 is God, as in 6:5. Verses 21–22 would strengthen this view. This is what "he who walks righteously . . ." (v. 15) will see, a vision of hope to balance the scenes of desolation and despair in the first half of the chapter. An alternative is to ignore any liturgical connection and see here instead a Messianic poem like the one in the previous chapter or those in 9:1–7 and 11:1–9. But this would leave the problem of who is being addressed unresolved.

If we follow the former view, then God in all his royal splendour, enthroned on high after defeating the powers of chaos (*eg* 52:7; Pss. 89; 93; 95–100), is compared first to "a land that stretches afar" (v. 17) and then later to "a place of broad rivers and streams" (v. 21). Verses 18–19 may well have been influenced

by the memory of the Assyrian oppressors, who demanded tribute (2 Kings 18:14–16) and whose ugly language is alluded to on
more than one occasion (*eg* 28:11; 36:11–13). But the overall
effect goes beyond any historical event, as some of the Zion
hymns beautifully illustrate (*eg* Pss. 46; 48; 122; cf. Isa. 24).

"The city of our appointed feasts" (v. 20) is a striking phrase:
the word for "city" is a poetic term recalling "the faithful city" of
chapter 1 (vv. 21, 26) and also the "city of chaos" in 24:10. The
mention of "feasts" reminds us that all worship involving sacrifices had to be at Jerusalem, and for the most part it was closely
linked with the agricultural year. Thus "the city of our appointed
feasts" in one stroke sketches a picture of continuous prosperity
and peace. Equally vivid are the images of a "quiet habitation"
(or better, "land of comfort", NEB) and an "immovable tent",
especially when we remember that the Hebrew word for "tent"
has all the overtones of our word "home" and has very little to do
with camping:

> You will know that all is well with your *household* [RSV "tent"],
> you will look round your home and find nothing amiss.
>
> (Job 5:24, NEB)

Verses 21–23 of Isaiah 33 contain an elaborate metaphor:
Jerusalem is compared to a ship borne along on the "broad rivers
and streams" of God's love. A similar way of thinking about the
city of God appears in 59:19 and Psalm 46:4. No foreign galley or
stately ship from Egypt (18:2) or Tarshish (23:14) or Babylon will
disturb the calm waters. Her sails will be filled with "the wind
of the Lord" (59:19). Verse 23 is a taunt hurled at Jerusalem
by her enemies. But it is a faint voice, already drowned by
the confidence of verse 22; an Isaianic version of the shout
of triumph in the so-called Enthronement psalms, "The Lord
reigns" (*eg* 93; 95–100).

The last word is about healing the sick and forgiving the sinner,
two processes intimately intertwined (38:16–17; Ps. 103:3; Matt.
9:2). "In abundance" (RSV 33:23) is based on a difficult Hebrew
text, and a minor emendation produces the following:

Then the blind man shall have a full share of the spoil
   and the lame shall take part in the pillage. (NEB)

Then the verse recalls the story of David's capture of Jerusalem:

The Jebusites, the inhabitants of the land . . . said to David, "You will
not come in here, but the blind and the lame will ward you off".
                                            (2 Sam. 5:6)

Mention of the blind and the lame, however, together with the
verse about healing the sick, comes as a rather unexpected ending
to a chapter about the dramatic struggle between the forces of
good and evil. It has been suggested, both here and in 2 Samuel 5,
that the word translated "blind" should be read as "guardian,
watcher" (the same word as in verse 8), and that "lame" should
be read as "protector". The word translated "spare" in 31:5
(NEB "standing over") is closely related to the word for "lame".
On this interpretation the "guardian angels" who protect
Jerusalem triumph in the end over the "destroyer". The covenants between man and nature are remade (v. 8), and the promise
to Abraham and his descendants fulfilled:

"To your descendants I give this land, from the river of Egypt to the
great river, the river Euphrates, the land of the Kenites, the
Kenizzites . . . and the Jebusites."
                                   (Gen. 15:18–21)

THE DAY OF JUDGMENT

Isaiah 34:1–17

  ¹Draw near, O nations, to hear,
     and hearken, O peoples!
  Let the earth listen, and all that fills it;
     the world, and all that comes from it.
  ²For the Lord is enraged against all the nations,
     and furious against all their host,
     he has doomed them, has given them over for slaughter.
  ³Their slain shall be cast out,
     and the stench of their corpses shall rise;
     the mountains shall flow with their blood.

⁴All the host of heaven shall rot away,
   and the skies roll up like a scroll.
All their host shall fall,
   as leaves fall from the vine,
   like leaves falling from the fig tree.

⁵For my sword has drunk its fill in the heavens;
   behold, it descends for judgment upon Edom,
   upon the people I have doomed.
⁶The Lord has a sword; it is sated with blood,
   it is gorged with fat,
   with the blood of lambs and goats,
   with the fat of the kidneys of rams.
For the Lord has a sacrifice in Bozrah,
   a great slaughter in the land of Edom.
⁷Wild oxen shall fall with them,
   and young steers with the mighty bulls.
Their land shall be soaked with blood,
   and their soil made rich with fat.

⁸For the Lord has a day of vengeance,
   a year of recompense for the cause of Zion.
⁹And the streams of Edom shall be turned into pitch,
   and her soil into brimstone;
   her land shall become burning pitch.
¹⁰Night and day it shall not be quenched;
   its smoke shall go up for ever.
From generation to generation it shall lie waste;
   none shall pass through it for ever and ever.
¹¹But the hawk and the porcupine shall possess it,
   the owl and the raven shall dwell in it.
He shall stretch the line of confusion over it,
   and the plummet of chaos over its nobles.
¹²They shall name it No Kingdom There,
   and all its princes shall be nothing.

¹³Thorns shall grow over its strongholds,
   nettles and thistles in its fortresses.
It shall be the haunt of jackals,
   an abode for ostriches.
¹⁴And wild beasts shall meet with hyenas,
   the satyr shall cry to his fellow;

yea, there shall the night hag alight,
and find for herself a resting place.

15There shall the owl nest and lay
and hatch and gather her young in her shadow;
yea, there shall the kites be gathered,
each one with her mate.
16Seek and read from the book of the Lord:
Not one of these shall be missing;
none shall be without her mate.
For the mouth of the Lord has commanded,
and his Spirit has gathered them.
17He has cast the lot for them,
his hand has portioned it out to them with the line;
they shall possess it for ever,
from generation to generation they shall dwell in it.

Picking up eschatological themes from the 'Isaiah Apocalypse' (chs. 24–27; see vol. 1) and introducing some of the powerful images and motifs to be developed later, the next two chapters describe how the anger of God will be directed against the nations, especially Edom (ch. 34), while God's people will return to Zion amid scenes of new life and everlasting joy (ch. 35).

Verses 1–4 suggest a trial scene in which the nations of the world are summoned to hear the sentences passed upon them. The legal vocabulary continues throughout the chapter: the sword of judgment (v. 5), the recompense and the cause of Zion (v. 8), and the lot-casting with which the passage ends (v. 17). 'The Day of Judgment' implies a just process whereby the wicked are condemned and the innocent acquitted: we are all ultimately answerable before God for our behaviour here on earth.

The crimes of the nations are not specified, although "for the cause of Zion" (v. 8) makes it obvious that they include crimes against God's people. The broad division of mankind into Israel and the nations (or the Church and the world) is a common one and not always qualified with references to good or evil:

Do not love the world or the things in the world. If any one loves the world, love for the Father is not in him.

(1 John 2:15; see also John 14:30; 2 Cor. 4:4)

Everything is black and white, and the language accordingly extreme.."Doomed" (v. 2) is a word from the ancient rules of war according to which no booty could be retained by a victorious army: every single man, woman, child and animal had to be "utterly destroyed" (*eg* Josh. 6:21; 7:1). It appears again in 34:5. "Slaughter" (v. 2) is a word used mainly in connection with butchery and cooking. The scene of carnage in verse 3 and later in verses 5–7 can only be compared to some of the gruesome images in artists' impressions of Hell.

The crumbling and the falling to earth of the stars (v. 4), like leaves off a tree, are regular motifs in Jewish Apocalyptic eschatology (*eg* 24:23; Joel. 2:10, 30–31; Mark 13:24–25), and anticipate the visions of a new heaven and a new earth in chapter 66 (also Rev. 21). The "scroll" in 33:4 is the same word as the one translated "book" in verse 16. Among the Dead Sea Scrolls, the Book of Isaiah is written on a parchment scroll over seven metres (24 feet) long by twenty-six centimetres (10 inches) wide. Just as the rich contents of so vast a work can be rolled up into an insignificant looking bundle, so the immense beauty of the starry skies will be transformed into a small grey lump.

The judgment of Edom is in two parts; the *first* describes the day of vengeance in terms of bloody slaughter (vv. 5–7) and unquenchable fire (vv. 9–10); the *second* brilliantly depicts animals and birds settling there, each one allocated a place, as the people of Israel had settled in the Promised Land (vv. 11–17). Human inhabitants (like the Canaanites, the Hittites and the Amorites) are seen there no more. Edom aroused almost as much bitterness in Judah as Babylon did, and is introduced here as an example. Just as Israel is a light to the nations, so Edom is held up as an illustration of what happens to the enemies of God. Probably these attitudes were sparked off in the sixth century B.C. by Edomite attempts to expand their territory at the expense of Judah. They are built up into the legends about enmity between Jacob and Esau (the ancestor of the Edomites; see Gen. 36) and recur in later texts such as Ecclesiasticus (*Sirach*) 50:25–26. The gory details of Edom's slaughter are filled out by reference to ritual sacrifice. The first few chapters of Leviticus describe this formally, but it is probably more appropriate to think in terms of polemical passages like Isaiah 1:11 and 66:3:

> He who slaughters an ox is like him who kills a man;
>   he who sacrifices a lamb, like him who breaks a dog's neck;
> he who presents a cereal offering, like him who offers swine's blood;
>   he who makes a memorial offering of frankincense, like him who
>   blesses an idol.
> These have chosen their own ways,
>   and their soul delights in their abominations.
>
> (Isa. 66:3)

For some, the carnage of ritual slaughter at the Temple was scarcely more acceptable than the atrocities of war.

Bozrah (v. 6), identified with Buseirah 27 miles south-east of the Dead Sea, was Edom's chief city, as recent excavations have impressively proved.

The fire and brimstone in verses 8–10 compares Edom to Sodom and Gomorrah (Gen. 19:24–29), just as Jerusalem is compared in Isaiah chapter 1. Verse 10 uses three different idioms to emphasize that Edom's downfall is final: "for ever . . . from generation to generation . . . for ever and ever". The poem is about Hell-fire and eternal damnation, not just a military defeat or natural disaster.

There is an eerie realism in the *second* part of this chapter (vv. 11–17). As a human kingdom, Edom is finished: "confusion" and "chaos" (Hebrew *tohu, bohu*) allude to primeval disorder (Gen. 1:2), and its new name (v. 12) is a parody of Ezekiel 48:35 ("The Lord is there"). Others translate verse 12 thus: "They shall call the nobles thereof to the kingdom, but none shall be there, and all her princes shall be nothing" (AV). But with its demise, new life appears, nature takes over in all its variety. Birds of prey (*eg* hawks, owls) and scavengers (*eg* hyenas, jackals) will be first on the scene. Nettles and briars will grow over the ruins. Verse 14 contains two words which may at one time have meant "he-goat" and "nightjar" (NEB) or "screech owl" (AV), but traditionally add a further demonic dimension to the description. The *first* is the word translated "satyr" in Leviticus 17:7, which refers to the wild spirits believed to inhabit trees and streams. The *second* is 'Lilith', the sinister "Nighthag" of Jewish legend, mentioned only here in the Bible, who was reputed to fasten onto anyone sleeping alone in a room, and steal new-born infants from their beds at night.

Verses 16–17 round off the description of Edom's destruction with two Parthian shots. *First*, these horrific events had been foretold in "the book of the Lord". What this refers to we can only guess: it could be to the words of God against Edom in other collections (*eg* Amos 1:11–12; Jer. 49:7–22; Ezek. 35); or to a similar prophecy from the earlier chapters of Isaiah, not specifically about Edom (*eg* 13:21–22); or even to the Flood story, the ruins of Edom serving as an ark in the wilderness for the animals to enter "two by two" (Gen. 7:2–3; see v. 15). *Second*, and finally, there is the truly cynical suggestion that Edom was the land promised to the beasts of the field and the birds of the air long ago, as Canaan was promised to Israel. Edom should never have been there in the first place, and now it is returned to its rightful owners for ever!

THE DAY OF REDEMPTION

Isaiah 35:1–10

> [1]The wilderness and the dry land shall be glad,
>> the desert shall rejoice and blossom;
> like the crocus [2]it shall blossom abundantly,
>> and rejoice with joy and singing.
> The glory of Lebanon shall be given to it,
>> the majesty of Carmel and Sharon.
> They shall see the glory of the Lord,
>> the majesty of our God.
> [3]Strengthen the weak hands,
>> and make firm the feeble knees.
> [4]Say to those who are of a fearful heart,
>> "Be strong, fear not!
> Behold, your God

will come with vengeance,
  with the recompense of God.
    He will come and save you."

⁵Then the eyes of the blind shall be opened,
    and the ears of the deaf unstopped;
⁶then shall the lame man leap like a hart,
    and the tongue of the dumb sing for joy.
  For waters shall break forth in the wilderness,
    and streams in the desert;
⁷the burning sand shall become a pool,
    and the thirsty ground springs of water;
  the haunt of jackals shall become a swamp,
    the grass shall become reeds and rushes.

⁸And a highway shall be there,
    and it shall be called the Holy Way;
  the unclean shall not pass over it,
    and fools shall not err therein.
⁹No lion shall be there,
    nor shall any ravenous beast come up on it;
  they shall not be found there,
    but the redeemed shall walk there.
¹⁰And the ransomed of the Lord shall return,
    and come to Zion with singing;
  everlasting joy shall be upon their heads;
    they shall obtain joy and gladness,
    and sorrow and sighing shall flee away.

The poem on Zion's redemption in chapter 35 takes up some early themes of hope, and leads into the story of Jerusalem's miraculous escape from the Assyrians in chapters 36–39 and thereafter to the "comfortable words" of chapters 40–55. It is thoroughly Isaianic in style, and, whether or not it is dependent on chapters 40–55, as some scholars argue, it is illuminating to keep them in mind as we read it.

Although the last few verses refer to the return of the exiles to Zion, the chapter is less explicitly tied to one historical event than the "Babylonian chapters" (especially chs. 40–48). It is in fact an anthology of short prophecies of salvation, applicable to any situation in which hope breaks through the darkness of despair. The eerie desolation of chapter 34 provides the background for the first of them (vv. 1–2). New life, colour, joy and singing will transform the wilderness into a place where God's glory will be revealed. In the new age barren hillsides will be covered with the majestic cedars of Lebanon (29:17, see vol. 1, p. 243) and richly carpeted with the vineyards and pastures of Carmel and Sharon, images already familiar to us.

The weak and afraid will be given new strength and courage (vv. 3–4). Verse 4 is rich in the theological idiom of the exile: "your God" (rather than "the Lord" or "the Lord of hosts"; see also 40:1); "the recompense of God", that is, his reward for being so steadfast in his love for wayward Israel (as in 40:10); and the verb "save", like the noun "salvation", which is rare in the early chapters, but very common in chapters 40–55 (see the commentary on 12:2—vol. 1, p. 129—and 43:3).

Disabilities will miraculously disappear (vv. 5–6): the blind will see, the deaf hear and the lame leap for joy. This was a recurring motif in Jewish eschatology, so that later it was believed that when these miracles started happening, the new age had dawned, and the kingdom was at hand (*eg* Matt. 11:1–6). These verses can also be taken metaphorically to refer to the release of prisoners from dark prisons, to the unreceptive beginning to listen to the word of God, and the like. The whole chapter lends itself to such a timeless and non-specific interpretation. Certainly the water in verse 6 is the same miraculous water that comes from the "wells of salvation" (12:3) and the New Exodus story (41:17–18; 48:21). The effect (v. 7) is to transform the burning sand into an oasis, and the grass that withers when the breath of the Lord blows upon it (40:7–8) into hardy reeds and bullrushes, the materials from which boats were made (*eg* 18:2; Exod. 2:3).

In the final scene (vv. 8–10) the exiles will return to Zion, free, safe and clean, along a specially built highway. Again there are many parallels later in the book (*eg* 40:3; 48:20–21; 52:11–12). The road is called the "Holy Way", using the model of the "holy city" (48:2; 52:1) to which it leads.

The second part of verse 8 is difficult but not meaningless. As it stands, it reads, "the unclean shall not pass over it; but it shall be for those; the wayfaring men, though fools, shall not err therein" (AV). "Those" refers to the blind and lame mentioned in verses 5–6, and the last clause means that even fools will not lose their way. The "Holy Way" will be so clearly marked and so free of obstacles, that nobody, however stupid or ignorant, blind or lame, will go wrong as they proceed to Zion. Wild beasts (v. 9) will be kept at bay, and the returning exiles will be protected, as they are in 52:12, by a God who is both vanguard and rearguard.

The last verse is identical with 51:11. Here it comes at the end of a motley series of prophecies describing the new age; in chapter 51 it is associated with the myth of God's victory over the monsters of the deep, and with the miraculous parting of the Red Sea to make a way for the ransomed to pass over on dry land (51:9–10). Such a passage draws together *creation, exodus* (from Egypt) and *return* (from Babylon) to Zion, and reminds us of the sheer scale of God's "mighty acts" on behalf of his people.

THE INVASION OF JUDAH—I

Isaiah 36:1–3

[1]In the fourteenth year of King Hezekiah, Sennacherib king of Assyria came up against all the fortified cities of Judah and took them. [2]And the king of Assyria sent the Rabshakeh from Lachish to King Hezekiah at Jerusalem, with a great army. And he stood by the conduit of the upper pool on the highway to the Fuller's Field. [3]And there came out to him Eliakim the son of Hilkiah, who was over the household, and Shebna the secretary, and Joah the son of Asaph, the recorder.

Chapters 36–39 are composed for the most part of prose narrative, telling the story of Sennacherib's invasion of Judah, Hezekiah's illness and the arrival of ambassadors from Babylon. The narrative re-appears almost word for word in 2 Kings 18:13–20:19, but there are two significant differences in the Isaianic version which indicate that our author was even less concerned with what actually happened than the author of Kings. In the *first* place, three revealing verses have been left out after 36:1. 2 Kings 18:14–16 tells how Hezekiah surrendered to the Assyrians:

> And Hezekiah king of Judah sent to the king of Assyria at Lachish, saying, "I have done wrong; withdraw from me; whatever you impose on me I will bear." And the king of Assyria required of Hezekiah king of Judah three hundred talents of silver and thirty talents of gold. And Hezekiah gave him all the silver that was found in the house of the Lord, and in the treasuries of the king's house. At that time Hezekiah stripped the gold from the doors of the temple of the Lord, and from the doorposts which Hezekiah king of Judah had overlaid, and gave it to the king of Assyria.

The Isaianic account tells only of victory. The *second* difference is the splendid psalm of thanksgiving in chapter 38 which does not appear in Kings.

It is an important feature of this narrative that it contains three prayers, including the long psalm just mentioned (37:16–20; 38:3; 38:10–26), and four prophecies (37:6–7; 37:21–35; 38:5–8; 39:6–7), so that we can hardly avoid approaching this section of the book as theological discourse rather than historical narrative. There is actually another account (2 Chron. chs. 29–32), in which the story of Hezekiah is rather differently elaborated. Not only is his ignominious surrender omitted altogether, as in the Isaianic account, but so also are his defeatism (Isa. 37:3–4) and the key role of Isaiah who is mentioned only once in passing (2 Chron. 32:20). The exciting events of Isaiah chapters 38–39 are reduced to passing references (2 Chron. 32:24–31), while a brief mention (not in Isa.) in 2 Kings 18:4 is expanded into three long chapters describing far-reaching religious reforms by Hezekiah (2 Chron. 29–31). The Chronicler moreover gives no dates after "the first year of his reign" (Chron. 29:3). Our concern, when we approach all three of these versions of events, must therefore be with what the individual authors are saying rather than with what actually happened, with timeless theology rather than ancient history. Especially is this so in the context of the Book of the Prophet Isaiah, where "the fourteenth year of King Hezekiah" (36:1) has to be taken in sequence with dates given in 1:1, 6:1 and 14:28.

All four chapters (36–39) are set in the same year. It was "in those days" that Hezekiah was given another fifteen years to live after his illness (38:1, 5), adding up to a total reign of twenty-nine years (2 Kings 18:2). It was also "at that time" that the arrival of the Babylonian ambassadors at Jerusalem prompted, we are meant to think, Isaiah's Babylonian prophecies (39:1, 5–7 and chs. 40–48). Yet the actual date of Sennacherib's invasion, according to the Assyrian records (preserved in the form of clay tablets written at the time), was 701 B.C., corresponding to the twenty-fourth year of Hezekiah's reign, not the fourteenth (v. 1). Perhaps the Old Testament preserves a memory of another Assyrian invasion in 713–711 B.C. (*ie*, the fourteenth year), referred to in chapter 20. There is, on the historical level, obviously some confusion; but it is not our task in this commentary to unravel it, but rather to take the book as we find it and concentrate on its religious message.

According to 2 Kings 18:7, Hezekiah led a heroic rebellion against the Assyrians and the invasion was therefore not unprovoked. The reign of Sennacherib (704–681 B.C.) is well-known to us both from contemporary Assyrian records such as the horrific portrayal of the capture of Lachish on wall-reliefs from Nineveh (now in the British Museum), and from legends both Biblical and apocryphal:

> The Assyrian came down like a wolf on the fold;
> His cohorts were gleaming with purple and gold.
>
> (Byron, *The Destruction of Sennacherib*)

Isaiah 5:26–30 and 10:27–32 have already given vivid glimpses into the effect his advancing army had on the citizens of Jerusalem.

The omission of any reference to peace negotiations (see 2 Kings 18:14–16) makes the sudden appearance (36:2) of an Assyrian, the "Rabshakeh", with a great army near the city, all the more effective. The precise reference (v. 2) to "the conduit of the upper pool on the highway to the Fuller's Field" recalls an earlier crisis when the heart of the king "and the heart of his people shook as the trees of the forest shake before the wind" (7:2–3).

The three Hebrew terms for the officials mentioned in verse 3 match the Assyrian "Rabshakeh". They are clearly arranged in descending order of importance (see 22:15–25) and the proposal that the third should be translated as "herald" rather than "recorder" is very attractive. The scene is being set for a confrontation between the people of God and the enemies of God.

THE INVASION OF JUDAH—II

Isaiah 36:4–22

[4]And the Rabshakeh said to them, "Say to Hezekiah, 'Thus says the great king, the king of Assyria: On what do you rest this confidence of yours? [5]Do you think that mere words are strategy and power for war? On whom do you now rely, that you have rebelled against me? [6]Behold, you are relying on Egypt, that broken reed of a staff, which will pierce the hand of any man who leans on it. Such is Pharaoh king of Egypt to all who rely on him. [7]But if you say to me, "We rely on the Lord our God," is it not he whose high places and altars Hezekiah has removed, saying to Judah and to Jerusalem, "You shall worship before this altar"? [8]Come now, make a wager with my master the king of Assyria: I will give you two thousand horses, if you are able on your part to set riders upon them. [9]How then can you repulse a single captain among the least of my master's servants, when you rely on Egypt for chariots and for horsemen? [10]Moreover, is it without the Lord that I have come up against this land to destroy it? The Lord said to me, Go up against this land, and destroy it.'"

[11]Then Eliakim, Shebna, and Joah said to the Rabshakeh, "Pray, speak to your servants in Aramaic, for we understand it; do not speak to us in the language of Judah within the hearing of the people who are on the wall." [12]But the Rabshakeh said, "Has my master sent me to speak these words to your master and to you, and not to the men sitting on the wall, who are doomed with you to eat their own dung and drink their own urine?"

[13]Then the Rabshakeh stood and called out in a loud voice in the language of Judah: "Hear the words of the great king, the king of Assyria! [14]Thus says the king: 'Do not let Hezekiah deceive you, for he will not be able to deliver you. [15]Do not let Hezekiah make you rely on the Lord by saying, "The Lord will surely deliver us; this city will not be

given into the hand of the king of Assyria." ¹⁶Do not listen to Hezekiah; for thus says the king of Assyria: Make your peace with me and come out to me; then every one of you will eat of his own vine, and every one of his own fig tree, and every one of you will drink the water of his own cistern; ¹⁷until I come and take you away to a land like your own land, a land of grain and wine, a land of bread and vineyards. ¹⁸Beware lest Hezekiah mislead you by saying, "The Lord will deliver us." Has any of the gods of the nations delivered his land out of the hand of the king of Assyria? ¹⁹Where are the gods of Hamath and Arpad? Where are the gods of Sepharvaim? Have they delivered Samaria out of my hand? ²⁰Who among all the gods of these countries have delivered their countries out of my hand, that the Lord should deliver Jerusalem out of my hand?'"

²¹But they were silent and answered him not a word, for the king's command was, "Do not answer him." ²²Then Eliakim the son of Hilkiah, who was over the household, and Shebna the secretary, and Joah the son of Asaph, the recorder, came to Hezekiah with their clothes rent, and told him the words of the Rabshakeh.

The battle of words between Assyria and Jerusalem is skilfully built up of allusive, emotive theological language. The Rabshakeh, who does most of the talking, quotes all kinds of Isaianic statements and claims. All that Eliakim, Shebna and Joah can do is plead with him to speak in a language their fellow citizens will not understand (v. 11), and silently rend their garments (vv. 21–22).

In his *first* speech, the Rabshakeh introduces the words of the king of Assyria as though they were the very words of God: "Thus says the great king . . ." (v. 4). The words for "rely" (v. 5) and "confidence" (v. 4) are drawn from earlier Isaianic tradition (*eg* 30:15; 31:1; 32:9–11, 17), and parodied by the Assyrian. Reliance on Egypt was condemned by Isaiah himself (30:1; 31:1), which makes the Assyrian's comments all the more forceful. The "broken reed" metaphor (v. 6), highly appropriate when applied by him to Egypt, is also used in a prophecy against Egypt by Ezekiel (29:6).

The tradition that Hezekiah removed the "high places and altars" (v. 7) is not recorded elsewhere in Isaiah, but is well-known from 2 Kings 18:4 and 2 Chronicles 29:3ff.; 31:21. The Assyrian's argument is thus ironically neutralized for the readers because they would be aware that it was just because Hezekiah *relied* on God that he carried out his reforms (2 Kings 18:5). In Isaiah 36:8 the Assyrian mocks Judah's lack of manpower, and in verse 9 the futility of relying on Egypt again. The double irony is once more evident since we know that, according to Isaianic teaching (*eg* 31:1–3), salvation comes neither from manpower nor from Egyptian horses and chariots, but from the Lord.

Finally, verse 10 brilliantly alludes to such passages as 10:5–6 and 7:17–20, in which Assyria is said to be acting under God's instructions. Thus the Rabshakeh's last argument is that he even has Judah's God on his side; but the readers would know differently.

The dramatic irony of the next incident is masterly too (36:11–12). Aramaic was the language of international diplomacy and would have been the normal medium of communication in such a situation. But it might also have had the effect of concealing from some of the bystanders what was actually going on. When the Assyrian insists on speaking Hebrew, the language of Judah, which everyone understands, and moreover speaking it "in a loud voice" (v. 13) for everyone to hear, we can enjoy anticipating the spectacle of him being humiliated later in full view of the citizens of Jerusalem. This takes the sting out of his disgusting allusion to the effects of a siege in verse 12.

The Rabshakeh's *second* speech (vv. 13ff.) recalls a similar situation thirty years before when Isaiah's task was to convince another king that faith in God is what is needed in times of crisis (ch. 7). But this time the threat is not the two little kingdoms on Judah's northern border—Ephraim and Syria—but the Great King, the king of Assyria himself, "the waters of the River, mighty and many" (8:7). The words of the Great King are introduced again as the word of God, as in verse 4. His arguments are simple and convincing; in human terms. Hezekiah is far too weak to withstand the might of Assyria (v. 14). The Lord is just one among many local deities who present no challenge whatever to the Assyrians (vv. 15, 18). Hamath and Arpad in Syria, and Samaria (whose God *was* the Lord), were captured by them within the space of a few years (vv. 19–20). Sepharvaim and the other names mentioned in parallel passages (37:13; 2 Kings 18:34) are unknown, but 2 Kings 17 tells us something about the false gods they worshipped (v. 31):

> And the Sepharvites burned their children in the fire to Adrammelech and Anammelech, the gods of Sepharvaim.

The term "deliver" used in Isaiah 36:15 by the Rabshakeh, a foreigner, and used elsewhere of idols and false gods (44:17), contrasts with the magisterial term "save" which Hezekiah (37:20) and Isaiah (37:35) use when they refer to what the Lord can do for his people.

In the middle part of his argument, the Assyrian tries to persuade Jerusalem to surrender by depicting how blissful life would be under Assyrian rule (v. 16). The word for such a "peace" in verse 16 is the one usually translated "blessing" (*eg* 44:3) and reflects a change of tone from abuse to cajoling. This is, after all, the voice of Satan trying everything to break the faith of God's people. "But they were silent" (37:21) signifies both deep anguish on the part of the three officials—this was how Job's comforters reacted (Job 2:13)—and at the same time an attempt to cling to their faith in God as in 30:15, and elsewhere:

> Be still, and know that I am God.

> (Ps. 46:10)

ISAIAH AND THE SALVATION OF JERUSALEM—I

Isaiah 37:1–20

¹When King Hezekiah heard it, he rent his clothes, and covered himself with sackcloth, and went into the house of the Lord. ²And he sent Eliakim, who was over the household, and Shebna the secretary, and the senior priests, clothed with sackcloth, to the prophet Isaiah the son of Amoz. ³They said to him, "Thus says Hezekiah, 'This day is a day of distress, of rebuke, and of disgrace; children have come to the birth, and there is no strength to bring them forth. ⁴It may be that the Lord your God heard the words of the Rabshakeh, whom his master the king of Assyria has sent to mock the living God, and will rebuke the

words which the Lord your God has heard; therefore lift up your prayer for the remnant that is left.'"

⁵When the servants of King Hezekiah came to Isaiah, ⁶Isaiah said to them, "Say to your master, 'Thus says the Lord: Do not be afraid because of the words that you have heard, with which the servants of the king of Assyria have reviled me. ⁷Behold, I will put a spirit in him, so that he shall hear a rumour, and return to his own land; and I will make him fall by the sword in his own land.'"

⁸The Rabshakeh returned, and found the king of Assyria fighting against Libnah; for he had heard that the king had left Lachish. ⁹Now the king heard concerning Tirhakah king of Ethiopia, "He has set out to fight against you." And when he heard it, he sent messengers to Hezekiah, saying, ¹⁰"Thus shall you speak to Hezekiah king of Judah: 'Do not let your God on whom you rely deceive you by promising that Jerusalem will not be given into the hand of the king of Assyria. ¹¹Behold, you have heard what the kings of Assyria have done to all lands, destroying them utterly. And shall you be delivered? ¹²Have the gods of the nations delivered them, the nations which my fathers destroyed, Gozan, Haran, Rezeph, and the people of Eden who were in Telassar? ¹³Where is the king of Hamath, the king of Arpad, the king of the city of Sepharvaim, the king of Hena, or the king of Ivvah?'"

¹⁴Hezekiah received the letter from the hand of the messengers, and read it; and Hezekiah went up to the house of the Lord, and spread it before the Lord. ¹⁵And Hezekiah prayed to the Lord: ¹⁶"O Lord of hosts, God of Israel, who art enthroned above the cherubim, thou art the God, thou alone, of all the kingdoms of the earth; thou hast made heaven and earth. ¹⁷Incline thy ear, O Lord, and hear; open thy eyes, O Lord, and see; and hear all the words of Sennacherib, which he has sent to mock the living God. ¹⁸Of a truth, O Lord, the kings of Assyria have laid waste all the nations and their lands, ¹⁹and have cast their gods into the fire; for they were no gods, but the work of men's hands, wood and stone; therefore they were destroyed. ²⁰So now, O Lord our God, save us from his hand, that all the kingdoms of the earth may know that thou alone art the Lord."

The king's reaction is in two parts. *First* he immediately acknowledges his own weakness. This he does through the usual ritual signs of penitence and self-abasement (v. 1). This is the nearest the present account comes to the story of Hezekiah's surrender to the Assyrians as recorded in 2 Kings 18:14–16, where he admits he was wrong. But these are the rituals of repentance which, as the Jonah story illustrates so graphically (chs. 3–4), are the prelude to salvation. That Hezekiah visits the Temple, rather than the "conduit of the upper pool on the highway to the Fuller's Field" (36:2), or his military headquarters, for an emergency meeting of his cabinet, symbolizes his rejection of the way of the flesh, and his acknowledgment of the power of the spirit (31:3, 40:6).

His *second* reaction is to turn to Isaiah the prophet (v. 2), and the rest of the story centres on this. The prophet's very name, which means "the Lord saves", reminds us that "salvation" is at hand and points forward to verses 20 and 35 of the present chapter, 38:20, and numerous passages in chapters 40–55, where the terms "save", "saviour" and "salvation" emerge as key words in Isaianic tradition.

Hezekiah's message to the prophet (vv. 3–4) begins with a proverb. The situation, he says, is like the critical moment in childbirth, when the baby is at the mouth of the womb but the woman is too weak to deliver it. Skilled obstetricians are urgently needed to save the baby. The word translated "birth" actually means "breaking-point" and perfectly links the two critical situations: the woman in labour and Jerusalem in danger.

Verse 4, beginning "It may be that...", gathers up three themes that together will answer the Rabshakeh and hold out hope for the city. It is the "living God" who has been insultingly compared to the false gods of Hamath and Arpad (36:19): the "living God" is Israel's God, and he has heard the Assyrian abuse; and Jerusalem is "the remnant" which embodies Israel's hope in so many contexts, some of them, like 1:9 and the present chapter (vv. 4, 31–32) associated with the Assyrian crisis. It will be recalled that "the remnant" was an idea built into the name of Isaiah's first son, *Shear-jashub*; "a remnant will return" (7:3).

The prophet's reply is in the form of a 'salvation oracle' (vv. 6–7; see the commentary on 41:8–10). It begins with the formula, "Fear not", goes on to comment upon the present situation (the Assyrian blasphemy), and then concludes with a prophecy foretelling the arrival of a rumour that causes the king of Assyria to withdraw suddenly, and his subsequent assassination. Verses 8–9 begin to unfold immediately how these prophecies were fulfilled—like those of the witches in *Macbeth*—as the story progresses. The invasion was continuing. Lachish had fallen and Sennacherib had moved on to the next city when the *first* part of the prophecy was fulfilled. Sennacherib's fate, like Macbeth's, was sealed. The "rumour" about Tirhakah, king of Ethiopia, and eventually of Egypt too, may reflect the fact that, at about the same time, Sennacherib defeated an Egyptian army at Eltekeh. But it is the dramatic effect of the rumour, coming so soon after Isaiah's prophecy, that is most impressive.

Before the *second* part of the prophecy about Sennacherib is fulfilled (in vv. 37–38), another story is told about the Assyrian crisis, comprising the same four elements as the one just finished: a taunting message from the Rabshakeh in almost the same words as he had used before (vv. 10–13); Hezekiah's reaction (vv. 14–20); a prophecy by Isaiah (vv. 21–35); and its fulfilment (v. 36). With this section must be taken another of Isaiah's prophecies, recorded in 31:8:

> And the Assyrian shall fall by a sword, not of man;
> and a sword, not of man, shall devour him.

Whether this *second* story, which adds to the account of Sennacherib's withdrawal (an account of a terrible slaughter among the Assyrians), is based on an alternative tradition of what happened in 701 B.C., or whether, with its strong hint of the miraculous (v. 36), it owes more to theological wishful thinking than to accurate historical memories, is a matter for strenuous argument among the scholars. It is not an argument into which we can meaningfully enter in this commentary; and, as so often, we are better advised to concentrate on the aims and interests of the author.

Once again the Rabshakeh's message focusses on a theological issue, categorizing the Lord as one of the false gods who had shown themselves incapable of defending some of the other nations invaded by the Assyrians. A number of other names are added to the earlier list (36:19) to heighten the effect (vv. 12–13).

Hezekiah's prayer in the Temple (vv. 16–20) recalls the great formal prayers of David (2 Sam. 7) and Solomon (1 Kings 8). *First*, it introduces the theme of *monotheism* (as in 2 Sam. 7:22), a theme which is to be greatly developed later (*eg* 45:5–6, 14, 21–22):

Thou art the God, thou alone, of all the kingdoms of the earth.

(Isa. 37:16)

Second, the belief that the Lord of hosts is creator of all things (also v. 16) makes nonsense of the comparison between him and the gods of wood and stone ridiculed even by the Rabshakeh here (v. 12) and frequently in the later Babylonian chapters (*eg* 44).

Two final theological points are made in verse 20: (1) the contrast between the hollow victories of Assyria over gods of wood and stone, in comparison with the power of "the Lord our God", is summed up in the choice of the loaded word "save", of which we were reminded at the beginning of the chapter (see the comment on v. 2); and (2) the ultimate purpose of God's intervention in the history of his people is not their safety or peace or happiness, but his own glory, a point made even more emphatically later in chapter 48 (see v. 11):

For my own sake, for my own sake, I do it . . . My glory I will not give to another.

ISAIAH AND THE SALVATION OF JERUSALEM—II

Isaiah 37:21–38

[21]Then Isaiah the son of Amoz sent to Hezekiah, saying, "Thus says the Lord, the God of Israel: Because you have prayed to me concerning Sennacherib king of Assyria, [22]this is the word that the Lord has spoken concerning him:
  'She despises you, she scorns you—
    the virgin daughter of Zion;
  she wags her head behind you—
    the daughter of Jerusalem.

[23]'Whom have you mocked and reviled?

Against whom have you raised your voice
  and haughtily lifted your eyes?
  Against the Holy One of Israel!
²⁴By your servants you have mocked the Lord,
  and you have said, With my many chariots
I have gone up the heights of the mountains,
  to the far recesses of Lebanon;
I felled its tallest cedars,
  its choicest cypresses;
I came to its remotest height,
  its densest forest.
²⁵I dug wells
  and drank waters,
and I dried up with the sole of my foot
  all the streams of Egypt.

²⁶'Have you not heard
  that I determined it long ago?
I planned from days of old
  what now I bring to pass,
that you should make fortified cities
  crash into heaps of ruins,
²⁷while their inhabitants, shorn of strength,
  are dismayed and confounded,
and have become like plants of the field
  and like tender grass,
like grass on the housetops,
  blighted before it is grown.

²⁸'I know your sitting down
  and your going out and coming in,
  and your raging against me.
²⁹Because you have raged against me
  and your arrogance has come to my ears,
I will put my hook in your nose
  and my bit in your mouth,
and I will turn you back on the way
  by which you came.'

³⁰"And this shall be the sign for you: this year eat what grows of itself, and in the second year what springs of the same; then in the third year sow and reap, and plant vineyards, and eat their fruit. ³¹And the

surviving remnant of the house of Judah shall again take root down-ward, and bear fruit upward; [32]for out of Jerusalem shall go forth a remnant, and out of Mount Zion a band of survivors. The zeal of the Lord of hosts will accomplish this.

[33]"Therefore thus says the Lord concerning the king of Assyria: He shall not come into this city, or shoot an arrow there, or come before it with a shield, or cast up a siege mound against it. [34]By the way that he came, by the same he shall return, and he shall not come into this city, says the Lord. [35]For I will defend this city to save it, for my own sake and for the sake of my servant David."

[36]And the angel of the Lord went forth, and slew a hundred and eighty-five thousand in the camp of the Assyrians; and when men arose early in the morning, behold, these were all dead bodies. [37]Then Sennacherib king of Assyria departed, and went home and dwelt at Nineveh. [38]And as he was worshipping in the house of Nisroch his god, Adrammelech and Sharezer, his sons, slew him with the sword, and escaped into the land of Ararat. And Esarhaddon his son reigned in his stead.

Most of this section of the narrative consists of Isaiah's long prophecy (vv. 21–35); there is then a brief appendix recording the three remaining events through which his prophecies were fulfilled and the Assyrian threat finally removed (vv. 36–38). Apart from 38:6 and a passing reference in 52:4, Assyria is not mentioned again. The prophecy is introduced initially by the common formula, "Thus says the Lord . . .". But in addition it is presented as the answer to a particular prayer "concerning Sennacherib king of Assyria".

The prophecy is in three parts. The *first* (vv. 22–29) is in the form of a taunt-song addressed to the king of Assyria, and may be compared to chapters 14 and 47 in which the king of Babylon is taunted in similar terms. It begins with a splendid image; in God's eyes Jerusalem is like a proud, courageous young woman dismiss-ing an unwelcome suitor with a scornful toss of her head (better than "wags her head", RSV). To Sennacherib she appears an easy conquest; while God recognizes fearlessness and invin-cibility in her, because to have designs on the Holy City (48:2; 52:1) is to have designs on the "Holy One of Israel" himself

(v. 23). It is not against flesh and blood that Sennacherib is fighting, but against the one true God.

Verses 24–25 contain the Assyrian's boast, corresponding to those of the king of Babylon in 14:13–14; five sentences beginning with "I". He claims to have climbed higher than the highest mountain, like the builders of the Tower of Babel (Gen. 11), and cut down the tallest cedars of Lebanon. Then he claims to have conquered Egypt with one contemptuous gesture (37:25), a reference to Eltekeh (see the comment on v. 9). Only the Lord can properly do such things (*eg* 51:10), and all along Assyria has been merely a tool in his hand, with which he chose to punish the nations of the world (10:5). The rise and fall of nations is God's handiwork, not man's (vv. 26–28). The similes for fading pomp in verse 27 anticipate a more famous passage in chapter 40: "All flesh is grass . . ." (v. 6). Everything is planned and controlled by God; verse 28 is a bitter parody of Psalm 121 and other passages, in which God's loving care for his people is transformed into a terrifying image of God as someone like "Big Brother" in Orwell's *Nineteen Eighty-four*. Job's parody of Psalm 8:4 is another poignant example (Job 7:17–18).

Final judgment is described (v. 29) in terms of taming a wild beast, like Leviathan, "king over all the sons of pride" (Job 41:34), in the spectacular climax of the speeches of the Lord in Job (41:1–34):

> Though the sword reaches him, it does not avail;
> nor the spear, the dart, or the javelin.
> He counts iron as straw,
> and bronze as rotten wood.
> The arrow cannot make him flee;
> for him slingstones are turned to stubble.
>
> (Job 41:26–28)

Such is the king of Assyria, and like Leviathan he will be tamed and dragged back to his lair (37:7, 34).

The *second* part of the prophecy addressed to Hezekiah (vv. 30–32) has the same form as one or two of those addressed earlier to Ahaz (*eg* 7:10–17; 8:1–8). It begins with a sign, concerned, like the Immanuel sign in 7:14, with the timing of events. Just as "what grows of itself" (a technical agricultural term from Lev. 25:5, 11) is enough to live on for two years, and normal crops will be harvested in the third, so the "remnant of the house of Judah" (v. 31) will have the strength and resilience to spring up again after the Assyrian threat is past.

The Zion prophecy beginning, "Out of Jerusalem . . ." (v. 32) is an effective variation of the one in 2:3 and Micah 4:2, and alluded to elsewhere (*eg* Amos 1:2; Joel 3:16). "The zeal of the Lord of hosts will accomplish this" occurs only here and in 9:7. With this flurry of "Zionist" fervour, we are in the mainstream of Isaianic tradition.

Curiously the *third* part of the prophecy (vv. 33–35) foretells nothing of the imminent bloody slaughter of the Assyrians in verse 36. We have already noted this omission and the problem it sets for historians. Perhaps the words recorded here are trying to put a favourable interpretation on what actually happened in 701 B.C. The real reason for Sennacherib's withdrawal without a blow being struck was that Hezekiah surrendered. This is recorded in 2 Kings 18:14–16, but, as we have seen, the Isaianic account omits any mention of it. Its purpose is to represent what happened as an act of divine intervention; notice especially how the theological key word "save" is reintroduced from 37:20.

Verse 36 then takes this theological line of interpretation still further by describing the divine victory in the most extreme terms, as befits the ultimate annihilation of evil. The "angel of the Lord" here, as in 63:9, is synonymous with the "Saviour": that is, God himself, who "saves" his people in his own way. Intrigued by this story, later tradition ingeniously sought to account for what happened in naturalistic terms: one tradition tells how a plague of field-mice invaded the Assyrian camp and gnawed through their bow-strings and shield-thongs (the two pieces of equipment mentioned in v. 33). But our text is more concerned to proclaim that, with God's help, people of faith like Isaiah and the citizens of Jerusalem, can conquer evil. The fate of the wicked, like a battlefield littered with corpses (66:24), is the sad corollary of a salvation such as the one envisaged in verses 30–32.

Finally verses 37–38 tell how the other part of Isaiah's prophecy in 37:7, which concerns the king of Assyria himself, was fulfilled. According to the Assyrian records, Sennacherib was killed twenty years after the invasion of Judah. His successor Esarhaddon is referred to in Ezra 4:2. Ararat (ancient Urartu) was a mountainous region north of Assyria, covering part of what is now Eastern Turkey and Armenia. From both a literary and a theological point of view, the concentration of strange Assyrian names fading away into the distance in these final verses, rounds off the story of Jerusalem's miraculous victory over the powers of evil.

THE RECOVERY OF KING HEZEKIAH

Isaiah 38:1–22

[1]In those days Hezekiah became sick and was at the point of death. And Isaiah the prophet the son of Amoz came to him, and said to him, "Thus says the Lord: Set your house in order; for you shall die, you shall not recover." [2]Then Hezekiah turned his face to the wall, and prayed to the Lord, [3]and said, "Remember now, O Lord, I beseech thee, how I have walked before thee in faithfulness and with a whole heart, and have done what is good in thy sight." And Hezekiah wept bitterly. [4]Then the word of the Lord came to Isaiah: [5]"Go and say to Hezekiah, Thus says the Lord, the God of David your father: I have heard your prayer, I have seen your tears; behold, I will add fifteen years to your life. [6]I will deliver you and this city out of the hand of the king of Assyria, and defend this city.

[7]"This is the sign to you from the Lord, that the Lord will do this thing that he has promised: [8]Behold, I will make the shadow cast by the declining sun on the dial of Ahaz turn back ten steps." So the sun turned back on the dial the ten steps by which it had declined.

[9]A writing of Hezekiah king of Judah, after he had been sick and had recovered from his sickness:
[10]I said, In the noontide of my days
    I must depart;
I am consigned to the gates of Sheol
    for the rest of my years.
[11]I said, I shall not see the Lord
    in the land of the living;

I shall look upon man no more
　　among the inhabitants of the world.
¹²My dwelling is plucked up and removed from me
　　like a shepherd's tent;
like a weaver I have rolled up my life;
　　he cuts me off from the loom;
from day to night thou dost bring me to an end;
¹³　I cry for help until morning;
like a lion he breaks all my bones;
　　from day to night thou dost bring me to an end.

¹⁴Like a swallow or a crane I clamour,
　　I moan like a dove.
My eyes are weary with looking upward.
　　O Lord, I am oppressed; be thou my security!
¹⁵But what can I say? For he has spoken to me,
　　and he himself has done it.
All my sleep has fled
　　because of the bitterness of my soul.

¹⁶O Lord, by these things men live,
　　and in all these is the life of my spirit.
　　Oh, restore me to health and make me live!
¹⁷Lo, it was for my welfare
　　that I had great bitterness;
but thou hast held back my life
　　from the pit of destruction,
for thou hast cast all my sins
　　behind thy back.
¹⁸For Sheol cannot thank thee,
　　death cannot praise thee;
those who go down to the pit cannot hope
　　for thy faithfulness.
¹⁹The living, the living, he thanks thee,
　　as I do this day;
the father makes known to the children
　　thy faithfulness.

²⁰The Lord will save me,
　　and we will sing to stringed instruments
all the days of our life,
　　at the house of the Lord.

²¹Now Isaiah had said, "Let them take a cake of figs, and apply it to the boil, that he may recover." ²²Hezekiah also had said, "What is the sign that I shall go up to the house of the Lord?"

This fascinating chapter contains two distinct types of material: a prose account of the words and actions of Isaiah and Hezekiah (vv. 1–8 and 21–22), and a beautiful psalm of thanksgiving written by Hezekiah on his recovery from illness (vv. 9–20). The scene is set in Jerusalem, during the Assyrian crisis (vv. 1, 6), and still further elaborates the theme of God's concern for Jerusalem and his servant David (37:35; 38:5, 20).

As in the previous story, we begin with a crisis: the "Lord's anointed" (Pss. 2:2; 89:51; 132:10) is going to die, and furthermore the prophet's initial reaction is judgmental. As when in the days of the judges a prophet told suffering and pleading Israel that they deserved all they got (Judg. 6:7–10), so now Isaiah tells the king he is doomed. Hezekiah's prayer in verse 2 contains no explicit repentance: instead he wins God's protection by his faithfulness and piety. He "turned" away from Isaiah and the others standing by his bedside—that is what "to the wall" means (1 Kings 21:4)—and "wept bitterly" as he prayed. But his prayer begins, "Remember now, O Lord": in these words we are to forget his panic of 37:3–4 (and his surrender in 2 Kings 18:14–16), and think instead of his reform in 2 Kings 18:1–8, omitted in Isaiah, but elaborately expanded in 2 Chronicles 29–31. See 2 Kings 18:5–6:

He trusted in the Lord the God of Israel; so that there was none like him among all the kings of Judah after him, nor among those who were before him. For he held fast to the Lord; he did not depart from following him, but kept the commandments which the Lord commanded Moses.

"Faithfulness" (v. 3) is what Isaiah called for in earlier crises (7:9; 30:15). It was a permanent characteristic of the ideal Jerusalem, "the city of righteousness, the faithful city" (1:21–26). "A whole heart" (38:3) meant single-minded devotion to God (1 Kings 8:61; 11:4).

So now the prophet foretells, in one breath (vv. 5–6), Hezekiah's recovery and the survival of Jerusalem; two of the main themes of this section of the book (37:35). Fifteen years' extension to Hezekiah's life, in the fourteenth year of his reign (36:1), adds up to the total of twenty-nine years given in 2 Kings 18:2. Far from reaching an untimely end "in the noontide of his days" (38:10), more than half of his reign is still to come.

In the Kings version (2 Kings 20:8) the king at this point asks for a sign in words very similar to those in verse 22, and experts have suggested that verse 22 should (with v. 21) be moved back to follow verse 6 (see NEB). But this still leaves the question of why verse 22 is placed where it is; and in any case it should be remembered that this would not be the first time that a king had refused to ask for a sign (7:12). However that may be, the sign that Isaiah gives has no parallel and defies natural explanation—as miracles should. The Hebrew of verse 8 is difficult. There is in fact no word for "[sun] dial" (RSV). The word translated "steps" usually refers to steps leading up to the Temple (*eg* Ezek. 40:6) or the altar (Ezek. 43:17) or Jerusalem (Neh. 3:15) or the like, and it is the same word as that translated "dial". But what the "steps of Ahaz" might have been is unknown. They sound like some architectural feature of the palace, visible from Hezekiah's bedroom. Whatever he actually saw the shadows doing, they demonstrated the power of a God who controls the movement of the heavenly bodies (40:26). See also Job 9:7, 9:

> Who commands the sun and it does not rise;
>   who seals up the stars . . .
> who made the Bear and Orion,
>   the Pleiades and the chambers of the south.

The same God who made the sun "stand still" for Joshua (Josh. 10:12–14) made it "turn back" for Isaiah. Hezekiah's recovery follows immediately (v. 9).

Hezekiah's thanksgiving is an impressive example of Hebrew religious poetry. Like other psalms it contains few references to any particular situation, let alone that of Hezekiah's illness, but it is not inappropriate. The crisis comes almost exactly at the midpoint—"noontide"—of his reign (v. 10). He thought he would never recover (vv. 10–13): God had told him this through the prophet Isaiah (v. 1). "Save" in verse 20 picks up the theological key-word from an earlier part of the Hezekiah story (37:20, 35), and the theme of *miraculous survival* is what the whole book is about. Maybe as we read verse 18 we are to think of the 185 000 Assyrian corpses (37:36) and the king of Babylon in *Sheol* (14:9–11). The psalm was written down (v. 9) perhaps to be placed with gratitude in the Temple (v. 20).

Like Jonah (2:2) Hezekiah begins by recalling how he felt when he first realized he was dying (vv. 10–11). "I thought" (NEB) is better than "I said" (RSV). Verses 12–14 each contain one or two images and an appeal to God. Verse 12 compares death to the sudden loss of one's home, or the irreversible cutting of the threads on a loom when the cloth is finished. Verse 13, as it stands, analyses the courageous effort to get through a night of pain and suffering. Both verses 12 and 13 end with a kind of refrain on the suddenness with which death would come upon Hezekiah. Verse 14 compares his cries of anguish to the incessant twittering and moaning of birds, and ends, like the two previous verses, with an appeal to God: "Be thou my security". In modern idiom this might be rendered, "Bail me out".

Verses 15–17 are difficult, but seem to move from reminiscing about the past, to present thanksgiving. *God has spoken . . . God has acted* (v. 15) surely refers to Isaiah's prophecy and the miracle of the sun turning back in verses 7–8. "All my sleep has fled" (RSV) is based on an emended text: Hebrew has "I shall walk humbly all my years because of the bitterness of my soul" (cf. AV). "By these things" in verse 16 again refers to the signs of divine intervention mentioned in the previous verse; and the haunting prayer for health and life corresponds to the mournful refrain at the end of verses 12 and 13. Verse 17 appears to tackle, albeit very briefly, the problem of suffering in the world. On the one hand, some good has come out of it insofar as the psalmist now experiences a new "welfare" (*shalom*) beyond his former bitterness. On the other hand, there is a connection between sin and disease since, like Jesus healing the paralytic (Matt. 9:1–8), God has healed the psalmist by first forgiving his sins (see also 33:24).

The psalm of thanksgiving ends, like Psalm 115, by contrasting the fate of the dead who do not know the joy of singing hymns of thanksgiving in the Temple, with that of the living, like Hezekiah, who do (vv. 18–20).

Verse 21 adds a couple of medical details to the story: Hezekiah had been suffering from a similar disease to that of Job (not just one "boil" as in the RSV!); and Isaiah, after the manner of Elisha (2 Kings 6:10) and Jesus (John 9:6–7), had prescribed a form of treatment for it.

Verse 22 does not need to be misplaced here (see comment on v. 6). Is it not an exclamation? "[What a miracle!] I shall go up to the house of the Lord."

AMBASSADORS FROM BABYLON

Isaiah 39:1–8

¹At that time Merodach-baladan the son of Baladan, king of Babylon, sent envoys with letters and a present to Hezekiah, for he heard that he had been sick and had recovered. ²And Hezekiah welcomed them; and he showed them his treasure house, the silver, the gold, the spices, the precious oil, his whole armoury, all that was found in his storehouses. There was nothing in his house or in all his realm that Hezekiah did not show them. ³Then Isaiah the prophet came to King Hezekiah, and said to him, "What did these men say? And whence did they come to you?" Hezekiah said, "They have come to me from a far country, from Babylon." ⁴He said, "What have they seen in your house?" Hezekiah answered, "They have seen all that is in my house; there is nothing in my storehouses that I did not show them."

⁵Then Isaiah said to Hezekiah, "Hear the word of the Lord of hosts: ⁶Behold, the days are coming, when all that is in your house, and that which your fathers have stored up till this day, shall be carried to Babylon; nothing shall be left, says the Lord. ⁷And some of your own sons, who are born to you, shall be taken away; and they shall be eunuchs in the palace of the king of Babylon." ⁸Then said Hezekiah to Isaiah, "The word of the Lord which you have spoken is good." For he thought, "There will be peace and security in my days."

The final story about Hezekiah leads us forward into the Babylonian chapters which follow (40ff.). It reminds us that, although Jerusalem survived the Assyrian invasion, it was to fall to the Babylonians, and that the prophet would then be called to comfort his people in exile (40:1).

"At that time" clearly places this incident in the same year as the preceding stories, "the fourteenth year of King Hezekiah" (36:1), which leaves him with fifteen years of "peace and security" (39:8). The experts tell us that the Babylonian king, Merodach-baladan's dates were 721–710 B.C., and that he made various attempts to stir up rebellion against the Assyrians. It is certainly more likely that he was trying to enlist Hezekiah's support for such an enterprise, than that he was merely sending him a letter congratulating him on his recovery. Or had he heard something of the astronomical phenomenon of 38:8?

The arrival of the ambassadors is reminiscent of the encounter between Solomon and the Queen of Sheba (1 Kings 10), and the arrival of the Ethiopians in chapter 18. The dramatic irony is obvious here: Hezekiah's innocent delight as he exposes all the treasures of his city to the Babylonians, is grimly overshadowed by the prophecy in verses 6 and 7, and the all too familiar tale of how Nebuchadnezzar carried off all the treasures of Jerusalem a century later (2 Kings 24:10–17).

Isaiah's appearance on the scene in verses 3–4, ignorant of what has happened, highlights Hezekiah's naïve optimism. It is noteworthy that Hezekiah is not guilty of any sin here: he is represented as totally innocent. The subsequent defeat of Jerusalem was not due to anything he had done, but to the abominations committed by his notorious successor, Manasseh (2 Kings 21:10–15). The fact that Hezekiah himself surrendered three hundred talents of silver and thirty talents of gold to the Assyrians (2 Kings 18:14–16) is not mentioned: God had "cast all [Hezekiah's] sins behind [his] back" (38:17). In Rabbinic tradition, however, Hezekiah's folly is compounded with arrogance and even deceit. When Isaiah asked him "What did these men say?" (v. 3), he did not answer directly, presumably ashamed of what he had done. Instead Hezekiah answered the second question ("And whence did they come to you?") with the boast, "They have come *to me* from a far country". Only later did he confess his political error (v. 4). For this he was punished by being forced to hear the ominous words of the prophecy in verses 5–7.

The prophecy is introduced by a conventional prophetic formula: "Hear the word of the Lord of hosts" (*eg* 1:10; Jer. 7:2; Ezek. 37:4). "Behold, the days are coming" is also a frequent formula, especially in Jeremiah (*eg* 7:32; 9:25; 31:31) and Amos (4:2; 8:11; 9:13).

No mention is made in this prophecy of the fall of Jerusalem or the destruction of the Temple. This may well be due to the fact that it was composed before the final blow fell in 587 B.C. This would agree with the appearance of the Jeremianic expressions in verses 5 and 6. Alternatively the author may have wished to concentrate on the fate of Hezekiah's treasure and his sons, rather than on what happened to the buildings. After all, possessions are a recurring theme in the Hezekiah narratives (2 Kings 18:14–16; 20:13; 2 Chron. 31:2–10).

Hezekiah's "sons" (39:7) include of course descendants of the royal line down to and including Josiah, who was mercifully delivered from the fate here prophesied (2 Kings 22:19–20), Jehoiachin who was taken prisoner by Nebuchadnezzar (2 Kings 24:12), and Zedekiah whose eyes were put out and who was bound in fetters and taken to Babylon (2 Kings 25:7). The humiliating term "eunuchs" (39:7) need not mean literally castrated, but rather stripped of their royal power and dignity and condemned to live, like any other foreign servant, at the court of the king of Babylon.

Verse 8 is in two parts. In the *first*, Hezekiah simply acknowledges that what Isaiah said is right, perhaps also admitting his mistake. This would have been an appropriate place at which to end the story of the Babylonian visit. The *second* part, however, appears to suggest that Hezekiah was rather callous; "thinking to himself that peace and security would last out his lifetime" (NEB). But surely it is more likely that the author is rounding off his account of Hezekiah's glorious reign in phraseology familiar from 30:15; 32:17; 38:3, 17 and elsewhere, without the least

intention of commenting on his character. The parallel in 2 Kings
20:19 is different, clearly more closely related to the preceding
story of political ineptitude, and it is followed by the usual conclusion: "The rest of the deeds of Hezekiah, and all his might . . ."
(2 Kings 20:20–21). Isaiah 39:8 has none of this.

Unimaginable "success and faithfulness" were the hall-marks
of Hezekiah's reign. Surely "peace and security" (RSV, NEB)
miss the miraculous and religious dimensions of the story. Chapter 32, and especially verses 16–20, fill in the details of such a
reign—in this world and the next.

COMFORT MY PEOPLE, SAYS YOUR GOD

Isaiah 40:1–11

¹Comfort, comfort my people,
  says your God.
²Speak tenderly to Jerusalem,
  and cry to her
 that her warfare is ended,
   that her iniquity is pardoned,
 that she has received from the Lord's hand
   double for all her sins.

³A voice cries:
 "In the wilderness prepare the way of the Lord,
   make straight in the desert a highway for our God.
⁴Every valley shall be lifted up,
   and every mountain and hill be made low;
 the uneven ground shall become level,
   and the rough places a plain.
⁵And the glory of the Lord shall be revealed,
   and all flesh shall see it together,
   for the mouth of the Lord has spoken."

⁶A voice says, "Cry!"
  And I said, "What shall I cry?"
 All flesh is grass,
   and all its beauty is like the flower of the field.
⁷The grass withers, the flower fades,

when the breath of the Lord blows upon it;
surely the people is grass.
⁸The grass withers, the flower fades;
but the word of our God will stand for ever.

⁹Get you up to a high mountain,
O Zion, herald of good tidings;
lift up your voice with strength,
O Jerusalem, herald of good tidings,
lift it up, fear not;
say to the cities of Judah,
"Behold your God!"
¹⁰Behold, the Lord God comes with might,
and his arm rules for him;
behold, his reward is with him,
and his recompense before him.
¹¹He will feed his flock like a shepherd,
he will gather the lambs in his arms,
he will carry them in his bosom,
and gently lead those that are with young.

Chapters 40–55 show a remarkable unity of style and theology, and the first words of chapter 40 announce their main theme: in the midst of sin there is forgiveness; in the desert, hope. The sufferings of God's people in Babylon, foretold in the previous chapter (39:6–7), are over, and, what is more important, they can be explained as divine punishment so that there is no question of God having forgotten his people: "the word of our God will stand for ever" (v. 8). Every word is selected to stress the same truths: "*your* God . . . *our* God" in verses 1, 3, 8 and 9, as opposed to "the Lord" or "the Lord of hosts", are particularly common in these chapters, and the terms "my people" (v. 1) and "his flock" (v. 11) make the same point. The triumphant procession of God back to Jerusalem after his victory over the enemy, when his royal glory will be revealed and the laws of nature suspended, is another theme to be taken up again later, as indeed the heralds dispatched to spread the news of victory throughout the ruined cities are as well (*eg* 52:7–12).

It has long been recognized that the author of these chapters is addressing an audience of Jewish exiles in Babylon, soon after the destruction of Jerusalem in 586 B.C. Incidental references to the ruined city of Jerusalem (44:28; 49:17; 52:9), Babylonian idols (46:1–2), Cyrus, King of the Medes and Persians (559–529 B.C.) (44:28; 45:1) and a Jewish colony in Egypt (49:12), make a sixth century B.C. date virtually indisputable. The explicit monotheism (*eg* 45:5–6, 14, 18, 21, 22), the ridicule of idols (*eg* 44:9–20), the daring 'New Exodus' motifs (*eg* 43:18–21) and the concept of vicarious suffering (53:4–6, 11–12) are closer to the theology of Jeremiah and Deuteronomy (cf. Deut. 4:35, 39; 32:39), than to that of the eighth century B.C. prophets. Just as a "Deuteronomic" hand shaped the history of Israel in Joshua–Kings in the light of the catastrophes of the sixth century B.C., so an exilic "Deutero-Isaiah" can be identified within the whole collection of Isaianic material.

The continuity of these Babylonian chapters with what precedes, however, is also unmistakable and must not be neglected. It is most unfortunate that modern commentaries normally divide the Book of Isaiah between chapters 39 and 40, giving the wholly misleading impression that chapters 1–39 are by "Isaiah of Jerusalem", an eighth century prophet, while chapters 40–55 are by a sixth century writer with little or no connection with the author of chapters 1–39. In fact chapters 1–39 are by no means a unity, as we have seen: some passages, such as chapters 24–27, are even later than "Deutero-Isaiah", while others, like chapters 13–14 and 34–35 are probably exilic and contemporary with him. In other words, whatever its date, "Deutero-Isaiah" is an integral part of the Book of Isaiah and must be studied in that context and not divorced from it.

Nowhere is this more important than in verses 1–8 of this chapter. In the mysterious scene represented here, the voice of God is overheard addressing his heavenly court. "Comfort" is plural, as in the Authorized Version and Handel's *Messiah* ("Comfort ye"), and cannot therefore be addressed to the prophet. In other words, we have another prophetic glimpse of heaven just like the one in chapter 6. The prophet overhears God calling to the angels, and the angels calling to one another (6:1, 3 and 6). He interrupts the heavenly dialogue ("What shall I cry?"—see 40:6), and receives his commission (v. 6). In both chapters the glory of God (6:3; 40:5) is contrasted with the condition of the people: their uncleanness and unreceptiveness in chapter 6 correspond to their frailty and sin in chapter 40. Forgiveness comes to the prophet alone in chapter 6, while in chapter 40 he is commissioned to proclaim forgiveness to the whole people. The pessimistic view of humanity in 40:6–8 (see also Ps. 39:4–6; Job 14) is reminiscent of chapter 6 too, but paradoxically it is a source of hope—if only you will put your faith in God. This too is a familiar eighth century Isaianic theme (7:9; 30:15; 31:1–5).

Verses 9–11 contain some exceptionally beautiful, tender imagery, typical of "Deutero-Isaiah" and conceivable only in conjunction with immense strength (v. 10): only someone with great mental and physical strength can show such gentleness. *First*, the people are addressed as "Zion" and "Jerusalem", as they are throughout the Babylonian chapters and beyond (cf. 49:14; 51:3, 17; 52:1–2, 7; 60:14; 62:6). Cities are feminine in Hebrew, and so the very grammar of the words has a tenderness unattainable in English. *Second*, the phrase "fear not" characteristically announces the appearance of God and the end of a period of anxious waiting. This was how the angels addressed Mary (Luke 1:30) and the shepherds (Luke 2:10); it runs like a golden thread through these chapters too (35:4; 41:10, 14; 43:1, 5, *etc*). *Third* and finally, there is the elaborate image of the good shepherd with his sheep, sensitive to their needs, feeding them, lifting up the lambs in his arms, and giving special protection to the ewes at lambing time (v. 11). The shepherd is a frequent image in Biblical tradition: John 10, Psalm 23 and Ezekiel 34 contain elaborate examples. On the one hand, the shepherd represents that combination of strength and tenderness just mentioned. But on the other hand, the leaders of society, and especially the king, were thought of as shepherds (*eg* 1 Kings 22:17; Jer. 23:1–4; 50:6; Ezek. 34:2), and so the good shepherd will be one who protects the vulnerable members of society from injustice and oppression, and ensures that the people live in "peace and security".

Verse 10 contains the engaging idea that God is going to be rewarded for the years of misery he has gone through while his wayward people suffered. Like Rachel weeping for her children, he will soon see his people returning to their own country—and that will be his reward (see Jer. 31:15–20). Our God is a God who weeps for us, suffers for us "like a woman in travail" (42:14) and glories in us (49:3).

CREATOR OF HEAVEN AND EARTH

Isaiah 40:12–31

> [12]Who has measured the waters in the hollow of his hand
>   and marked off the heavens with a span,
>   enclosed the dust of the earth in a measure
>   and weighed the mountains in scales
>   and the hills in a balance?
> [13]Who has directed the Spirit of the Lord,
>   or as his counsellor has instructed him?
> [14]Whom did he consult for his enlightenment,
>   and who taught him the path of justice,
>   and taught him knowledge,
>   and showed him the way of understanding?
> [15]Behold, the nations are like a drop from a bucket,
>   and are accounted as the dust on the scales;
>   behold, he takes up the isles like fine dust.
> [16]Lebanon would not suffice for fuel,
>   nor are its beasts enough for a burnt offering.
> [17]All the nations are as nothing before him,
>   they are accounted by him as less than nothing and emptiness.
>
> [18]To whom then will you liken God,
>   or what likeness compare with him?
> [19]The idol! a workman casts it,
>   and a goldsmith overlays it with gold,
>   and casts for it silver chains.
> [20]He who is impoverished chooses for an offering
>   wood that will not rot;

he seeks out a skilful craftsman
 to set up an image that will not move.

²¹Have you not known? Have you not heard?
 Has it not been told you from the beginning?
 Have you not understood from the foundations of the earth?
²²It is he who sits above the circle of the earth,
 and its inhabitants are like grasshoppers;
who stretches out the heavens like a curtain,
 and spreads them like a tent to dwell in;
²³who brings princes to naught,
 and makes the rules of the earth as nothing.

²⁴Scarcely are they planted, scarcely sown,
 scarcely has their stem taken root in the earth,
when he blows upon them, and they wither,
 and the tempest carries them off like stubble.
²⁵To whom then will you compare me,
 that I should be like him?
  says the Holy One.
²⁶Lift up your eyes on high and see:
 who created these?
He who brings out their host by number,
 calling them all by name;
by the greatness of his might,
 and because he is strong in power
 not one is missing.

²⁷Why do you say, O Jacob,
 and speak, O Israel,
"My way is hid from the Lord,
 and my right is disregarded by my God"?
²⁸Have you not known? Have you not heard?
 The Lord is the everlasting God,
 the Creator of the ends of the earth.
He does not faint or grow weary,
 his understanding is unsearchable.
²⁹He gives power to the faint,
 and to him who has no might he increases strength.
³⁰Even youths shall faint and be weary,
 and young men shall fall exhausted;
³¹but they who wait for the Lord shall renew their strength,

they shall mount up with wings like eagles,
they shall run and not be weary,
they shall walk and not faint.

The imperatives of the *first* part of this chapter, "Comfort
... prepare ... cry ... get you up ... fear not", contrast with the
rhetorical questions of the *second* (vv. 12–31). The logical connection between the two parts is the deliberate contrast between,
on the one hand, the frailty of chastened, frightened Jerusalem,
and on the other, the incomparable power of God as revealed in
the sheer cosmic scale of his creative activity. Put your faith in the
former and you will wither like grass (vv. 6–7; cf. 24); put your
faith in God and you will "mount up with wings like eagles" (v.
31).

As though to inspire that faith, a series of powerful arguments
from the nature of the universe is presented to prove the omnipo-
tence of God and the power of those who trust in him. This type of
argumentation is a regular feature of Old Testament prophecy,
but especially of "Deutero-Isaiah" (cf. 41; 49:14–50:3). The
appeal to nature as an argument for belief in God appears frequently too, especially in the Psalms and Job (*eg* Pss. 8; 19; Job
38–41). The fundamental argument here is that God is unique and
that his authority, over all creation, is consequently un-
challengeable. Explicit monotheism—the belief that no other
gods exist beside Israel's God—does not seem to have been
articulated in ancient Israel until the Babylonian exile; but then it
is emphatically and repeatedly proclaimed (see Isa. 43:10; 44:6,
8; 45:5–6, 14, 18, 21, 22; 46:9; and "Deuteronomic" passages
such as Deut. 4:35; 2 Sam. 7:22; 1 Kings 8:60). It is one way of
expressing total commitment to one's God, as creator and ruler of
the universe.

Verse 12 focuses on the immense scale of things: however great
our idea of the universe—and our twentieth century view is in
many ways infinitely greater than the Old Testament's—God is
greater. Psalm 93:3–4 expresses this magnificently:

The floods have lifted up, O Lord,
the floods have lifted up their voice,
the floods lift up their roaring.

Mightier than the thunders of many waters,
  mightier than the waves of the sea,
  the Lord on high is mighty.

Next comes the fantastic intricacy of the world about us. Job, chapters 38–41, lists numerous examples of the wonders of nature, and challenges Job to explain them. Nowadays the more scientific explanations we are given, the more incredible the picture becomes. Again, however amazing the scientific knowledge we amass about the universe, the wisdom of God is more amazing still (vv. 13–14). In verse 14, "the path of justice" comes close to the idea of order in the universe: the word translated "justice" is translated "pattern" in Exodus 25:9 and elsewhere. Another element in the argument from nature is the beauty of the universe. The sky is stretched out like a curtain (v. 22) and the stars parade before our eyes like a magnificent army in all its splendour (v. 26). More is made of this in Psalm 8, Job 38 and elsewhere, but it is part of "Deutero-Isaiah"'s argument too.

The main argument, however, is about strength: who is stronger—the God whose greatness, wisdom and beauty are revealed in the universe, or the nations which caused Israel's suffering, or the ridiculous idols, or the princes and rulers of the earth, or even the stars? Initially (vv. 15–17), the nations are dismissed as "less than nothing and emptiness" (the latter word appears also in Gen. 1:2, "without form"). No doubt we are intended to think of Egypt, Assyria, Babylon and Persia in the ancient world, as well as the United States and the Soviet Union in our own day. The cedars of Lebanon in all their glory provide an effective symbol of size, abundance, strength and economic power, which mean nothing to God.

Verses 18–20 contain the first of several passages in which idolatry is ridiculed (see also 41:7; 44:9–20; 46:1–2). Extravagant language is used; to make one idol, three men are required, one of whom cannot even afford the expense; human craftsmanship is mockingly compared to God's. Such passages are attacks on misdirected effort and devotion to false gods, whatever they may be, from one's personal appearance or private swimming pool, to race-horses or even cruise missiles. Princes and rulers are next in line for ridicule (vv. 21-24), with Nebuchadnezzar and Cyrus in mind, no doubt. From God's point of view, they are like grasshoppers; small, funny-looking, insignificant, powerless to change anything; or like plants, scarcely planted, when they are blown away in the wind. Finally, in case anyone should think of putting his faith in the stars, it is as well to remember that they too are mere numbers in a heavenly host, created and marshalled by God (vv. 25-26).

The chapter ends with an appeal to Israel to trust in the Lord. Faced with such spectacular evidence of God's wisdom and power (vv. 28-29), how can you doubt? Verse 27 is drawn from the psalms of lamentation (eg Ps. 88:14), and poignantly expresses Israel's doubts, dispelled at once by reference to the arguments from creation just presented. The last four verses address in particular the problem of faintness and weariness (the terms are repeated in every verse), and answer it with statements about God's power and the strength of those who trust in him. With typical brilliance the rabbis applied verse 31 to their own experience: "they shall mount up with wings like eagles" refers to the Exodus from Egypt (cf. Exod. 19:4; Deut. 32:11); "they shall run and not be weary" refers to the wanderings in the wilderness; and "they shall walk and not faint" refers to life in the Promised Land. This is the kind of interpretation which reminds us of the need to remove these texts from sixth century B.C. Babylon and make them our own.

LORD OF HISTORY

Isaiah 41:1-7

1Listen to me in silence, O coastlands;
    let the peoples renew their strength;
  let them approach, then let them speak;
    let us together draw near for judgment.

2Who stirred up one from the east
    whom victory meets at every step?

He gives up nations before him,
    so that he tramples kings under foot;
he makes them like dust with his sword,
    like driven stubble with his bow.
³He pursues them and passes on safely,
    by paths his feet have not trod.
⁴Who has performed and done this,
    calling the generations from the beginning?
I, the Lord, the first,
    and with the last; I am He.

⁵The coastlands have seen and are afraid,
    the ends of the earth tremble;
    they have drawn near and come.
⁶Every one helps his neighbour,
    and says to his brother, "Take courage!"
⁷The craftsman encourages the goldsmith,
    and he who smooths with the hammer him who strikes the anvil,
saying of the soldering, "It is good";
    and they fasten it with nails so that it cannot be moved.

Once again the prophet is not content to address his audience directly: in chapter 40 he began with God's words to the angels; in chapter 1, he summoned heaven and earth to listen to the word of the Lord (see also Deut. 32:1). Here, as in chapters 34 and 49, he calls on the nations of the world to bear witness to the mighty acts of God in history.

The scene (as in vv. 21–29 later in the ch.) is a trial scene: "set forth your case" (v. 21); "let us together draw near for judgment" (v. 1). But we are not to envisage a formal, modern law court: in ancient Israel, justice was dispensed "at the gate" (cf. Job 5:4; 29:7; Amos 5:12), in the hurly-burly of the busiest part of the city, where an injured party had to summon all the help he could get from friendly witnesses and supporters. Only as a last resort could he appeal to the king for help (*eg* 2 Sam. 14:4). Such trial scenes are frequently used by the prophets as a medium for their message. Amos 3:9–11 is an effective example, in which witnesses are called, accusations made, and finally the sentence pronounced with the formula, "Therefore thus says the Lord

God . . .". In the present context, the prophet, with characteristic originality, uses the trial speech to convince his audience of the truth of his prophecies of salvation. He challenges them to produce witnesses to prove him wrong. The best witnesses are the nations of the world; they have seen for themselves the terrifying power of God in their own history, and cannot deny it. God's power in history is as indisputable as his power in creation (ch. 40).

The actual example quoted by the prophet is that of Cyrus the Great, king of the Medes and Persians (550–530 B.C.). Verses 2, 3, 5 and 25 allude to his spectacular military successes; in particular, perhaps in Asia Minor, one of the "coastlands" (v. 5). Later, Cyrus is hailed as the Lord's *anointed* (45:1). It was he who was to conquer Babylon and liberate the exiles. His proclamation is cited at the end of the long history of the decline and fall of Jerusalem in 1 and 2 Chronicles as a ray of hope after the fall of Jerusalem and the desolation of the Promised Land:

> Now in the first year of Cyrus, king of Persia . . . the Lord stirred up the spirit of Cyrus king of Persia so that he made a proclamation throughout all his kingdom and also put it in writing: "Thus says Cyrus king of Persia, 'The Lord, the God of heaven, has given me all the kingdoms of the earth, and he has charged me to build him a house at Jerusalem, which is in Judah. Whoever is among you of all his people, may the Lord his God be with him. Let him go up.'"
>
> (2 Chron. 36:22–23)

A clay cylinder with the actual words of Cyrus' proclamation written on it in Babylonian was discovered in the last century. The Chronicler's version just quoted, and the Ezra version which embroiders the text still further (Ezra. 1:2–4), may not correspond entirely to historical fact, but they make the same point as "Deutero-Isaiah". The spectacular victories of Cyrus the Great, conqueror of Babylon and liberator of the Jews, were initiated by the Lord: it was he who "stirred up one from the east" (v. 2), "stirred up the spirit of Cyrus" (2 Chron. 36:22; cf. Ezra. 1:1), and said to Cyrus, "I will go before you" (45:1–2). Just as Assyria was the big stick with which God punished Israel in the eighth century (10:5), so now Cyrus is the instrument of their salvation in the Babylonian period. Such a view of history may not, when put so crudely, be acceptable to us today; but one has to admire the faith which can see in disaster evidence of God's love, and attribute to him the credit for events that are wholly good.

The word translated "victory" (Hebrew *tsedek*) in verse 2 (and again in v. 10) is the same great theological term which is translated as "righteousness" elsewhere (*eg* 42:6), and "triumphs" in the Song of Deborah (Judg. 5:11). It is a favourite Isaianic term, associated with Jerusalem (1:26), and denotes a victory that only God can win; one that brings with it *justice* and *salvation* (cf. 45:8; 51:5, 6, 8). The difficulty involved in translating the word is evident in the variety of translations offered for verse 2: *eg* "Who raised up the righteous man from the east . . .?" (AV). This could suggest an alternative interpretation of the verse. Taken with verse 8, it could refer to the story of Abraham, who was called by God from roughly the same part of the world as Cyrus (Gen. 12:1–4) and who, according to Genesis 14, was able to trample kings under foot too. And, of course, Abraham's righteousness was legendary (Gen. 15:6). This is possible; but a reference to Cyrus, based on contemporary history, is more convincing.

Verse 3 describes the speed of his campaigns: his feet hardly touch the ground. The same detail is given in Daniel's visionary description of Alexander the Great as a "he-goat coming from the west across the face of the whole earth, without touching the ground" (Dan. 8:5). Only God's anointed servant (45:1) could travel so fast or so successfully.

The end of the first argument from history comes in verse 4 with the divine statement, repeated over and over again in these chapters, and in John 8:58, Revelation 1:8 and elsewhere: "I am He". *First* of all, we are surely intended to think of the Burning Bush story and the meaning of the name of God (Exod. 3:14). It means "the One who is", that is to say, "the One who is active in history", since in Hebrew the verb "to be" (*hayah*) is very much more dynamic and concrete than "to be" in English. *Second*, this first "I am" saying begins a series of theological statements: "I am God" (43:13); "I am the Lord" (43:11); "I am the Creator of

Israel, your King" (43:15) *etc*, which, on the one hand, bring God
and his people as close to one another as Moses and the Burning
Bush or Jesus and his disciples, and on the other hand, imply
"There is no other god besides me" (45:21, 22) or, in Christian
terms, "No one comes to the Father, but by me" (John 14:6). In
verse 4 as well, there is the formula, "I am the first and the last",
repeated again later in these chapters (44:6) and in a Greek form
in Revelation 1:8: "I am the Alpha and the Omega".

Like the argument from creation in 40:12–17, and the second
argument from contemporary history to come in 41:25–29, this
one closes with another mocking glance at the misguided efforts
of idol-worshippers (vv. 6–7). No less than four men are pictured
earnestly discussing their work. Having once glimpsed a world-
view like that of "Deutero-Isaiah", one can hardly take such a
scene very seriously.

FEAR NOT, CHILDREN OF ABRAHAM

Isaiah 41:8–20

8But you, Israel, my servant,
    Jacob, whom I have chosen,
        the offspring of Abraham, my friend;
9you whom I took from the ends of the earth,
    and called from its farthest corners,
    saying to you, "You are my servant,
        I have chosen you and not cast you off";
10fear not, for I am with you,
    be not dismayed, for I am your God;
    I will strengthen you, I will help you,
        I will uphold you with my victorious right hand.

11Behold, all who are incensed against you
    shall be put to shame and confounded;
    those who strive against you
        shall be as nothing and shall perish.
12You shall seek those who contend with you,
    but you shall not find them;
    those who war against you

shall be as nothing at all.
¹³For I, the Lord your God,
hold your right hand;
it is I who say to you, "Fear not,
I will help you."

¹⁴Fear not, you worm Jacob,
you men of Israel!
I will help you, says the Lord;
your Redeemer is the Holy One of Israel.
¹⁵Behold, I will make of you a threshing sledge,
new, sharp, and having teeth;
you shall thresh the mountains and crush them,
and you shall make the hills like chaff;
¹⁶you shall winnow them and the wind shall carry them away,
and the tempest shall scatter them.
And you shall rejoice in the Lord;
in the Holy One of Israel you shall glory.

¹⁷When the poor and needy seek water,
and there is none,
and their tongue is parched with thirst,
I the Lord will answer them,
I the God of Israel will not forsake them.
¹⁸I will open rivers on the bare heights,
and fountains in the midst of the valleys;
I will make the wilderness a pool of water,
and the dry land springs of water.
¹⁹I will put in the wilderness the cedar,
the acacia, the myrtle, and the olive;
I will set in the desert the cypress,
the plane and the pine together;
²⁰that men may see and know,
may consider and understand together,
that the hand of the Lord has done this,
the Holy One of Israel has created it.

Between the two arguments from history in verses 1–7 and 21–29, we come to the *first* of what are called 'salvation oracles', a favourite type of prophecy in these chapters. These were originally the answers given to people in need or danger or doubt, who came to "consult the oracle"; that is, they journeyed to a sacred site, such as Delphi in ancient Greece, or Bethel in Israel, and, in answer to their question, received a divine response either in a dream, like Jacob (Gen. 28:12–15), or mediated to them by a priest or prophet, or a prophetess like Deborah (Judg. 4:4–5). Such responses or 'oracles' came to be composed in a conventional form and incorporated into the liturgy. Psalm 60 may be an example, where the people cry for help in time of need ("O God, thou hast rejected us..."), and then in response, God utters a salvation oracle in colourful, rather enigmatic language (vv. 6–8). In some Psalms there seems to be a gap where such an oracle is missing: Psalm 22, for example, begins "My God, my God, why hast thou forsaken me?" and continues "[Praise the Lord]... glorify him... for he has not despised or abhorred the affliction of the afflicted" (vv. 22–31). "Deutero-Isaiah" has preserved many such missing salvation oracles. Just imagine the effect of hearing the words, "Fear not, you worm Jacob... I will help you" (v. 14) after the cries of dereliction in Psalm 22: "But I am a worm, and no man" (vv. 6ff.).

There are two examples in the present section, verses 8–10 and 14–16. Both demonstrate the three main features of the salvation oracle: (1) "fear not"; (2) a statement about the nature of God or what he has done ("I chose you... redeemed you... called you..."); and (3) a promise or prophecy about happier times in the future ("I will help you... I will strengthen you... you shall rejoice in the Lord"). Often the last part is expanded, as in verses 11–13 and 17–20, with extended poems on the theme of salvation for Israel, and destruction for her enemies. No more appropriate framework could be imagined for our author to present his gospel to the exiles in, than the salvation oracle. For other clear examples of salvation oracles see 43:1–7 and 54:4–8.

"The servant of the Lord" in Isaianic idiom usually means Israel (v. 8), whereas elsewhere in the Old Testament it normally refers to Moses (*eg* Deut. 34:5) or David (*eg* Ps. 18) or the prophets (*eg* Jer. 7:25). This is one more indication of the originality of these chapters. In later passages, notably the famous passage 52:13 to 53:12, "the servant of the Lord" may have to be interpreted differently, but normally it is applied to God's people

Israel. The people are frequently addressed as an individual: "Zion" (see on 40:9), "Israel" or "Jacob" (vv. 8, 14), "my servant", and the like, to emphasize the close bond between God and his chosen people. Abraham is called the "friend of God" in James 2:23 as well, and Al Khalil, "the Friend", is now the chief name for Abraham (Ibrahim) in Islam. Verses 9–10 allude to the patriarchal traditions in Genesis: the appearance of God to Abraham, for example, in 15:1, and to Isaac in 26:24. "The ends of the earth . . . its farthest corners" (Isa. 41:9), however, go beyond the stories of Abraham, Isaac and Jacob, and include the contemporary situation as well: even though you may be scattered to the four corners of the earth, Babylon, Egypt or the coastlands, I am with you, I have not "cast you off". On the meaning of "my victorious right hand", see above on verse 2.

The poem in verses 11–13 is in the form of a lament over the fate of the wicked. We shall discuss the sometimes brutal corollaries of the salvation oracles later (see 49:23, 26; 51:23). Notice the intimacy in verse 13 again: God takes his people by the hand.

The *second* salvation oracle (vv. 14–16) moves from the image of Israel as a worm—powerless, insignificant, primitive, blind (see above on the connection with Psalm 22)—to that of Israel as a "threshing sledge". These were heavy implements, made of wooden boards with metal or flint teeth set in them, and dragged round and round the threshing floor by a donkey or an ox; often a boy sat on it to drive it and to give it extra weight. The image is a gruesome one when applied to the punishment of one's enemies (see also Amos 1:3), but very powerful. Some recent scholars ingeniously argue that the rather unusual phrase translated "men of Israel" in verse 14, should be translated "poor louse" (NEB) or "puny mite"(JB), but as it stands it picks up a highly appropriate theme from Deuteronomy 26:5, one of its very few occurrences in the Bible: "A wandering Aramean was my father; and he went down into Egypt and sojourned there, few in number; and there he became a nation, great, mighty, and populous" (cf. Ps. 105:12).

Almost as if the author wishes to wash away the stains of his people's savage victory described in verses 15 and 16 (as in 63:1–6), he appends (vv. 17ff.) another exquisite poem about

water in the desert (see above on 35:1–4). In a way the exiles are
back in the wilderness again, without a city, without a Temple,
without a homeland, as they were during the forty years that
passed between the Exodus and the settlement in Canaan. The
prophet tells them in effect to remember "the Rock of their
salvation"; to remember who "found them in a desert land, and in
the howling waste of the wilderness...", and who is "like an
eagle that stirs up its nest, that flutters over its young, spreading
out its wings, catching them, bearing them on its pinions", and to
remember who "alone did lead them" (Deut. 32:10–13). That
first time, Moses struck one rock and one stream of water gushed
out for the people to drink from (Exod. 17; Num. 20). This time
rivers, fountains, pools and springs will appear everywhere
(v. 18); the whole wilderness will become a lush, wooded place
(v. 19); and the poor and needy will have shade, timber, fruit and
all the water they need (v. 17). This is nothing short of a "new
creation", a complete break with the past; something which will
go beyond anything that has ever happened before, because "the
Holy One of Israel has created it" (v. 20). "All things are possible
to him who believes" (Mark 9:23).

THE IMPOTENCE OF FALSE GODS

Isaiah 41:21–29

> [21]Set forth your case, says the Lord;
>   bring your proofs, says the King of Jacob.
> [22]Let them bring them, and tell us
>   what is to happen.
>   Tell us the former things, what they are,
>   that we may consider them,
>   that we may know their outcome;
>   or declare to us the things to come.
> [23]Tell us what is to come hereafter,
>   that we may know that you are gods;
>   do good, or do harm,
>   that we may be dismayed and terrified.
> [24]Behold, you are nothing,

and your work is naught;
an abomination is he who chooses you.

25I stirred up one from the north, and he has come,
from the rising of the sun, and he shall call on my name;
he shall trample on rulers as on mortar,
as the potter treads clay.
26Who declared it from the beginning, that we might know,
and beforetime, that we might say, "He is right"?
There was none who declared it, none who proclaimed,
none who heard your words.
27I first have declared it to Zion,
and I give to Jerusalem a herald of good tidings.
28But when I look there is no one;
among these there is no counsellor
who, when I ask, gives an answer.
29Behold, they are all a delusion;
their works are nothing;
their molten images are empty wind.

In the second of the two trial scenes in this chapter, the false gods
are on trial, with God as judge (see 41:1–7). He challenges them
to prove their divinity by predicting the future (vv. 22–23), or by
telling us how things began (v. 22), or by doing anything at all,
good or evil, to demonstrate their power. God is given the unusual title "King of Jacob" for two reasons. *First*, it was the king
who acted as ultimate court of appeal in ancient Israel, and it
is in that context that we are surely intended to understand the
words of this trial speech: God speaks here as supreme judge.
The *second* association that this phrase "King of Jacob" has, is
with the so-called Enthronement psalms, which describe God's
victory over the powers of evil—symbolized by floods or sea
monsters or the like—and then hail him as king. Psalm 74:
12–17 is a good example:

Yet God my King is from old,
working salvation in the midst of the earth.
Thou didst divide the sea by thy might;
thou didst break the heads of the dragons on the waters.
Thou didst crush the heads of Leviathan,

thou didst give him as food for the creatures of the wilderness.
Thou didst cleave open springs and brooks;
   thou didst dry up ever-flowing streams.
Thine is the day, thine is also the night;
   thou hast established the luminaries and the sun.
Thou hast fixed all the bounds of the earth;
   thou hast made summer and winter.

Psalms 89, 93, 95–100 contain other examples, as, in a prophetic dress, does Isaiah 52:7–10. Genesis 1 probably goes back to the same way of thinking, although there God's enemies have been deprived of their power and their personality, and the climax is sabbath rest instead of enthronement. In the present context, God's victory includes his past defeat of the Egyptians which led to the creation of Israel (see 51:9–10), as well as the primeval struggle which led to the creation of heaven and earth. And it implies the future defeat of the Babylonians and the "new creation" of which we have been speaking.

Verses 22–23 contain some interesting time terminology. The author uses it here to praise God and restore his people's faith. Ecclesiastes draws very different conclusions from the same phenomena, as in 3:11 (NEB):

He [God] has made everything to suit its time; moreover he has given men a sense of time past and future, but no comprehension of God's work from beginning to end.

Verse 22 of Isaiah 41 contains four terms which came to have a precise philosophical meaning. The *first* term, the verb translated "happen", belongs to the same way of thinking as Ecclesiastes' famous poem beginning "For everything there is a season, and a time for every matter under heaven" (3:1–9). The word for "fate" comes from the same root (Eccl. 2:14), and further emphasizes the point that, whatever happens, only God knows why. The *second* term is "the former things". This must denote, in the light of what we have been arguing so far, everything since creation, and again it is in the Wisdom literature that we get a clue to what is meant. Job chapter 38, like Ecclesiastes chapters 1–3, applies the same argument to the contrast between man and God (see 38:4):

> Where were you when I laid the foundation of the earth?
> Tell me, if you have any understanding.

The *third* of these time words, translated "their outcome", originally simply meant, "what comes later", virtually indistinguishable from its parallel in the next line, "the things to come". But in the light of such influential passages as the Blessing of Jacob (Gen. 49:1), Balaam's "Star prophecy" (Num. 24:14), the Zion prophecy in Isaiah 2:2 (also Mic. 4:1) and Daniel's eschatological visions (8:19; 10:14), texts like this were soon understood to refer to the end of time: "how things will end" corresponding to "how things began". *Fourth* and finally "the things to come" returns to familiar prophetic language concerning prediction, which, according to Mosaic law (Deut. 18: 21–22), was the proper criterion for distinguishing between true and false prophecy.

The verdict on the impotent gods is expressed in two ways. One is by a series of words for "nothing", "delusion", or the like: there are six of them, two in verse 24 and four in verse 29. In verse 24, "nothing" means simply something that does not exist: it occurs no less than five times in verses 26 and 28 as well. It is the word translated "there is none" in all those emphatic monotheistic statements in chapter 45 and elsewhere to which we have already drawn attention (vv. 5–6, 14, 21–22, *etc*). Other gods just do not exist. The word translated "naught" occurs only here in the Bible. Some maintain that it is a scribal error for that reason, but, whether or not it started life in that way, it has the effect of building up a case against the false gods to almost absurd proportions. "Abomination" comes from the context of cultic and social legislation (*eg* Lev. 20:13; Deut. 24:4; Isa. 1:13).

The *first* of the four "nothing" words in verse 29 ("delusion") is associated above all with the expression "evildoers" in the Psalms (*eg* 5:5; 6:8; 14:4; 28:3, *etc*), where it certainly suggests danger and sinister power. In Isaianic idiom it appears in the phrases "iniquitous decrees" (Isa. 10:1; cf. 32:6), "the unrighteous man" (55:7), and "an idol" (66:3). The translation "delusion" is an attempt to capture the idea that the seeming power of the false gods is an illusion: in fact they do not exist. The *second* word is the numeral "zero": thus their works are of no account. *Third* and *fourth*, in the phrase "empty wind" are the two most colourful terms in the series, literally "wind" and "formlessness". Ecclesiastes uses the former: "Behold, all is vanity and a striving after wind" (1:14, 17, *etc*). The latter, from Genesis 1:2, removes the false gods from the rank of creator, and places them instead in the primeval chaos that preceded creation. The hyperbole by which the author refutes their claims is a model of prophetic rhetoric: who now would put their faith in such idols?

The other way in which the verdict against idols is expressed brings in Cyrus (v. 25), the "one from the north" (see above on v. 2). There is a story that Croesus, king of Lydia, consulted an oracle before engaging in battle with Cyrus. He was told that if he fought, he would destroy a great empire. But of course the oracle meant his own, and in 547 B.C. Cyrus conquered Lydia. It is not impossible that this passage indirectly alludes to that story, and makes an additional point that, as well as engineering Cyrus' victories, the Lord knew the course of history beforehand, unlike Croesus and his advisers.

Verse 27 in Hebrew reads literally: "First to Zion, behold, behold them, and to Jerusalem I give a herald of good tidings". This implies that news of Cyrus' victories, and indeed of all God's mighty acts, reaches his own people first:

> Surely the Lord God does nothing,
> without revealing his secret
> to his servants the prophets.

> (Amos 3:7)

These are the words of a people secure in their faith.

"He shall call on my name" (v. 25) implies that Cyrus too will recognize the supremacy of the Lord, as he does in Chronicles (2 Chron. 36:23; cf. Ezra 1:2), and as the "coastlands" will (41:5), and eventually the whole world will (11:9; 49:6), "beginning from Jerusalem" (Luke 24:47).

A LIGHT TO THE NATIONS—I

Isaiah 42:1–13

[1]Behold my servant, whom I uphold,
  my chosen, in whom my soul delights;
 I have put my Spirit upon him,
  he will bring forth justice to the nations.
[2]He will not cry or lift up his voice,
  or make it heard in the street;
[3]a bruised reed he will not break,
  and a dimly burning wick he will not quench;
  he will faithfully bring forth justice.
[4]He will not fail or be discouraged
  till he has established justice in the earth;
  and the coastlands wait for his law.

[5]Thus says God, the Lord,
  who created the heavens and stretched them out,
  who spread forth the earth and what comes from it,
 who gives breath to the people upon it
  and spirit to those who walk in it:
[6]"I am the Lord, I have called you in righteousness,
  I have taken you by the hand and kept you;
 I have given you as a covenant to the people,
  a light to the nations,
[7] to open the eyes that are blind,
 to bring out the prisoners from the dungeon,
  from the prison those who sit in darkness.
[8]I am the Lord, that is my name;
  my glory I give to no other,
  nor my praise to graven images.
[9]Behold, the former things have come to pass,
  and new things I now declare;
 before they spring forth
  I tell you of them."

[10]Sing to the Lord a new song,
  his praise from the end of the earth!
 Let the sea roar and all that fills it,
  the coastlands and their inhabitants.

¹¹Let the desert and its cities lift up their voice,
    the villages that Kedar inhabits;
  let the inhabitants of Sela sing for joy,
    let them shout from the top of the mountains.
¹²Let them give glory to the Lord,
    and declare his praise in the coastlands.
¹³The Lord goes forth like a mighty man,
    like a man of war he stirs up his fury;
  he cries out, he shouts aloud,
    he shows himself mighty against his foes.

One of the major Isaianic themes, introduced in chapter 1 and appearing at memorable points all through the book, is the plight of the poor and vulnerable:

seek justice,
  correct oppression;
defend the fatherless,
  plead for the widow.
                   (Isa. 1:17; cf. 11:1–9; 26:6; 35:5–6; 61:1–2)

The *first* and *second* parts in this section contain two more excellent examples: the servant of the Lord's mission is to "[establish] justice in the earth" (vv. 1–4), and to be "a light to the nations" (vv. 5–9). Just as the lamb and the kid and the little child in chapter 11 are protected in the new age from the savagery of wolves and leopards, so now the servant will discriminate in favour of the poor, who are fragile as a "bruised reed", and those with hardly a spark of hope, like a flickering lamp in which the wick has all but burnt out (v. 3). He will "open the eyes that are blind" and "bring out the prisoners from the dungeon" (v. 7) (cf. 35:5–6; 61:1–2). Who the servant is matters very much less than what he does, as the magnificent hymn of praise and thanksgiving, which constitutes the *third* part of the section (vv. 10ff.) indicates. It is God's will to bring good news to the poor and to bind up the broken-hearted (61:1–2 quoted in Luke 4), and that is cause for universal jubilation (v. 10):

Sing to the Lord a new song,
  his praise from the end of the earth.

The *first* prophecy (vv. 1–4) is reminiscent of the Messianic language of chapter 11, and of some of the Royal psalms, such as 2, 45, 72, 89, 110 and 132. The servant is God's "chosen one" (Ps. 89:3; see also 1 Chron. 28:5), in whom he is well pleased (Mark 1:11). The "spirit" of God will rest upon him, and chapter 11 explains what that means: "the spirit of wisdom and under-standing, the spirit of counsel and might, the spirit of knowledge and the fear of the Lord" (11:2); "with righteousness he shall judge the poor..." (11:4; cf. Ps. 72:1–4).

This passage is usually taken along with the other three so-called "servant songs" (49:1–6; 50:3–9; 52:13–53:12); these four passages being regarded as special "Messianic" composi-tions. Chapter 42:1–4 would then introduce this special servant, and his later life story would be told in the three subsequent poems. Its link with these later passages, however, is tenuous, and the force of its present context should not be overlooked. Following on from chapter 41, and taking into account later passages like 44:28 and 45:1–4, the author—and the reader—must surely have Cyrus in mind as the primary agent of God's justice and salvation for the nations in the author's own day. But it is entirely natural that Jews and Christians should also apply such language to him who fulfils their Messianic expectations (*eg* Matt. 12:18–21; Mark 1:11), long after Cyrus was dead and buried.

Verse 2 is commonly understood to imply that the Messiah will be a humble, gentle person, rather than a conquering hero; an interpretation which may have been influenced by such familiar texts as Zechariah 9:9 (Matt. 21:5; John 12:15), or Isaiah 53:7–9. But originally it probably meant, "there will be no crying or lifting up of the voice...in the street". In other words, no-one in the Messianic kingdom will be heard crying for help: everyone will be safe and content. Revelation 21:4 is a good parallel.

The *second* prophecy (vv. 5–9) is introduced by the formula, "Thus says God, the Lord", a unique variant of the usual "Thus says the Lord", coupled with a kind of creed, a concise statement of faith in God as Creator of heaven and earth and all that is therein, not forgetting the two most important elements in creation; the *breath of life* and the *human spirit* (see 1 Kings 10:5 for an illustration of this meaning of "spirit"). The prophecy is addressed by God to his servant, but this time the language seems to recall texts like 41:8–10, where the servant is Israel. Some commentators, ancient and modern, conclude that verses 1–4 are also about Israel, not the Messiah. Certainly we should try to maintain the sense of continuity between verses 1–4 and 5–9: it is the same Lord, and there is the same objective, "to bring forth justice to the nations" (v. 1) or "to bring out the prisoners from the dungeon" (v. 7). On "righteousness" (v. 6) see 41:21.

The word "covenant" (v. 6) is relatively rare in Isaiah, occurring only four times in chapters 40–55; twice in the phrase, "a covenant to the people" (42:6; 49:8). The other two occurrences (54:10; 55:3), together with the occurrence of the word in the patriarchal stories (*eg* Gen. 15), give us the key to how it is to be understood here. It means an act of divine compassion: what God promised to Abraham and David is to be extended to the rest of the world. The "people" (v. 6) clearly refers back to the people upon the earth in the previous verse, and the tortuous attempts to explain the phrase otherwise (*eg* "a covenant people" or "a vision to the peoples" or "a light to all peoples", NEB) are unnecessary. Like the grandiloquent phrase, "a light to the nations", it takes up the theme of chapter 2: "out of Zion shall go forth the law . . .". "Those who sit in darkness" (v. 7) recalls the imagery of 9:1–7 as well.

The hymn in verses 10–13 responds to the idea of something totally new happening in verse 9; see also 43:18–19, 65:17 and Revelation 21:1–2. It is written in the style of the Enthronement psalms which celebrate the Lord's victory over the powers of chaos (*eg* Pss. 96; 98); see the commentary on 41:21ff. Those who go down to the sea (v. 10) (RSV "Let the sea roar" is an emendation derived from Pss. 96:11 and 98:7), like the sailors on Jonah's ship (Jon. 1:14–16), join with the people of the coastlands and of the desert (v. 11) in worshipping the Lord. For the fabulous cities of the Arabian desert, such as Palmyra and Petra, see 21:16 (vol. 1, p. 188).

The battle images in verse 13 allude to the Song of the Sea in Exodus 15, itself modelled on the Enthronement Psalms. God's victory over primeval chaos (Ps. 93), the Egyptians (Exod. 15), Babylon (Isa. 47) or, for that matter, death (Isa. 25:8) and the Devil (Rev. 20:7–10), is celebrated in the words, "The Lord will reign for ever and ever" (Exod. 15:18; Rev. 22:5).

The term translated here "fury" (v. 13) is the same as the one translated "zeal" in 9:7, 37:32 and also, in a marvellously wistful vision of God the Father, in 63:15–16. It denotes the sheer energy and dynamism that distinguishes the power of God—and that of those who believe in him—from false gods and their devotees. The prophet summons us to join in the New Exodus which, by God's power, will bring us through the weakness (v. 3) and darkness (v. 7) of our present plight, and into the Promised Land.

GOD AS MOTHER

Isaiah 42:14–25

¹⁴For a long time I have held my peace,
    I have kept still and restrained myself;
now I will cry out like a woman in travail,
    I will gasp and pant.
¹⁵I will lay waste mountains and hills,
    and dry up all their herbage;
I will turn the rivers into islands,
    and dry up the pools.
¹⁶And I will lead the blind
    in a way that they know not,
in paths that they have not known
    I will guide them.
I will turn the darkness before them into light,
    the rough places into level ground.
These are the things I will do,
    and I will not forsake them.
¹⁷They shall be turned back and utterly put to shame,
    who trust in graven images,

who say to molten images,
  "You are our gods."

18Hear, you deaf;
  and look, you blind, that you may see!
19Who is blind but my servant,
  or deaf as my messenger whom I send?
Who is blind as my dedicated one,
  or blind as the servant of the Lord?
20He sees many things, but does not observe them;
  his ears are open, but he does not hear.
21The Lord was pleased, for his righteousness' sake,
  to magnify his law and make it glorious.
22But this is a people robbed and plundered,
  they are all of them trapped in holes
  and hidden in prisons;
they have become a prey with none to rescue,
  a spoil with none to say, "Restore!"
23Who among you will give ear to this,
  will attend and listen for the time to come?
24Who gave up Jacob to the spoiler,
  and Israel to the robbers?
Was it not the Lord, against whom we have sinned,
  in whose ways they would not walk,
  and whose law they would not obey?
25So he poured upon him the heat of his anger
  and the might of battle;
it set him on fire round about, but he did not understand;
  it burned him, but he did not take it to heart.

Picking up a theme from the previous prophecy, before the hymn
in verses 10–13, the last part of chapter 42 focusses on blindness
(see above vv. 6 and 7). It consists of two sections. The *first* is a
prophecy in which a new age is envisaged when the blind will see
light and go along paths they had not thought possible before
(vv. 14–17), and the *second* explains in truly Isaianic idiom what
that blindness refers to (vv. 18–25).

The prophecy first begins with the striking image of God as a
mother, gasping, panting and crying out in the pains of childbirth.
This is one of the verses which may be quoted as an antidote to the

predominantly masculine imagery of God in the Bible. Deuteronomy 32:18 is another, as are the beautiful images of the "Spirit" (a feminine noun) of God, hovering like a bird over the face of the waters at the beginning of Genesis (1:2); and that of God as an eagle "fluttering" (RSV; it is the same word as in Gen. 1:2) over her young at the end of Deuteronomy (32:11), *ie* at the beginning and end of the *Torah* (Law). It is also worth remembering in this connection that, according to Genesis 1:27, God created both male and female "in his own image". Here in Isaiah 42, as in Romans 8:22, the birth of a new age is painful, especially for the one who gives it birth. It is perhaps significant that several words for "love" and "compassion" in Hebrew are related to the word for "womb" and have in them the concept of a mother's love. As the seven year old daughter of a colleague told me once, "God is mother and father of us all".

The pain and agony of change is further described in terms of laying waste to mountains, drying up the grass, and turning rivers into islands (v. 15). But it leads to new possibilities: the blind will be able to go to places they have never been to before, their darkness will be changed into light, and rough places will be made level for their safety (v. 16). As in our society, institutions go to considerable expense to build ramps for wheel-chairs and to design special routes for the disabled; in a like manner, God will care for his people.

Verse 17 gives the tragic other side of the picture: the more appealing the images of heaven, the more distasteful the images of Hell: look at my comments on 25:6–12 (vol. 1, pp. 213–214) and, later, on 49:23 and 26.

The *second* section answers the question: who are the blind? In verse 18 the prophet recalls the hard words of chapter 6 (v. 9):

Hear and hear, but do not understand;
see and see, but do not perceive.

He makes it clear that he is thinking of his own people, unreceptive and faithless as ever. Israel, the servant of the Lord, sees but does not observe; his ears are open but he does not hear (v. 20).

In verse 19, three terms are applied to the people of God.

Although blind and deaf, Israel is nevertheless the servant of the Lord, chosen and not cast off (41:8–9). He is also "my messenger" (*malachi* in Hebrew), sent into the world like Malachi (Mal. 3:1), and Isaiah himself (6:8–9), with a message to be a "light to the nations" (42:6). In 6:9ff., the prophet is sent to his people with a message of doom; now he bears a message of hope. The last term, translated "my dedicated one" (RSV), is actually a proper name, "Meshullam", quite frequent in the family trees at the beginning of Chronicles, where it is the name of a son of the Davidic king, Zerubbabel (1 Chron. 3:19), and of a son of Zadok, a priest (1 Chron. 9:11). It probably means simply "hired" or "commissioned" (NEB). On the basis of its obvious etymological connection with *shalom* ("peace") it has been explained as, "the one who has been granted my covenant of peace", but this is unlikely, however theologically attractive. Another suggestion is, "the one for whom God has paid the price", alluding to passages like 40:2 and 43:3.

Verses 21–25 provide a historical account of how the people came to be in their present plight. God chose them and gave them his law, his *Torah*, at Sinai (v. 21). But they sinned against him and did not obey his law (v. 24), and that is why they have now been "robbed and plundered" (v. 22). God punished them by war and fire, but they would not take it to heart (v. 25). Of course the fire in verse 25 recalls the siege of Jerusalem in 586 B.C.:

And they burned the house of God, and broke down the wall of Jerusalem, and burned all its palaces with fire, and destroyed all its precious vessels.

(2 Chron. 36:19; see also 2 Kings 25:9)

In the more theological and poetic language of Lamentations we have (4:11; cf. 2:3–5):

The Lord gave full vent to his wrath,
he poured out his hot anger;
and he kindled a fire in Zion,
which consumed its foundations.

The stern message of these verses, more characteristic of eighth century prophecy than their present context, is softened by the prophecies of hope, both before and after, that the time of punishment is ended, and by the note of repentance in verse 24: "We have sinned". Even the godless Ninevites were forgiven when they repented (Jon. 3:10; 4:11): how much more the people of God! Most important of all, this interpretation of history, according to which even catastrophes like the fall of Jerusalem are interpreted as part of God's plan, means that God is in control; and therefore there is no reason ever to despair. Even the blind have hope, if God loves us and suffers for us like a mother.

I AM YOUR SAVIOUR

Isaiah 43:1–13

¹But now thus says the Lord,
    he who created you, O Jacob,
    he who formed you, O Israel:
 "Fear not, for I have redeemed you;
    I have called you by name, you are mine.
²When you pass through the waters I will be with you;
    and through the rivers, they shall not overwhelm you;
 when you walk through fire you shall not be burned,
    and the flame shall not consume you.
³For I am the Lord your God,
    the Holy One of Israel, your Saviour.
 I give Egypt as your ransom,
    Ethiopia and Seba in exchange for you.
⁴Because you are precious in my eyes,
    and honoured, and I love you,
 I give men in return for you,
    peoples in exchange for your life.
⁵Fear not, for I am with you;
    I will bring your offspring from the east,
    and from the west I will gather you;
⁶I will say to the north, Give up,
    and to the south, Do not withhold;
 bring my sons from afar
    and my daughters from the end of the earth,

⁷every one who is called by my name,
  whom I created for my glory,
  whom I formed and made."

⁸Bring forth the people who are blind, yet have eyes,
  who are deaf, yet have ears!
⁹Let all the nations gather together,
  and let the peoples assemble.
 Who among them can declare this,
  and show us the former things?
 Let them bring their witnesses to justify them,
  and let them hear and say, It is true.
¹⁰"You are my witnesses," says the Lord,
  "and my servant whom I have chosen,
 that you may know and believe me
  and understand that I am He.
 Before me no god was formed,
  nor shall there be any after me.
¹¹I, I am the Lord,
  and besides me there is no saviour.
¹²I declared and saved and proclaimed,
  when there was no strange god among you;
  and you are my witnesses," says the Lord.
¹³"I am God, and also henceforth I am He;
  there is none who can deliver from my hand;
  I work and who can hinder it?"

Another salvation oracle (see on 41:8–10) is introduced by the usual formula, "Thus says the Lord", but also by the emotive, "But now", like Paul's "But now [*ie* as things are in the new age]" (*eg* Gal. 3:25). Again the formation of Israel out of the chaos of oppression is compared to an act of creation (see on 51:9–10).

"Fear not" is the *first* element in the salvation oracle, and references to what God has done for his people in the past is the *second*. Here legal terminology is applied, as so often in Biblical language, to these mighty acts of God. At first he "redeemed" his people; that is to say, rescued them or protected them as their kinsman in law (cf. Ruth chs. 2–4). Next, he named them, as their legal parent or guardian (*eg* Gen. 21:3; 41:51–52; Isa. 7:14). Last, he ransomed them (vv. 3–4). Many other legal terms are applied to the saving actions of God: "covenant", "righteousness", "vindicate" (*eg* Ps. 43:1), and "contend" (Ps. 35:1) are a few examples.

"Saviour" (vv. 3 and 11) is another word with legal connections (*eg* Deut. 22:27; "deliverer", or better, "saviour", or "judge"; Judg. 3:9 parallel to Judg. 2:16, 17). Verse 12 indicates that "saving" can consist of speaking up on behalf of someone like an advocate in a court of law. Two passages from Samuel and Kings make the legal associations of the verb "to save" even more obvious. In these passages, people in legal disputes appeal to the king for justice in the formula, "Help, my lord, O king!" (2 Kings 6:26; 2 Sam. 14:4). This formula then appears in the language of prayer addressed to God (*eg* Ps. 118:25), and, because of the certainty that God, and God alone, will answer the prayer, the formula functions even as a cry of triumph, "Hosanna!" (*eg* Matt. 21:9, 15).

Verse 2 alludes to Israel's victory at the Red Sea (Exod. chs. 14–15), but the word "rivers" points to realities beyond history. It is the word used in the Enthronement psalms (*eg* 93), translated "floods", symbol of all that is evil in the world, and conquered by God (see the comments on 41:21ff.). Similarly no doubt the "fire" in the same verse alludes to the "iron furnace" of Egyptian slavery and oppression (Deut. 4:20; Isa. 48:10; Jer. 11:4), and to the siege of Jerusalem just referred to in 42:25; but again it goes beyond that to include the "burning fiery furnace" of suffering and martyrdom (*eg* Dan. 3) in all ages. It can even be interpreted as an instrument for testing or refining us, as, for example, in Psalm 66:10, 12:

> For thou, O God, hast tested us;
>   thou hast tried us as silver is tried . . .
> thou didst let men ride over our heads;
>   we went through fire and through water;
> yet thou hast brought us forth to a spacious place.

Verses 3–4 represent the "Saviour" arranging a legal transaction by which Cyrus is to get Egypt, with Ethiopia and Seba to the south thrown in, in exchange for Israel's freedom. From a historical point of view, it was actually not Cyrus, but his son Cambyses who conquered Egypt in 525 B.C. But as an expression of God's love for his people, "precious in his eyes, and honoured" (v. 4), the prophecy serves its purpose well. God goes to endless lengths to get his people back from exile.

The ingathering of the exiles (vv. 5–6) is a favourite theme of "Deutero-Isaiah" (see also 49:12, 18, 22), and one which again transcends the facts of ancient history, since not until modern times did the Jews of the Diaspora return to Israel in large numbers. Since the Zionist movements of the last century, such texts have been applied to the immigration of Jews from South America, China, the United States, Russia and almost every other part of the world. The word translated "gather" in verse 5 is derived from the same root as the modern Hebrew word *kibbutz* or "collective settlement".

The trial speech in verses 8–13 develops the legal imagery of verses 3–4 and uses it to argue that there is no saviour apart from the Lord. Whereas his people were blind, now they see (v. 8), and are now witnesses before the nations of the world, to bear witness to his unique saving power. Notice the contrast between "deliver" (v. 13), used of unbelievers and false gods, and "save" and "saviour", used almost exclusively of "God" (v. 11): see the commentary on 37:11–12, 20.

"Believe" in verse 10, alongside "understand [and see]", picks up a major Isaianic theme from the earlier chapters of the book: "the faithful city" in chapter 1, for instance, or the famous pun in 7:9, or the beautiful prophecy in 30:15:

In returning and rest you shall be saved;
in quietness and trust shall be your strength.

Verses 10–13 constitute one of the most emphatic statements of monotheism in these chapters (like ch. 45). *First*, they deny that any man-made object can be a god (v. 10), and then, *second*, state that there is no other "saviour" (*ie* god) apart from the Lord. Unlike Islam, where the denial of the existence of other gods is a central doctrine, even appearing as it does on the flag of some Islamic countries, Old Testament theology is not so much concerned with the status of other gods beside Yahweh, as with single-minded commitment and devotion to him. The *Shema*, chief daily prayer of Jews to this day, sums this up as follows:

> Hear, O Israel: The Lord our God, the Lord is one, and you shall love the Lord your God with all your heart ....
>
> (Deut. 6:4–5)

The word "one" comes from the language of love-poetry, such as the Song of Solomon (6:9), rather than from philosophical discourse. To love God, to trust him completely, is to love him and trust him as though he were the only one in existence. Idols and false gods are irrelevant.

THE NEW EXODUS

Isaiah 43:14–28

14Thus says the Lord,
>   your Redeemer, the Holy One of Israel:
>   "For your sake I will send to Babylon
>   and break down all the bars,
>   and the shouting of the Chaldeans will be turned to lamentations.
15I am the Lord, your Holy One,
>   the Creator of Israel, your King."
16Thus says the Lord,
>   who makes a way in the sea,
>   a path in the mighty waters,
17who brings forth chariot and horse,
>   army and warrior;
>   they lie down, they cannot rise,
>   they are extinguished, quenched like a wick:
18"Remember not the former things,
>   nor consider the things of old.
19Behold, I am doing a new thing;
>   now it springs forth, do you not perceive it?
>   I will make a way in the wilderness
>   and rivers in the desert.
20The wild beasts will honour me,
>   the jackals and the ostriches;

for I give water in the wilderness,
    rivers in the desert,
to give drink to my chosen people,
²¹ the people whom I formed for myself
that they might declare my praise.

²²"Yet you did not call upon me, O Jacob;
    but you have been weary of me, O Israel!
²³You have not brought me your sheep for burnt offerings,
    or honoured me with your sacrifices.
I have not burdened you with offerings,
    or wearied you with frankincense.
²⁴You have not bought me sweet cane with money,
    or satisfied me with the fat of your sacrifices.
But you have burdened me with your sins,
    you have wearied me with your iniquities.

²⁵"I, I am He
    who blots out your transgressions for my own sake,
    and I will not remember your sins.
²⁶Put me in remembrance, let us argue together;
    set forth your case, that you may be proved right.
²⁷Your first father sinned,
    and your mediators transgressed against me.
²⁸Therefore I profaned the princes of the sanctuary,
    I delivered Jacob to utter destruction
    and Israel to reviling."

The short prophecy on the fall of Babylon in verses 14–15, introduced by a characteristic formula (compare it with 42:5 and 43:1), contains an unusually colourful scene, so unusual that modern commentators and translators (including RSV, NEB) modify it by emending the text. In addition to the surprise appearance of a besieging army ("I will send to Babylon"), the Hebrew text seems to describe the panicking Babylonians (or Chaldeans, as they are often called) fleeing in ships. It reads literally (cf. AV):

For your sake I sent to Babylon,
    and I defeated them all as they fled,
    the Chaldeans shouting in the ships.

No doubt details in the original description of an event as yet in the future, were modified by what actually happened. According to Herodotus, during the siege of Babylon Cyrus diverted the Euphrates so that his troops could enter the city along the river bed. There may be allusions to this tradition in Jeremiah's spectacular taunt-song about Babylon (chs. 50–51):

> O you who dwell by many waters,
>   rich in treasures,
> your end has come,
>   the thread of your life is cut (51:13)

> A drought upon her waters,
>   that they may be dried up! (50:38)

> . . . his city is taken on every side;
>   the fords have been seized,
> the bulwarks are burned with fire,
>   and the soldiers are in panic (51:31–32)

We must remember that we are not dealing with history, but with prophecy; and that being so, perhaps the most illuminating texts for comparison are the story of Balshazzar's feast in Daniel 5, and the vision of St John in Revelation 18:

> Fallen, fallen is Babylon the great!
> . . . .
> And in her was found the blood of prophets and of saints,
>   and of all who have been slain on the earth.
>
> (Rev. 18:2, 24)

Babylon came to be a symbol of all that is godless and materialist—(see Ps. 137) and its downfall became a symbol of victory for the faithful. Hence the more conventional parts of this short prophecy—"for your sake" (v. 14)—removes the event from the context of ancient history and applies it to the experience of the living community. It is a demonstration of God's creative power, and so he is hailed as "your King" (v. 15), as in the Song of the Sea (Exod. 15) and the Enthronement psalms (*eg* Ps. 93).

Verses 15–21 break new ground in Biblical tradition. Instead of celebrating or reliving the Passover, as is done by Jews every spring-time to this day, the prophet calls upon them to forget

the old story of the Red Sea miracle (v. 16) and the defeat of
Pharaoh's horses and chariots (v. 17). A New Exodus through the
wilderness is about to happen, and rivers are going to appear in
the desert "to give drink to my chosen people" (vv. 18–20).
Coupled with verses 14–15, this refers to an exodus from the
Babylonian captivity (48:20–21 is another example), but it can
also express the hopes of the "Church of the Poor" in parts of
Latin America, and of Jews in the Soviet Union, today. For
commentary on the contrast between the old Exodus and the
new, see also 41:17–20.

The next section (vv. 22–28) suggests that an exodus from the
slavery of sin and punishment is also included in these prophecies.
The God who brings back his people from exile in Babylon,
brings them back also from the captivity of sin (v. 25). Sin is
defined, as in earlier prophetic tradition (*eg* Isa. 1; Amos 4) in
ritual terms. With extreme irony the prophet charges his people
with having failed to satisfy God with the elaborate rituals of the
Temple: "burnt-offerings", in which the whole beast is ritually
burnt; "sacrifices", in which part of the beast is burnt, but most of
it eaten in a communion meal (see Lev. 7:15–18); "offerings",
which are of grain or wine or anything else apart from beasts
(Lev. 2); and "frankincense" and "sweet cane", luxury imports
used in the making of incense (for which the recipe is given in
Exod. 30:34–38). Jeremiah uses the same argument, without the
irony (Jer. 6:20):

> To what purpose does frankincense come to me from Sheba,
>   or sweet cane from a distant land?
> Your burnt offerings are not acceptable,
>   nor your sacrifices pleasing to me.

The author's purpose is made clear in verses 27–28, where the
destruction of the Temple establishment is attributed to a more
fundamental cause; the sin of "your first father". The most natural way of taking this is as a reference to what happened in the
Garden of Eden (Gen. 3), a universal phenomenon as in Job
(4:17–19):

Can mortal man be righteous before God?
    Can a man be pure before his Maker?
Even in his servants he puts no trust,
    and his angels he charges with error;
how much more those who dwell in houses of clay . . .

But probably we are intended to think rather of Israel's own
tragic history, and therefore of Jacob, who from the beginning
was a cheat, just as from the beginning, God's people, the twelve
sons of Jacob, were dishonest and faithless. Hosea makes a similar point, alluding to the story of how Jacob "supplanted" Esau
his elder brother (Gen. 25:21–34; Hos. 12:2–4). With such a
father, it would have been hard for Israel to be anything other
than sinful.

The "mediators" probably include, *first*, the prophets, who
with a few notable exceptions, led Israel astray. There is a tale of
how, in the days of Jehoshaphat, the king of Judah, four hundred
prophets prophesied lies, and only one the truth (1 Kings 22). The
same could be said, *second* and *third*, of Israel's kings and priests
as well. However, this is not brought up here primarily as a
rebuke, but as an explanation of why Jerusalem was lying in ruins,
an explanation that gave hope, since the punishment was now
over and a New Exodus about to begin.

OUR ROCK AND OUR REDEEMER

Isaiah 44:1–8

1"But now hear, O Jacob my servant,
    Israel whom I have chosen!
2Thus says the Lord who made you,
    who formed you from the womb and will help you:
 Fear not, O Jacob my servant,
    Jeshurun whom I have chosen.
3For I will pour water on the thirsty land,
    and streams on the dry ground;
 I will pour my Spirit upon your descendants,
    and my blessing on your offspring.

⁴They shall spring up like grass amid waters,
>   like willows by flowing streams.
⁵This one will say, 'I am the Lord's,'
>   another will call himself by the name of Jacob,
>   and another will write on his hand, 'The Lord's,'
>   and surname himself by the name of Israel."

⁶Thus says the Lord, the King of Israel
>   and his Redeemer, the Lord of hosts:
>   "I am the first and I am the last;
>   besides me there is no god.
⁷Who is like me? Let him proclaim it,
>   let him declare and set it forth before me.
> Who has announced from of old the things to come?
>   Let them tell us what is yet to be.
⁸Fear not, nor be afraid;
>   have I not told you from of old and declared it?
>   And you are my witnesses!
> Is there a God besides me?
>   There is no Rock; I know not any."

"But now", that is to say (as in 43:1), in the new age, descendants of sinful Jacob (43:27–28), are addressed in the comfortable words of a salvation oracle. Whatever they have done in the past, they are still God's "servant", chosen by him, made by him. "From the womb" (v. 2) means even before they were born, just as, even before Jeremiah was born, he was appointed as a prophet to the nations (Jer. 1:5), and Paul was set apart to "preach him [Christ] among the Gentiles" (Gal. 1:15–16).

"Fear not" (v. 2) is a regular motif in this type of oracle, as we have seen (41:8–10; 14–16). "Jeshurun" is a rare name for Israel. Like the image of God as a Rock (44:8) and as a mother (42:14), and the explicit monotheism (*eg* 43:10–11), and other expressions in these chapters, "Jeshurun" appears only here and in the poems at the end of Deuteronomy (Deut. 32 and 33):

> There is none like God, O Jeshurun,
>   who rides through the heavens to your help,
>   and in his majesty through the skies.

(33:26)

Associated as it is with sinful Jacob (43:27), both here and in Deuteronomy 32:15, perhaps the name carries sinful overtones. Alternatively, since it seems to be connected with words for "straight" and "upright" (*eg* Job 1:1), it could be intended to balance Jacob, a name associated with words for "crooked" and "deceitful" (*eg* Jer. 17:9). Either way, the point is that God showed his love to Israel "while [they] were yet sinners" (Rom. 5:8), and that by his grace, "the crooked [*ie* Jacob] shall be made straight [*ie* Jeshurun], and the rough places plain" (40:4, AV).

Verses 3–5 of Isaiah 44 contain the *third* element in the salvation oracle, namely God's promise. They recall the promise to Abraham and his seed for ever:

> And I will make of you a great nation, and I will bless you, and make your name great, so that you will be a blessing . . . and by you all the families of the earth shall bless themselves.
>
> (Gen. 12:2–3)

Verse 3 speaks of the growth of a nation: to use another famous image from the same century, out of the valley of dry bones "an exceedingly great host" arises (Ezek. 37:10). The dry ground here means the dry bones of Israel, stranded in a foreign land without hope; and the streams that revitalize them are the "Spirit" of God and his blessing (v. 3). The spirit of God brings life to the dying—cf. the following:

> I will put my Spirit within you, and you shall live, and I will place you in your own land.
>
> (Ezek. 37:14)

To understand the next term—"blessing"—we may look at the lists of blessings that await God's people when they obey the covenant:

> And all these blessings shall come upon you and overtake you, if you obey the voice of the Lord your God. Blessed shall you be in the city, and blessed shall you be in the field. Blessed shall be the fruit of your body, and the fruit of your ground, and the fruit of your beasts, the

increase of your cattle, and the young of your flock. Blessed shall be your basket and your kneading-trough. Blessed shall you be when you come in, and blessed shall you be when you go out.

(Deut. 28:2–6)

In the new age, their "warfare ended" and their "iniquity pardoned" (40:2), all this will be theirs.

Verse 5 goes beyond the boundaries of Israel and envisages citizens of the world acknowledging the Lord as their God. The sacred name *Yahweh*, rendered "the Lord" in most modern English translations, and known as the *tetragrammaton* because it is spelt with four letters in Hebrew, embodies the essence of Old Testament theology, as the name *Jesus* does in the New (Eph. 1:21; Phil. 2:9–10); and to bear it, written on one's hand as here, or on one's forehead as in the Apocalypse (Rev. 14:1; 22:4), symbolizes commitment to him and membership of his people Israel.

The trial speech in verses 6–8 contains familiar themes already discussed: the kingship of God; the Redeemer metaphor; monotheism; and God's control of history. "The Lord of hosts" (v. 6), however, is rare in "Deutero-Isaiah": it recalls Isaiah's vision of God's Temple and the members of his heavenly court (6:3), as well as "the heavens and the earth . . . and all the host of them" within the created universe (Gen. 2:1; Isa. 40:26).

The other new term here is the "Rock" (v. 8), a frequent image for God, especially in the Psalms (*eg* 18:2, 31, 46; 19:14; 28:1; 62:2, 6) and Deuteronomy 32:4, 15, 18, 30–31. It comes nearer to English "bedrock" or *terra firma* or even "ground" (Prov. 30:19), than to the isolated rock of refuge in a stormy sea. It is the base on which a wise builder lays his foundations (Matt. 7:24), and hence the name "Peter", the rock on which Jesus founded the Church (Matt. 16:18). In the Exodus imagery, the Rock also provides water in the wilderness (Exod. 17:6; Ps. 105:41; Isa. 48:21), and in a memorable passage quoted above in connection with 42:14ff., the Rock is like a mother to Israel (Deut. 32:18).

Verse 7 in Hebrew contains a detail of the creation story, removed by the RSV translators. It reads literally:

Let him declare it and set it all before me,
from the time when I placed the ancient people there.

In other words, can anyone else apart from God claim to understand the whole of human history, from the beginning up to the present, since the time he placed Adam in the garden of Eden (Gen. 1:8), "rejoicing in his inhabited world and delighting in the sons of men" (Prov. 8:31)?

THE FOLLY OF IDOLS

Isaiah 44:9–20

9All who make idols are nothing, and the things they delight in do not profit; their witnesses neither see nor know, that they may be put to shame. 10Who fashions a god or casts an image, that is profitable for nothing? 11Behold, all his fellows shall be put to shame, and the craftsmen are but men; let them all assemble, let them stand forth, they shall be terrified, they shall be put to shame together.

12The ironsmith fashions it and works it over the coals; he shapes it with hammers, and forges it with his strong arm; he becomes hungry and his strength fails, he drinks no water and is faint. 13The carpenter stretches a line, he marks it out with a pencil; he fashions it with planes, and marks it with a compass; he shapes it into the figure of a man, with the beauty of a man, to dwell in a house. 14He cuts down cedars; or he chooses a holm tree or an oak and lets it grow strong among the trees of the forest; he plants a cedar and the rain nourishes it. 15Then it becomes fuel for a man; he takes a part of it and warms himself, he kindles a fire and bakes bread; also he makes a god and worships it, he makes it a graven image and falls down before it. 16Half of it he burns in the fire; over the half he eats flesh, he roasts meat and is satisfied; also he warms himself and says, "Aha, I am warm, I have seen the fire!" 17And the rest of it he makes into a god, his idol; and falls down to it and worships it; he prays to it and says, "Deliver me, for thou art my god!"

18They know not, nor do they discern; for he has shut their eyes, so that they cannot see, and their minds, so that they cannot understand. 19No one considers, nor is there knowledge or discernment to say, "Half of it I burned in the fire, I also baked bread on its coals, I roasted flesh and have eaten; and shall I make the residue of it an abomination? Shall I fall down before a block of wood?" 20He feeds on ashes; a deluded mind has led him astray, and he cannot deliver himself or say, "Is there not a lie in my right hand?"

The powerless charlatans challenged in the preceding trial speech (vv. 7–8) are now identified with the makers of idols in a long colourful passage distinguished from the rest of these chapters by the fact that it is in prose. The introduction (vv. 9–11) contains sarcastic allusions to the creativity of Almighty God: "make" and "fashion" are words used in verse 2; "nothing" comes from Genesis 1:2 ("without form", RSV); and "their witnesses" contrasts with God's witnesses, that is to say, his people Israel (v. 8). In 43:10, the claim that any other god could be "formed" is scornfully rejected, and here is an elaborate account of craftsmen actually trying to do that. Such efforts will achieve nothing (vv. 9–10). They lead only to *shame* and *fear* (vv. 9 and 11).

Verses 12–17 give a blow by blow account of how an idol is made—with frequent, pointed references to human frailty. The craftsman feels hungry and is faint (v. 12); he warms himself (v. 15); he never thinks about what he is doing or how ridiculous he is (vv. 18–20). There are many difficulties in the Hebrew, but the general picture is clear. The Hebrew text of verses 12–13 makes no mention of smiths and carpenters as the RSV suggests, although it does describe the craftsmen working in metal and wood.

Verse 13 seems more sympathetic to the craftsman's art, and raises the question of what exactly is the prophet's attitude towards art objects. Among the relics of ancient near eastern idolatry are some exquisite pieces in ivory, wood, gold, silver and so on; graced, we must assume, like some of the great Christian works of art, by the artists' religious devotion. Passages like the present one, however, come dangerously near to what is known as *iconoclasm*, an abhorrence of all idols and images, which at many times in the history of Christianity (including, *eg*, the era of Cromwell and the Puritans) has led to the mass destruction of works of religious art. The ban on images, like the sabbath law, unique in the history of religion, is one of the Ten Commandments (Exod. 20:4–6; Deut. 5:8–10), and must be seen in its proper context. On the one hand, visible images of God may have been banned, but this had little effect on the religious imagination of Old Testament writers, including "Deutero-Isaiah": verbal images of God as king, shepherd, lion, father, mother, *etc*, are integral to Old Testament theology.

On the other hand, the objection to an idol is that it can become an end in itself: the craftsmen in this chapter cannot see beyond the object they have made to what it represents. Or, at any rate, the prophet cannot see beyond the object; and for him the use of idols in worship is pointless. Not every student of religion would share this negative view either of the value of statues, or stained-glass windows, or icons, or even of the status of religions other than their own. See my comments on 43:10–11. But few would deny the reality of the temptation to worship the art or the sculpture or the music or the poetry of religion as ends in themselves, at the expense of the moral and spiritual purpose for which they were produced.

The climax of the passage is in verse 17, where the man "falls down to it and worships it; he prays to it and says, 'Deliver me, for thou art my god!' " In addressing a piece of wood as "God", he finally reveals his utter stupidity. Of course it is possible to fall down before a statue of Christ, whether crucified or in his risen glory, and pray to him (*not* the statue), "Deliver me, for thou art my God". It is also possible to fall down before a statue of the Virgin Mary, and ask her (*not* the statue) to intercede for us. It is also possible to see only the statue, the work of art, and forget the heavenly reality beyond, and it is not always easy for the observer, as it clearly was not easy for the author of this scathing attack on idol-worshippers, to tell the difference. George Herbert puts it this way (in the poem *Teach me, my God and King*):

A man that looks on glass
   On it may stay his eye;
Or if he pleaseth, through it pass,
   And then the heaven espy.

The delusion of those who see only the objects and not what they represent is summed up in verses 18–20. They cannot know how tragically mistaken they are.

JERUSALEM SHALL BE REBUILT

Isaiah 44:21–28

21Remember these things, O Jacob,
　　and Israel, for you are my servant;
I formed you, you are my servant;
　　O Israel, you will not be forgotten by me.
22I have swept away your transgressions like a cloud,
　　and your sins like mist;
return to me, for I have redeemed you.

23Sing, O heavens, for the Lord has done it;
　　shout, O depths of the earth;
break forth into singing, O mountains,
　　O forest, and every tree in it!
For the Lord has redeemed Jacob,
　　and will be glorified in Israel.

24Thus says the Lord, your Redeemer,
　　who formed you from the womb:
"I am the Lord, who made all things,
　　who stretched out the heavens alone,
　　who spread out the earth—Who was with me?—
25who frustrates the omens of liars,
　　and makes fools of diviners;
who turns wise men back,
　　and makes their knowledge foolish;
26who confirms the word of his servant,
　　and performs the counsel of his messengers;
who says of Jerusalem, 'She shall be inhabited,'
　　and of the cities of Judah, 'They shall be built,
　　and I will raise up their ruins';
27who says to the deep, 'Be dry,
　　I will dry up your rivers';
28who says of Cyrus, 'He is my shepherd,
　　and he shall fulfil all my purpose';
saying of Jerusalem, 'She shall be built,'
　　and of the temple, 'Your foundation shall be laid.' "

A call to remember what God has done for his people (vv. 21–22),

together with a short but splendid hymn of praise (v. 23), introduces the next prophecy which foretells the imminent success of
Cyrus and the rebuilding of Jerusalem (vv. 24–28).

Memory plays a very important part in religion and it is unlikely
that "these things" (v. 21) refer merely to the pathetic behaviour
of idolatrous craftsmen in the previous verses. This is surely a call
to remember the stories of the creation of heaven and earth, the
Exodus, and the other mighty acts of God, as recorded, for
example, in the Psalms (*eg* 89; 103–107). Part of 'remembering' in
worship is to allow ourselves to be caught up in past events so as to
let our salvation history affect our lives now. This is what happens
in the Eucharist for Christians, and in the Passover meal for Jews.
Baptism is another example. "Fortified by our baptism," as
Luther put it, we experience the forgiveness of our sins, and are
able to obey God's call (see v. 22):

Return to me, for I have redeemed you.

At first sight it appears that the hymn in verse 23 follows the
usual pattern (see 42:10ff.; 45:8): all nature bursts into song to
celebrate the redemption of Israel. But it actually goes further
than that. In this little hymn, heaven and hell join the jubilant
choir as well: "the depths of the earth" refers to the underworld,
or "Sheol" as it was called, where the dead lead a colourless and
shadowy existence. We know from passages like Amos 9:2 and
Psalm 139:7–12 that even Sheol is under the jurisdiction of God:

If I ascend to heaven, thou art there!
If I make my bed in Sheol, thou art there!

(Ps. 139:8)

Once more our author's vision pushes the frontiers of our faith
and imagination to their limits.

The form of the prophecy in verses 24–28 is strikingly effective:
it is composed of one main clause, "I am the Lord"—the fundamental truth on which the whole book is based—and a large
number of relative clauses such as, "who made all things . . . who
stretched out the heavens . . . who says of Cyrus . . .", *etc*. These
move from statements about the creation of heaven and earth in
the past to their climax in prophecies about Cyrus and the rebuild-

ing of Jerusalem in the present. Verses 25–26 concern the distinction between false prophets and the prophets of God, and recall the stories of Joseph at the court of Pharaoh (Gen. 41:8; 44:15) and Daniel at the court of Nebuchadnezzar (Dan. chs. 1–2). The problem is also dealt with in Deuteronomic law (Deut. 18:9–22) and Jeremiah 23:9–22. Isaiah 55:10–11 is another statement on the infallibility of God's word.

The primary criterion for distinguishing true prophecy from false is whether it is fulfilled or not. The six prophecies listed here (vv. 26–27) all came true within a generation or so of the time when the author uttered them. In fact, anyone with a smattering of the language of Isaianic faith must have believed that the destruction of Jerusalem could not be the end, and that somehow she would be rebuilt. Jewish daily prayer still contains the same hopes for the city that fell again in A.D. 70:

> Rebuild the city of righteousness soon in our days,
>   and may it be a centre of prayer for all people.
> Blessed art thou, O Lord, who rebuildest Jerusalem.

Nor would it have been hard to guess that it was Cyrus who was going to be Judah's ally in conquering Babylon and making it possible for the Jews to return to their homeland. But we must remember that the author wishes us to imagine that this is a prophecy of Isaiah, delivered in the eighth century B.C., just like the last few verses of the Book of Amos (9:11ff.), and if that is so, then we are dealing with a truly miraculous prophet of the Lord (v. 26);

> who confirms the word of his servant
>   and performs the counsel of his messengers.

"The rivers" in verse 27 are, first of all, the primeval floods, familiar from the Enthronement psalms (*eg* 93; 98), and representative of evil and destruction in general, so that the prophecy heralds a new era of safety and hope. But the particular victory over evil in everyone's mind as we read these chapters, is the fall of Babylon, and we are entitled to relate the words of this verse to Cyrus' famous strategy mentioned in the discussion of 43:14.

In verse 28 Cyrus is mentioned by name for the first time, although we have already met two references to him as the one whom God "stirred up . . . from the east, whom victory meets at every step" (41:2; 41:25). He is described here as God's "shepherd". Like the term "anointed" in the next chapter, this was regularly applied to kings and rulers in the ancient near east, but in addition to the notion of authority vested in such a leader by God, we are no doubt also intended to think of the care and protection devoted by a good shepherd to his sheep (see the commentary on 40:11).

The last verse was partially fulfilled under Cyrus in 538 B.C. when the foundations of the second Temple were laid (Ezra. 5:16). The Temple, however, was not completed until 515 B.C. (Ezra. 6:13–15), and Jerusalem itself still lay in ruins half way through the next century, as Nehemiah recalls (Neh. 2:3–5; 7: 1–4). But the grammar of verse 28 is odd: the two verbs ("shall be built" and "shall be laid") are feminine agreeing with "Jerusalem" (cities are always feminine in Hebrew). It has therefore been suggested that the word "temple" (which is masculine) is a later insertion, introduced by a pro-temple party. Certainly the Temple does not seem to have been a central theme in these chapters; this is the only mention of it apart from the ironical allusions in 43:22–24. Later there is even an emphatic rejection of the whole institution (66:1–3). It seems likely that there were already, among the exiled Jews, some who saw beyond actual buildings to a temple not "made with hands" (Mark 14:58; 2 Cor. 5:1). Perhaps "Deutero-Isaiah" was one of them.

CYRUS THE LORD'S ANOINTED

Isaiah 45:1–7

[1]Thus says the Lord to his anointed, to Cyrus,
   whose right hand I have grasped,
to subdue nations before him
   and ungird the loins of kings,
to open doors before him
   that gates may not be closed:

2"I will go before you
   and level the mountains,
I will break in pieces the doors of bronze
   and cut asunder the bars of iron,
3I will give you the treasures of darkness
   and the hoards in secret places,
that you may know that it is I, the Lord,
   the God of Israel, who call you by your name.
4For the sake of my servant Jacob,
   and Israel my chosen,
I call you by your name,
   I surname you, though you do not know me.
5I am the Lord, and there is no other,
   besides me there is no God;
   I gird you, though you do not know me,
6that men may know, from the rising of the sun
   and from the west, that there is none besides me;
   I am the Lord, and there is no other.
7I form light and create darkness,
   I make weal and create woe,
   I am the Lord, who do all these things."

Two extravagant prophecies about the coming victories of Cyrus lead to further statements on the uniqueness of God—"there is no other" (vv. 5 and 6)—and the condemnation of any who challenge his claim to control history (vv. 9ff.). Between them, like the chorus in a Greek drama, there is another magnificent hymn on the theme of *salvation* (v. 8).

The *first* prophecy is addressed to Cyrus, king of the Medes and Persians. This is in itself remarkable, although elsewhere, as we saw (41:2; 2 Chron. 36:22), writers could express the belief that the Lord "stirred up the spirit of Cyrus", which is a not dissimilar idea. Elsewhere too he is called God's "shepherd" (44:28), and in the proclamation put into his mouth by the Chronicler, he acknowledges the authority of the God of Israel:

"The Lord, the God of heaven, has given me all the kingdoms of the earth, and he has charged me to build him a house at Jerusalem, which is in Judah. Whoever is among you of all his people, may the Lord his God be with him. Let him go up."

(2 Chron. 36:23)

It is historically unlikely that Cyrus had even heard of *Yahweh* (the Lord), the God of one of the least among the nations in his vast empire, let alone communicated with him or his prophets in any way. This manner of speaking is merely a way of stressing the close, personal involvement of God in contemporary affairs. He also grasps Cyrus by the right hand (45:1). Cyrus was in any case the greatest statesman of his day. His own people called him "father", the Jews called him "the Lord's anointed"; even the Babylonians welcomed him as the one who liberated them from the unpopular, eccentric king, Nabonidus, and the Greeks hailed him as "master and lawgiver".

The "anointed one", *Messiah* in Hebrew, is a term applied to two other historical persons by sixth century B.C. prophets: Zerubbabel, the Davidic prince and Joshua the High Priest (see Zech. chs. 3–4). It is normally reserved for kings of Israel, from Saul (1 Sam. 24:10) onwards, especially descendants of David (see Pss. 2:2; 89:38; 132:10), and so the term *Messiah* came to be applied to the ideal "son of David", the Saviour who was to bring peace and justice in the "Messianic" age. Old Testament passages about this Saviour figure, such as Isaiah 9:1–7; 11:1–9 and 42:1–4, do not use the term; it was later interpreters who made the connection, as we have seen (see commentary on 42:1ff.). (The Greek for "anointed" is *Christ*.) When the prophet uses the term here, he is thus not expressing the belief that Cyrus is the Messiah, but that, like a Davidic king, he has a special role to play in history, to build Jerusalem and set the exiles free (v. 13). Cyrus is not being represented as a fulfilment of Messianic prophecies like the ones just referred to from earlier chapters of Isaiah, as Zerubbabel apparently was for a brief period after the exile, or, indeed, as Jesus of Nazareth was. Some have even suggested that the words, "to Cyrus", were inserted after the event, just as, perhaps, the word "temple" was inserted in 44:28. But at whatever date the connection between Jewish Messianic hopes and Cyrus was made, Cyrus certainly came to be regarded by them as a "saviour", as 2 Chronicles 36, Ezra 1, and many other later references, make abundantly clear. God used Assyria as a big stick to punish Israel with (Isa. 10:5), and Nebuchadnezzar, "the

king of Babylon, my servant'', for a similar purpose (Jer. 25:9).
Cyrus is another example of how God controls history for his own
ends; only, in his case, it was for a positive end.

Verses 1–3 depict Cyrus' progress in powerful military language: nations and their kings will fall before him (like the kingdoms of Asia Minor, including Croesus, king of Lydia); gates of
bronze and iron bars will not be able to keep his armies at bay
(Sardis fell in 547 B.C., and Babylon in 539 B.C.); and no treasures
will be hidden from his victorious army (like the gold and silver
vessels from Jerusalem which he retrieved from the Babylonians
and gave back to the Jews: see Ezra 5:14–15).

The *second* part of the Cyrus prophecy explains that the purpose behind his call is two-fold: on the one hand, it is all for
Israel's sake (v. 4), and on the other, it is to reveal, both to Cyrus
himself and to all the nations of the world, that, ''I am the Lord
and there is no other'' (vv. 5 and 6).

Verse 7 is of immense theological interest. In contrast to
Genesis 1:2, where formless earth, darkness, the deep and the
waters are all present before God says ''Let there be light'' (his
first creative act), here any trace of dualism—the belief in something outside of God's creation—is ruled out: ''light'', ''darkness'', ''weal'' and ''woe''(RSV) or ''peace'' and ''evil'' (AV), are
created by God—and there is no other power. John 1:3 puts it
thus:

> All things were made through him, and without him was not anything
> made that was made.

God must then be the creator of evil. Faced with disease,
drought, earthquake or any other ''woe'' or ''evil'' not of human
origin, we must either say it is created and controlled by God, or
else postulate some other power apart from God; a devil, a
capricious god of the Sea or the like. This chapter admits no other
power apart from God, so that evil must be part of God's plan
somehow or other, to educate us, to punish us, or, as the author of
the Book of Job argues, for some other purpose too difficult for
our finite human minds to conceive of:

Whence then comes wisdom?
  And where is the place of understanding?
It is hid from the eyes of all living,
  and concealed from the birds of the air.
Abaddon and Death say,
  'We have heard a rumour of it with our ears'.
God understands the way to it,
  and he knows its place.
For he looks to the ends of the earth,
  and sees everything under the heavens.

(Job 28:20–24)

There are other Old Testament texts where a battle rages between God and some other power: the flood (Ps. 93), a dragon (Ps. 89) or some other embodiment of evil. It is a battle which God wins, but which is real enough. Neither of these two Old Testament views of evil can claim to embody the whole truth, so complex is the nature of God, and so variegated the nature of human experience.

WILL YOU CRITICIZE THE CREATOR?

Isaiah 45:8–13

8"Shower, O heavens, from above,
  and let the skies rain down righteousness;
let the earth open, that salvation may sprout forth,
  and let it cause righteousness to spring up also;
  I the Lord have created it.

9"Woe to him who strives with his Maker,
  an earthen vessel with the potter!
Does the clay say to him who fashions it, 'What are you making'?
  or 'Your work has no handles'?
10Woe to him who says to a father, 'What are you begetting?'
  or to a woman, 'With what are you in travail?' "
11Thus says the Lord,
  the Holy One of Israel, and his Maker:
  "Will you question me about my children,

or command me concerning the work of my hands?
¹²I made the earth,
    and created man upon it;
  it was my hands that stretched out the heavens,
    and I commanded all their host.
¹³I have aroused him in righteousness,
    and I will make straight all his ways;
  he shall build my city
    and set my exiles free,
  not for price or reward,"
    says the Lord of hosts.

The theme of the hymn in verse 8 is again "righteousness" (*tsedek*) and "salvation" (*yesha*). These two terms are not abstract terms, but refer to concrete realities, as visible as the sky above, and as tangible as the earth beneath. They are acts of God, righteous acts ("triumphs" Judg. 5:11), by which he conquers evil and establishes peace; acts of divine intervention in which he creates order out of chaos, Israel out of Egyptian slavery (43:1), a new Jerusalem out of the ruins of the old (65:18). The whole universe eloquently demonstrates such mighty acts of God.

The woe-sayings in verses 9–10 recall the attacks on social and moral evils in the earlier chapters of the book (*eg* 5; 10; 29–31), but are here directed at theological errors. Woe to the men of clay who criticize their Maker! We have met this idea already in 10:15, where Assyria, the rod of God's anger, is accused of challenging the one who wields it. Here no doubt we are to recognize the reaction of the prophet's audience, who would not believe that Cyrus could conceivably be the "Lord's anointed". How could a pagan king be God's servant? It was surely a sort of blasphemy even to suggest that he was. The prophet rebukes their arrogance. God is like a potter who has total control of his clay; he is like a father or a mother, and what they produce cannot be changed or influenced by anyone else—before the advent of genetic engineering, that is.

Verse 11 takes up the argument of Job 38: do you know better? Could you do better yourselves? This is the theological answer given to those who say: what have I done to deserve this? or who ask, like the famous question that appeared amongst the graffiti at the scene of a mining disaster: where was God? Trust God; he is omniscient and omnipotent: as Paul puts it, "All things work together for good to them that love God" (Rom. 8:28, AV).

Notice how, according to verse 11, all the people of the world (even Medes and Persians) are "children" of God. Verse 12, like so many other Isaianic passages, seems to be dependent on Genesis 2:1–9: the earth, the heavens and "all the host of them", from verse 1, and the creation of man upon the earth from verses 7–8.

Finally, the whole section is summed up in a rich and allusive verse (45:13). The first few words are already familiar: "aroused" here is the same Hebrew word as "stirred up" in 41:2, 25. "Righteousness" (*tsedek*) means "victory" here as in 41:2. "I will make straight" occurred in 40:3 as well as more recently in 45:2 (RSV, "level"). *Building Jerusalem* and *setting the exiles free* are also themes we have met already, but the subject here is explicitly Cyrus, as nowhere else, and the personal expressions "my city" and "my exiles" (God is speaking) are uniquely moving. "The city of God" is an epithet for Jerusalem in Psalm 46:4, Hebrews 12:22 and elsewhere.

The word translated "exiles" is a singular noun, meaning literally "captivity" or "exile", not common in Biblical Hebrew (only here, and in Isaiah 20:4), but later to become the normal, emotive Jewish term, in Yiddish as well as Hebrew, for the diaspora (*Golah*). It is applied also to the "expulsion of the Jews from Spain", an event that occurred in A.D. 1492.

At the last, the whole operation is to be without price or reward. The doctrine of unmerited grace is a major one in Biblical theology, even though in this context it is rather inconsistent with what has been said already in 40:1–2 and 43:3. It is the basis of all those stories about God's choice of the weaker or less worthy person—for example, Jacob instead of Esau, David not Saul—and is best expressed (as so often) in Deuteronomic idiom (see Deut. 7:6–8):

> For you are a people holy to the Lord your God; the Lord your God has chosen you to be a people for his own possession, out of all the

peoples that are on the face of the earth. It was not because you were more in number than any other people that the Lord set his love upon you and chose you, for you were the fewest of all peoples; but it is because the Lord loves you ... that the Lord has brought you out with a mighty hand, and redeemed you from the house of bondage.

THERE IS NO OTHER GOD BESIDES ME

Isaiah 45:14-25

[14]Thus says the Lord:
  "The wealth of Egypt and the merchandise of Ethiopia,
    and the Sabeans, men of stature,
shall come over to you and be yours,
    they shall follow you;
    they shall come over in chains and bow down to you.
They will make supplication to you, saying:
    'God is with you only, and there is no other,
    no god besides him.' "
[15]Truly, thou art a God who hidest thyself,
    O God of Israel, the Saviour.
[16]All of them are put to shame and confounded,
    the makers of idols go in confusion together.
[17]But Israel is saved by the Lord
    with everlasting salvation;
you shall not be put to shame or confounded
    to all eternity.

[18]For thus says the Lord,
  who created the heavens
    (he is God!),
  who formed the earth and made it
    (he established it;
  he did not create it as a chaos,
    he formed it to be inhabited!):
  "I am the Lord, and there is no other.
[19]I did not speak in secret,
    in a land of darkness;
I did not say to the offspring of Jacob,
    'Seek me in chaos.'

I the Lord speak the truth,
  I declare what is right.

20"Assemble yourselves and come,
  draw near together,
  you survivors of the nations!
They have no knowledge
  who carry about their wooden idols,
and keep on praying to a god
  that cannot save.
21Declare and present your case;
  let them take counsel together!
Who told this long ago?
  Who declared it of old?
Was it not I, the Lord?
  And there is no other god besides me,
a righteous God and a Saviour;
  there is none besides me.

22"Turn to me and be saved,
  all the ends of the earth!
For I am God, and there is no other.
23By myself I have sworn,
  from my mouth has gone forth in righteousness
  a word that shall not return:
'To me every knee shall bow,
  every tongue shall swear.'

24"Only in the Lord, it shall be said of me,
  are righteousness and strength;
to him shall come and be ashamed,
  all who were incensed against him.
25In the Lord all the offspring of Israel
  shall triumph and glory."

Verses 14–25 are a rich collection of prophecies and declarations on the monotheistic theme introduced in verses 5–6. First (v. 14), Egyptians, Ethiopians and Sabeans, adopt a monotheistic religion, a curious prophecy when one considers the fact that, with the spread of Islam in the seventh century A.D., this is exactly what happened. The Muslim majority in these three regions of

Africa and Arabia and elsewhere, five times a day, recite the *Shahada*, one of the "Pillars" of Islam: "There is no god but God, and Muhammad is his prophet". The wealth and merchandise referred to would include horses and chariots from Egypt (1 Kings 10:28–29); and spices, gold and precious stones from Sheba (1 Kings 10:2). The reference to the impressive appearance of these handsome peoples recalls the exciting description of the arrival of Ethiopian envoys at Jerusalem in chapter 18.

The other detail in verse 14 is less appealing. These proud peoples will be in chains when they acknowledge the one true God, and will bow down in subservience to Jerusalem. This is the dark side of Jerusalem's triumph. It is indeed disturbing to think of the black slave trade that flourished in East Africa for many centuries, as in any way a fulfilment of this prophecy. But there are some even more gruesome examples of this ferocious rejection of the enemies of Israel, such as 49:23, 26 and the last verse of Psalm 137, and we must not dream of taking them literally. Egypt stands for oppression (Exod. 1:8–14), and in more recent history it was an Egyptian Pharaoh who killed Judah's last great king (2 Kings 23:29–30). Ethiopians and Sabeans were under Egyptian control during much of the Biblical period, and were thus frequently bracketed with Egypt: in Genesis 10:6–7, Cush (*ie* Ethiopia) and Egypt are brothers (sons of Ham), and Seba (*ie* Sabeans) is one of the sons of Cush (see also my comments on chs. 17 and 20 in vol. 1, pp. 166ff., 178ff.).

Verses 15–17 develop the theme of judgment on those who reject God: "everlasting salvation" for Israel means shame and confusion for the rest of the nations. God is the Saviour of Israel, but hidden from the nations. Like Augustine's conclusion that an unbaptized baby is condemned to Hell-fire, this attitude to the nations who reject God arises from attempts to force God's wisdom into the strait-jacket of human logic. Surely we must in fact leave room for God's love, and for the mystery of his wisdom which is hidden from us too, especially in times of dark despair.

In the second statement of monotheism (vv. 18–19) it is the one true God himself who is speaking. If by God we mean the ultimate source of all that exists in heaven and in earth, then there can, by definition, be only one God; and for Biblical writers this one God is *Yahweh* (the Lord), "and there is no other" (v. 18). "Chaos", a fundamental part of the creation story (Gen. 1:2: translated "without form", RSV), is twice mentioned here: *first*, in connection with the order inherent in the universe, because it was out of chaos that God formed the inhabited world as we know it (v. 18); and *second*, in connection with the revelation of God's will through the prophets, which has nothing to do with chaos (v. 19). The truth is not hard to grasp: it is simple and direct. God does not confuse us or hide himself from us (see Deut. 30:12–14):

> It [God's commandment] is not in heaven, that you should say, "Who will go up for us to heaven, and bring it to us, that we may hear it and do it?" Neither is it beyond the sea, that you should say, "Who will go over the sea for us, and bring it to us, that we may hear it and do it?" But the word is very near you; it is in your mouth and in your heart, so that you can do it.

Verses 20–21 constitute another trial speech, in which the idol-worshippers are challenged to put their case. Idols can do nothing by themselves: they have to be carried around (see also 46:1–4). They cannot save: God is "a righteous God and a Saviour". This word-pair is similar to the one in the hymn in verse 8 and elsewhere: "righteous" (Hebrew *tsaddik*) means both "just" and "victorious" (see my discussion of 41:2). It also includes being active in the operation to save Israel, and therefore overlaps with the other term "Saviour" (Hebrew *moshia*, from the same root as *yesha*), which is properly used only of the activities of God or his appointed agents. We might put it this way: the Saviour is just and righteous, and the righteous God is triumphant and saving . . . and there is no other "righteous God and Saviour" besides the Lord.

Verses 22–23 contain a prophecy which helps to dispel the awful darkness of verse 14. All the nations of the earth are invited to "turn to [God] and be saved"; not just to watch as blessings are showered upon Israel, but to share in the victory themselves. The subservience now is to God, not Israel, and an astonishing prophecy of universal salvation, which cannot be argued away, clinches the matter (v. 23):

To me every knee shall bow,
every tongue shall swear.

The passage is frequently quoted, from Romans 14:11 and Philippians 2:10–11 on. Imperialistic it may be in regard to other religions, but it expresses a single-minded commitment to the God and Father we know, which cannot be wrong. The status of other religions and other gods is another question, on which perhaps passages like Malachi 1:11 have something to say.

The noun *tsedek* and the related verb (*tsadak*) are the subject of the final prophecy in the series as well (vv. 24–25), but the meaning of the Hebrew words is hard to represent in English. For the noun, translated "righteousness" (RSV), is actually plural, and must be more concrete or active than the abstract term "righteousness" suggests. The Jerusalem Bible and the New English Bible have "victory", as in 41:2 (RSV), but this still does not represent the plural. This is the word translated "triumphs" in Judges 5:11, and surely it should be so rendered here, especially when the related verb is translated "shall triumph" in the next verse. This prophecy is about the power of God to intervene on our behalf, in situations of danger or injustice, and to triumph in a way that only he can do.

THE FALSE GODS OF BABYLON

Isaiah 46:1–13

¹Bel bows down, Nebo stoops,
their idols are on beasts and cattle;
these things you carry are loaded as
burdens on weary beasts.
²They stoop, they bow down together,
they cannot save the burden,
but themselves go into captivity.

³"Hearken to me, O house of Jacob,
all the remnant of the house of Israel,
who have been borne by me from your birth,

carried from the womb;
4even to your old age I am He,
and to grey hairs I will carry you.
I have made, and I will bear;
I will carry and will save.

5"To whom will you liken me and make me equal,
and compare me, that we may be alike?
6Those who lavish gold from the purse,
and weigh out silver in the scales,
hire a goldsmith, and he makes it into a god;
then they fall down and worship!
7They lift it upon their shoulders, they carry it,
they set it in its place, and it stands there;
it cannot move from its place.
If one cries to it, it does not answer
or save him from his trouble.

8"Remember this and consider,
recall it to mind, you transgressors,
9   remember the former things of old;
for I am God, and there is no other;
I am God, and there is none like me,
10declaring the end from the beginning
and from ancient times things not yet done,
saying, 'My counsel shall stand,
and I will accomplish all my purpose,'
11calling a bird of prey from the east,
the man of my counsel from a far country.
I have spoken, and I will bring it to pass;
I have purposed, and I will do it.

12"Hearken to me, you stubborn of heart,
you who are far from deliverance:
13I bring near my deliverance, it is not far off,
and my salvation will not tarry;
I will put salvation in Zion,
for Israel my glory."

In the *first* section (vv. 1-7) the prophet takes up a theme from the previous chapter (45:20), and contrasts the scene of heavy idols being carried through the streets of Babylon by weary beasts of burden, with that of his own people being carried by God—"on eagles' wings" (Exod. 19:4), as it were—out of Egypt, through the Red Sea and the wilderness, into the Promised Land. He *made* them and will *carry* them and *save* them (v. 4); man-made objects have to be carried by men because they have no life of their own, and they can do nothing to save others.

Bel is the Babylonian form of the Canaanite name *Baal*, and appears in the name of Babylon's last king, Belshazzar (Dan. 5). It means "lord" and was a title of Marduk, chief among the gods of Babylon. Marduk was represented as a king standing on the back of the sea-monster Tiamat, whom he defeated in Babylon's creation myth, and on ceremonial occasions he was led along the "Processional Way" from the Gate of Ishtar (goddess of love), past the Hanging Gardens, to the main Temple area in the centre of the city. As in chapter 44, the author's view of what must obviously have been a splendid spectacle, and one that expressed deeply held beliefs about Babylon's guardian deity, is coloured by his monotheism. However impressive, the rituals are to him meaningless and do nothing for the worshippers. It may of course be that he was no less disillusioned about the rituals of his own Temple (43:22–28; cf. 1:10–17; 66:1–4).

Nebo, Marduk's son, was god of the scribal art, and his name appears frequently in other personal names, like Nebuchadnezzar and Nebuzaradan (2 Kings 25:8).

The words of God in verses 3–4 contain some interesting expressions. "The remnant of the house of Israel" is a powerful theme from the eighth century B.C. on, and can be used in prophecies both of judgment (*eg* Amos 3:12) and salvation (Isa. 37:31–32). In the present context it represents a source of hope. The phrase translated "from your birth" is in fact the same as the one translated "from the womb" in 44:2, *ie* before birth. In view of the bold imagery of 42:14 and Deuteronomy 32:18, is it not conceivable that the image of God as a mother, carrying a child in her womb, occurs here also? The word here translated "womb" is a rare word (it occurs only here in Isaiah), but it is closely related to words for "love", "mercy" and "compassion" (*eg* 49:13, 15;

54:7; 55:7; 63:15). Old age, the other end of life, is just as much in God's hands as the beginning (v. 4).

Verse 5 is still concerned with the contrast between the God of Israel and the false gods of Babylon. But it also raises the question discussed above (in the commentary on 44:13) of how God is to be envisaged, if at all: as king, shepherd, judge, father, mother, lion or any other creature. The three words "liken", "make equal" and "compare", are all different. The *first* (see also 40:18) occurs in a liturgical context in the sense of imagining or recalling or even re-enacting instances of God's love for his people:

> We have *thought on* thy steadfast love, O God,
> in the midst of thy temple.
>
> (Ps. 48:9)

This must surely be a legitimate part of worship (see on 44:21). The *second* question, "To whom will you . . . *make* me *equal*?", however, must be answered in the negative (45:5–6, 14). The *third* is a more intellectual term and, like the *first*, may invite a positive answer. In theological discourse, as in worship, our human minds have to envisage God in human terms, because we have no other language to use. Every image can tell us something about the nature of God, but no image must be allowed to become an end in itself or delude us into believing God is knowable through it alone. God is both lord and cheated husband (Hosea chs. 1–3), both father and mother, and much more besides.

In addition to regular language for the manufacture and worship of idols, verses 6–7 draw on two other sources for effect. On the one hand, commercial language is used to parody the wasted effort of the business: gold, silver, purse, weighing, scales, hire. On the other hand, the last sentence applies the highly charged language of formal prayer to the absurd activities of the idol-worshipper: he "cries" for help, as the Israelites "cry" to God (*eg*. Judg. 6:6); the idol does not "answer" as God "answers" Jonah (Jon. 2:2); "trouble" or "distress" is the term so frequent in the Psalms (*eg* 4:1; 20:1; 22:11), and "save" is the theological term used only of God and, by definition, can never have an idol as the subject (Isa. 45:15, 17).

The *second* part of the chapter is addressed to "transgressors" (v. 8) and "you stubborn of heart" (v. 12). "Remember" at the beginning sounds a note of caution and rebuke, and only secondarily appeals to the evidence of what God has done for them (as in 44:21). The "transgressors" may include those taken in by the allure of idol worship (48:3–4), but more likely they are disbelievers, those who know better than God; those who cannot accept that Cyrus is God's servant, the one who is going to rescue them.

The vocabulary of verse 10 is familiar already from 41:22 and gathers together into one sentence the whole of history, from beginning to end, as masterminded by God. Cyrus is one example of God's plans and how they are revealed to the prophets (see 44:25–6). The "bird of prey" (v. 11) recalls the image of the eagle bearing Israel on her wings (Exod. 19:4) and hovering over her young (Deut. 32:11), but also no doubt the speed and ferocity of Cyrus' victories (41:2–3). Speed is also the subject of the last brief prophecy (vv. 12–13) in which the themes of *righteousness* ("deliverance", RSV) and *salvation* are once more woven together (as in 45:24–25) in a final appeal to disbelievers and cynics.

THE FALL OF BABYLON

Isaiah 47:1–15

> [1]Come down and sit in the dust,
>   O virgin daughter of Babylon;
> sit on the ground without a throne,
>   O daughter of the Chaldeans!
> For you shall no more be called
>   tender and delicate.
> [2]Take the millstones and grind meal,
>   put off your veil,
> strip off your robe, uncover your legs,

pass through the rivers.
³Your nakedness shall be uncovered,
    and your shame shall be seen.
 I will take vengeance,
    and I will spare no man.
⁴Our Redeemer—the Lord of hosts is his name—
    is the Holy One of Israel.

⁵Sit in silence, and go into darkness,
    O daughter of the Chaldeans;
 for you shall no more be called
    the mistress of kingdoms,
⁶I was angry with my people,
    I profaned my heritage;
 I gave them into your hand,
    you showed them no mercy;
 on the aged you made your yoke
    exceedingly heavy.
⁷You said, "I shall be mistress for ever,"
    so that you did not lay these things to heart
    or remember their end.
⁸Now therefore hear this, you lover of pleasures,
    who sit securely,
 who say in your heart,
    "I am, and there is no one besides me;
 I shall not sit as a widow
    or know the loss of children":
⁹These two things shall come to you
    in a moment, in one day;
 the loss of children and widowhood
    shall come upon you in full measure,
 in spite of your many sorceries
    and the great power of your enchantments.

¹⁰You felt secure in your wickedness,
    you said, "No one sees me";
 your wisdom and your knowledge
    led you astray,
 and you said in your heart,
    "I am, and there is no one besides me."
¹¹But evil shall come upon you,

for which you cannot atone;
disaster shall fall upon you,
    which you will not be able to expiate;
and ruin shall come on you suddenly,
    of which you know nothing.

12Stand fast in your enchantments
    and your many sorceries,
    with which you have laboured from your youth;
perhaps you may be able to succeed,
    perhaps you may inspire terror.
13You are wearied with your many counsels;
    let them stand forth and save you,
those who divide the heavens,
    who gaze at the stars,
who at the new moons predict
    what shall befall you.

14Behold, they are like stubble,
    the fire consumes them;
they cannot deliver themselves
    from the power of the flame.
No coal for warming oneself is this,
    no fire to sit before!
15Such to you are those with whom you have laboured,
    who have trafficked with you from your youth;
they wander about each in his own direction;
    there is no one to save you.

The long taunting poem about the fall of Babylon is written, with bitter sarcasm, in the form of a lament. Where conventionally tragic details would be catalogued to elicit sympathy from the mourners (as in lamentations over the fall of Jerusalem: *eg* Lam. 1), here they are translated into vulgar gloating language, so bitter and violent that one might be forgiven for asking how it can have been included in scripture. A number of points must be borne in mind, however.

First, this poem, like Psalm 137 and other passages (*eg* Isa. 45:14; 49:23, 26), was undoubtedly composed at a time when bitterness and defeat brought out the worst in God's people.

There is no way we can justify these attitudes, but equally it ill becomes any of us to pretend that such vindictiveness does not exist or that we have never felt it ourselves. It warrants our sympathy, not only our condemnation. It is a measure of the breadth of vision in scripture that even our worst failings are not covered up but frankly displayed for all to see. All human experience, not just the nice parts of it, has, so to speak, been "canonized" to indicate that even people with such grotesquely "unchristian" failings can, by the grace of God, be accepted within God's people.

Second, we must remember that similar vicious language was directed against Jerusalem in earlier chapters of this book (*eg* 3:16–26). In other words, any who are guilty of acts of brutal violence, against the poor (as in Isa. 3) or against the peoples of conquered nations (as in the case of Babylon's crimes), will be severely punished. It matters not whether they are God's people or a foreign people. There is justice in that.

Third, Babylon is a symbol of evil—here as in Revelation 18—and it is surely acceptable that the intensity of feeling that revels in visions of the everlasting bliss in store for the righteous, should also be directed at the evil in the world. Babylon claimed to be the one true God (v. 8), and that was unforgivable. There is much in the Old Testament about forgiveness: *eg* even Assyria is forgiven in the Book of Jonah (4:11), and Egypt in Isaiah 19: 24–25. But Babylon remains the symbol of what is unforgivable, and this passage is a stern reminder of the reality of evil and the ultimate answerability of evil-doers to God.

The fall of Babylon is dramatically couched in terms of the contrast between a lady seated in all her elegance, and a slave-girl forced to strip off her clothes and then raped (vv. 1–5). The terrifying suggestion in verse 3 is that God himself is the subject of these verses. After all, it was he who treated Jerusalem in this way (*eg* Lam. 1): how much more her unregenerate enemies!

Verses 6–11 go back over the reasons for Babylon's downfall. She was given the task of punishing God's people. Through her, God "profaned [his] heritage" (v. 6), an expression wistfully recalling the promises to Abraham and his seed for ever. But she went too far: she showed them no mercy, she was especially brutal towards the elderly, and finally she began to think she was God. She even used the monotheistic formula, exclusively reserved for *Yahweh*: "I am, and there is no one besides me" (vv. 8, 10). Her downfall was inevitable therefore. Again the special grief of women—the loss of their children and their husbands—would come upon her (v. 9). There would be no escape. She would not be able to buy God off. "Atone" and "expiate" (v. 11) are possibly correct translations, but in view of texts like 43:3, probably "ransom" and "buy off" are better, suggesting a commercial transaction rather than a religious one.

The word "ruin" in verse 11 came to be the Modern Hebrew term for the Holocaust, the destruction of six million Jews in Nazi Europe.

Verses 9*b* and 12–13 refer sarcastically to Babylonian astrology, a speciality of the city's science. The word "Chaldeans" (v. 5), a synonym for Babylonians, actually came to mean *sages, magicians*, and *soothsayers*, as in Daniel 2:2–11. "Let them [your enchantments]...save you" (47:13) is another instance of the intentionally improper use of that special theological term, *hoshia* (45:15–17).

Finally Babylon would be consumed by fire (v. 14), like stubble. Perhaps the author is sarcastically recalling the scene in chapter 44, where a Babylonian idol-maker is warming himself at the fire: "Aha, I am warm, I have seen the fire!" (44:16). Babylon's final conflagration would be "no fire to sit before" (47:14).

The *traffickers* in verse 15 constitute one of the main themes in the great poem on the doom of "Babylon" in Revelation 18 (see vv. 15–17):

> The merchants of these wares, who gained wealth from her, will stand far off, in fear of her torment, weeping and mourning aloud, "Alas, alas, for the great city...laid waste".

The fall of Babylon in Revelation affects the whole world. Here the point is rather that she who once had many friends, is abandoned by them all in her hour of need: "there is no-one to save you" (Isa. 47:15). The lament is, in effect, a song of triumph: evil has been overcome and the people are free (cf. 48:20–21).

A REBEL FROM BIRTH

Isaiah 48:1–11

> [1]Hear this, O house of Jacob,
>> who are called by the name of Israel,
>> and who came forth from the loins of Judah;
> who swear by the name of the Lord,
>> and confess the God of Israel,
>> but not in truth or right.
> [2]For they call themselves after the holy city,
>> and stay themselves on the God of Israel;
>> the Lord of hosts is his name.
>
> [3]"The former things I declared of old,
>> they went forth from my mouth and I made them known;
>> then suddenly I did them and they came to pass.
> [4]Because I know that you are obstinate,
>> and your neck is an iron sinew
>> and your forehead brass,
> [5]I declared them to you from of old,
>> before they came to pass I announced them to you,
> lest you should say, 'My idol did them,
>> my graven image and my molten image commanded them.'
>
> [6]"You have heard; now see all this;
>> and will you not declare it?
> From this time forth I make you hear new things,
>> hidden things which you have not known.
> [7]They are created now, not long ago;
>> before today you have never heard of them,
>> lest you should say, 'Behold, I knew them.'
> [8]You have never heard, you have never known,
>> from of old your ear has not been opened.
> For I knew that you would deal very treacherously,
>> and that from birth you were called a rebel.
>
> [9]"For my name's sake I defer my anger,

> for the sake of my praise I restrain it for you,
> that I may not cut you off.
> [10]Behold, I have refined you, but not like silver;
> I have tried you in the furnace of affliction.
> [11]For my own sake, for my own sake, I do it,
> for how should my name be profaned?
> My glory I will not give to another."

Before the nine magnificent chapters (40–48) we have been studying are rounded off with the call, "Go forth from Babylon", the prophet in this chapter draws together for the last time his main themes: the appeal to past prophecy; the distinction between the former things and the new things; the victories of Cyrus; the fall of Babylon; the false gods; and the one true God who is creator of all. But in addition, and with the same devastating effect as Nathan's "*You* are the man" (2 Sam. 12:7), he suddenly and unexpectedly turns on his audience, "who are called by the name of Israel" (v. 1), and says to them in effect: "*you* are the idol-worshippers (v. 5)! *you* are the false prophets (v. 7)! *you* are the rebels (v. 8)!" Their sufferings in the "furnace of affliction" (v. 10) are not for their sake, to improve them or punish them for their own good, but (and the prophet is of course speaking for God) "for my own sake, for my own sake" (v. 11). If God had restrained his anger, it was for his own name's sake, not Israel's (v. 9).

Verses 1–11 are thus unique in these chapters. Nowhere else does the prophet attack his audience with such vehemence. There was a note of rebuke in 46:8, but nothing so ferocious as this. Some scholars have noted discrepancies of style between these verses and the rest of the book: the phrase "for my *name's* sake", for example, occurs only here in Isaiah, and the familiar theological term *tsedaka*, "righteousness", occurs in an un-Isaianic sense "in [truth or] right" in verse 1. In some respects the verses come closer to Ezekiel (*eg* Ezek. 20) than to Isaiah. One explanation of this could be that the passage was composed for delivery on some solemn occasion such as the Day of Atonement; a day of confession and self-examination (Lev. 16:29–31). However that may be, it adds a telling new dimension to the Babylonian chapters of the book. Acknowledging the sinful nature of his people, rebels from birth, the prophet argues nonetheless that God will redeem them. The wistful tone of verse 18—"O that you had hearkened to my commandments!"—reminds us that this is a God who loves us and will not let his people down.

The first two verses of chapter 48 are heavy with irony. The people of Judah are addressed as those who *claim* to be God's people, called by the name "Israel" just because they are descended from an Israelite tribe, but "not in truth or right". The distinction is drawn between inherited genes and personal acts of faith, between race and religion. Instead of "loins of Judah" (RSV), the Hebrew actually has "waters of Judah", and may contain an allusion to Psalm 68:26, where the people are described as "you who are of Israel's fountain", or perhaps to Balaam's celebrated prophecy:

How fair are your tents, O Jacob,
  your encampments, O Israel!
Like valleys that stretch afar,
  like gardens beside a river,
like aloes that the Lord has planted,
  like cedar trees beside the waters.
Water shall flow from his buckets,
  and his seed shall be in many waters.

(Num. 24:5–7)

At all events the issue is obvious. Who are God's people? Is it enough to be descended from Abraham, as the Jews in Jesus' time argued: "We are descendants of Abraham" (John 8:33)? The answer is clear: "Jew" is not a racial term, except in Hitler's demonic vocabulary. You need only walk along a street in Jerusalem today to see the infinite variety of races embraced by the term "Jew". The same applies to "Israel", the "people of God", and to the "Church". An act of personal commitment is required: "swearing by the name of the Lord" is one expression for this (Deut. 6:13; 10:20); another is confessing the "God of Jacob"—that is, invoking his name in hymns and prayers (see Psalm 20). It can never be enough to be born into a faith: you must work at it to make it your own.

"The holy city" (v. 2; 52:1) is a rare name for Jerusalem before the exile, but it eventually became, like "the Holy Land", one of the commonest (*eg* Matt. 4:5).

Prophecy and fulfilment is the familiar theme of the next part of the rebuke (vv. 3–5). We are of course intended to imagine that an eighth century B.C. prophet foresaw in the fall of Jerusalem and the coming of Cyrus (vv. 14–16) in the sixth century, more evidence of the power of God over and against the false gods and their idols.

Stubbornness is represented in verse 4 by the hard neck that does not respond to the oxherd's goad, and a "brass forehead" (like a "brass neck" in English idiom!) stands for impudence or effrontery:

> Yet you have a harlot's brow;
>   you refuse to be ashamed.
>
> (Jer. 3:3)

"New things", things hidden from you until now, things created for the first time before your eyes, things you have never heard of, are about to happen. This theme (vv. 6ff.) comes near Paul's "things that cannot be told, which man may not utter" (2 Cor. 12:4), and heralds the dawning of a new age revealed first to prophets and visionaries.

The history of Israel has been one of treachery and rebellion from the beginning (v. 8). While he was still in the womb, Jacob (*ie* Israel) struggled to outdo his twin brother Esau (Gen. 25:22–26). God punished them in the "furnace of affliction" (v. 10): *first* Egypt (Deut. 4:20; 1 Kings 8:51), and *second*, Babylon (Isa. 47:6). But he restrained his anger so that they were never totally destroyed (v. 9), and moreover, they have been refined, purified by their sufferings (v. 10), a powerful image hammered out of the experience of martyrdom (Dan. 11:35; Zech. 13:9; Mal. 3:2–3).

Verse 11 returns to the rebuke theme once more: the ultimate goal of Israel's history is not the salvation of God's people, which is only the means to an end, but the glory of God.

GO FORTH FROM BABYLON!

Isaiah 48:12–22

¹²"Hearken to me, O Jacob,
    and Israel, whom I called!
I am He, I am the first,
    and I am the last.
¹³My hand laid the foundation of the earth,
    and my right hand spread out the heavens;
when I call to them,
    they stand forth together.

¹⁴"Assemble, all of you, and hear!
    Who among them has declared these things?
The Lord loves him;
    he shall perform his purpose on Babylon,
    and his arm shall be against the Chaldeans.
¹⁵I, even I, have spoken and called him,
    I have brought him, and he will prosper in his way.
¹⁶Draw near to me, hear this:
    from the beginning I have not spoken in secret,
    from the time it came to be I have been there."
And now the Lord God has sent me and his Spirit.

¹⁷Thus says the Lord,
    your Redeemer, the Holy One of Israel:
"I am the Lord your God,
    who teaches you to profit,
    who leads you in the way you should go.
¹⁸O that you had hearkened to my commandments!
    Then your peace would have been like a river,
    and your righteousness like the waves of the sea;
¹⁹your offspring would have been like the sand,
    and your descendants like its grains;
their name would never be cut off
    or destroyed from before me."

²⁰Go forth from Babylon, flee from Chaldea,
    declare this with a shout of joy, proclaim it,
send it forth to the end of the earth;

say, "The Lord has redeemed his servant Jacob!"
²¹They thirsted not when he led them through the deserts;
    he made water flow for them from the rock;
    he cleft the rock and the water gushed out.
²²"There is no peace," says the Lord, "for the wicked."

The climax of chapters 40–48 consists initially of three short, but magnificent, prophecies, linked by a common structure and a common theme:

   (a) I am the One who *called* all things into being (vv. 12–13);
   (b) I am the One who *called* Cyrus (vv. 14–16);
   (c) I am the One who leads his people, "Israel, whom I *called*" (vv. 17–19).

After the striking change of style and tone in verses 1–11, we are back again in the mainstream of our author's teaching. He who called Israel (v. 12) is the same God who called the earth and the heavens into being. Creation by the Word is a favourite Biblical theme, indicating the effortlessness of God's creative acts and his commanding authority over all that exists (*eg* Ps. 33:6–9):

By the word of the Lord the heavens were made,
    and all their host by the breath of his mouth.
He gathered the waters of the sea as in a bottle;
    he put the deeps in storehouses.
Let all the earth fear the Lord,
    let all the inhabitants of the world stand in awe of him!
For he spoke, and it came to be;
    he commanded, and it stood forth.

He is also the One who called Cyrus (41:2, AV). Verses 14–16 constitute the last trial speech in this section of the book; and as before (*eg* ch. 41), the evidence of history—especially the correspondence between eighth century prophecy and its fulfilment in the sixth—is put forward as proof of God's power. The success of Cyrus, in particular his conquest of Babylon, is foretold again, and yet another extravagant expression is used to describe him: the Lord's "anointed" (45:1), his "shepherd" (44:28), "man of [God's] counsel" (46:11), and now the one whom "the Lord loves" (v. 14).

The last line in verse 16 is one of several Isaianic texts about the prophet's mission: from "Here am I! Send me" in 6:8 to "he has sent me to bind up the brokenhearted" in 61:1. No doubt 40:3 is also in mind. The "Spirit" is the spirit which inspired the prophets (*eg* Num. 11:24–30; Joel 2:28–29; Zech. 7:12; Acts 2), but cannot be separated from the spirit which gave Gideon his courage (Judg. 6:34), Samson his strength (Judg. 14:6, 19) and the Davidic saviour his wisdom (Isa. 11:2) and justice (42:1). It comes here not only as a comment on the rest of verses 14–16, but also as a kind of signature at the end of chapters 40–48; balancing 40:1–8 as it were, and pointing forward to 49:1–6.

Another short prophecy in verse 17, introduced by one of the regular Isaianic formulas (cf. 43:14), turns from the created universe and world history, to what God has done for his own people. He is their teacher and their guide: his teaching, at Sinai and through his servants the prophets, was for their own good, for their "profit" (RSV is ambiguous!); and his guidance, out of exile and through the wilderness, will bring them to the Promised Land. Verse 18 envisages God wistfully longing for his people to obey him. It is reminiscent of the familiar words in Psalm 95:7, but Job 14 contains a more poignant parallel. In comparison with his present suffering, Job imagines the peace and tranquillity of Sheol, the abode of the dead, and God's voice reaching him there (Job 14:15):

> Thou wouldest call, and I would answer thee;
>> thou wouldest long for the work of thy hands.

Our God is no distant, impersonal power, unmoved by our condition: he is a God who suffers with us and because of us. In the pained cries of Jesus over Jerusalem, we can hear that longing again (see Matt. 23:37):

> "O Jerusalem, Jerusalem, killing the prophets and stoning those who are sent to you! How often would I have gathered your children together as a hen gathers her brood under her wings, and you would not!"

The images chosen to describe what might have been, are marvellously effective. "Peace" (*shalom*) (v. 18) is not only absence of war, but also denotes health, security and prosperity. And "righteousness" in its normal Isaianic sense (unlike its use in verse 1), includes victory and salvation (see also 41:2). The word for "river" (Hebrew *nahar*) is elsewhere translated "flood" (*eg* Ps. 93:3; see Isa. 43:2), and means a substantial river, one that flows all the year round, like the Jordan or the Euphrates or the Nile; more like the waves of the sea than the seasonal *wadis* that pass for streams in Israel. Job 6:15–20 is a dramatic description of such a wadi. "The actual history of Israel had been like the wadis of Judaea, transient gleams of prosperity being interrupted by long intervals of misfortune; the river suggests to the writer an image of . . . boundless and unfailing blessedness" (J. Skinner, *Isaiah XL–LXVI*, p. 86). Amos imagines a wadi that never dries up (5:24):

> But let justice roll down like waters,
>   and righteousness like an everflowing stream [*ie* wadi].

Verse 19 looks back to the promise to Abraham and his seed for ever (*eg* Gen. 22:17; Hos. 1:10). It is significant that such a promise makes no mention of the "land", and can be fulfilled even at times when there is no Jewish homeland.

Finally we have the first of two calls to leave captivity behind and to set out into the world again, free, jubilant, trusting in a God who can lead his people Israel through deserts and make water flow for them from the rock (vv. 20–22; 52:11–12). Babylon is not mentioned again in the Book of Isaiah: Israel is free. Let the whole world know that "the Lord has redeemed his servant Jacob!" (v. 22). Notice the singular again, "his servant"; a way of emphasizing at the same time the oneness of Israel, and the close personal relationship between his people and God.

Verse 22, which appears in a more obviously logical context at the end of chapter 57, is an isolated proverb marking the division between chapters 40–48 and 49–55. It is also a comment on the theme of failure in verse 18 and the peace that could have been Israel's had they not rebelled. The visions of a new age in chapters

40–48 have not yet been fulfilled: there is still much to say on the subject of Israel's salvation.

A LIGHT TO THE NATIONS—II

Isaiah 49:1–6

¹Listen to me, O coastlands,
　and hearken, you peoples from afar.
The Lord called me from the womb,
　from the body of my mother he named my name.
²He made my mouth like a sharp sword,
　in the shadow of his hand he hid me;
he made me a polished arrow,
　in his quiver he hid me away.
³And he said to me, "You are my servant,
　Israel, in whom I will be glorified."
⁴But I said, "I have laboured in vain,
　I have spent my strength for nothing and vanity;
yet surely my right is with the Lord,
　and my recompense with my God."

⁵And now the Lord says,
　who formed me from the womb to be his servant,
to bring Jacob back to him,
　and that Israel might be gathered to him,
for I am honoured in the eyes of the Lord,
　and my God has become my strength—
⁶he says:
"It is too light a thing that you should be my servant
　to raise up the tribes of Jacob
　and to restore the preserved of Israel;
I will give you as a light to the nations,
　that my salvation may reach to the end of the earth."

In chapters 34 and 41 the nations are addressed, but here there is a great difference. *First*, it is "the servant of the Lord" who is speaking, and not God; this is not a trial speech or an oracle, but the servant's own testimony about his call and his mission to bring salvation to the ends of the earth (v. 6). *Second*, it introduces a new section (chs. 49–55) in which there is no mention of Babylon or of Cyrus, very little about idols and the wonders of creation, and a new interest in the "servant", to whom three magnificent poems are devoted in the space of five chapters (49:1–6; 50:4–9; 52:13–53:12). When we remember how chapter 48 ended with a final summons to "go forth from Babylon" (48:20) and an isolated proverb that seems to have a rounding-off function (v. 22), it is tempting to suppose that chapters 49–55 were composed after the fall of Babylon and reflect rather different social and religious conditions. There is more about rebuilding ruins, for example, and about returning exiles. Thanksgiving that suffering and humiliation have been replaced by exaltation becomes central. These and other themes, familiar enough to us already from the earlier chapters, are from now on developed to new heights of poetic power.

Verses 1–6 have long been known as the second 'servant song' and are often discussed as one in a series of separate 'Messianic' poems, rather than within their actual context at the beginning of chapter 49 (see my comments on 42:1–4). As they stand, the servant is identified with Israel (v. 3), called from the womb as in 44:2 and 48:1, and thus they highlight a central Isaianic theme, namely, Israel's mission to the world (see 2:3):

And many peoples shall come, and say;
"Come, let us go up to the mountain of the Lord,
    to the house of the God of Jacob;
that he may teach us his ways
    and that we may walk in his paths."
For out of Zion shall go forth the law,
    and the word of the Lord from Jerusalem.

Those who delete the word "Israel" from (49:3) seek to identify the servant with an individual saviour figure as he is in 42:1 and 52:13 (where the word "Messiah" appears in some ancient Jewish versions). All we can do here, as in so many other Biblical texts, is to enjoy the various levels of interpretation and listen sensitively to their individual voices.

The servant is depicted as a prophet, called, like Jeremiah (Jer. 1:5) and Paul (Gal. 1:15), to be God's missionary before he was born. God's call to Israel is described elsewhere thus: God is Israel's father and mother (44:1–2; 46:3), and therefore the one who named him when he was born—as he now does in verse 3 ("Israel, in whom I will be glorified"). Verse 2 develops the prophetic model in two ways. On the one hand, the word of God is like a sharp sword, symbol of power and decisiveness (see Jer. 23:29):

Is not my word like fire, says the Lord, and like a hammer which breaks the rock in pieces.

The word of the Lord destroys the wicked on the Day of Judgment (Hos. 6:5; Rev. 19:15, 21) and gives courage to "an ambassador in chains" (Eph. 6:17, 20). On the other hand, this devastating power of God is concealed, like an arrow in the quiver, until the moment of truth. In later Apocalyptic writings Isaiah 8:16 was interpreted in this way and may be compared to Daniel 12:4. Our author's intention is that we should imagine that Isaiah was called in the eighth century B.C., but that the true meaning of his prophecies was not revealed until after the fall of Babylon in the sixth century.

In verse 3 God addresses the servant directly in the familiar language of the Royal psalms (*eg* 2:7; 89:4; 110:4; 132:11) and the Baptism story (Mark 1:11), where the Lord's *anointed*, the Messiah, is commissioned. The plain meaning of the Hebrew text is that it is Israel which is being commissioned as God's servant, to be a light to the nations. But in view of what has been said above about individual interpretations, it is worth mentioning that Israel could be an epithet for an individual saviour, the Messiah. He is "Israel", the embodiment of God's people, the saving remnant. As when all his disciples had forsaken him, Christ on the cross was the only faithful representative of God's people on earth, and the focal point of a new age about to dawn; so here the servant of the Lord embodies Israel's hopes.

Like Jeremiah and Elijah, the servant feels alone, cut off from his people (v. 4); at times, like Jesus on the cross, afraid that he had been forsaken (Matt. 27:46). The suffering of the lonely prophet in a hostile world was poignantly described in chapter 6. The two halves of verse 4 marvellously combine such doubts and fears with a courageous statement of faith and commitment to God. The same relationship between faith and doubt underlies the Passion narrative (*eg* Mark 14:35–36). The word translated "nothing" in 49:4 is the same as the word for "chaos" in 45:18 and "without form" in Genesis 1:2. But there is no chaos so formless or so meaningless that God cannot impose order upon it. As so often in Isaiah, salvation is represented in legal terms ("my right"; cf. 40:27).

The conclusion in verses 5–6 returns to the universal context with which the poem begins. The servant's first mission, like that of Moses, Elijah and Isaiah (ch. 6), had been to his own people (v. 5), to bring them back to God from exile; the exile of disobedience and sin as well as the Babylonian exile. The Hebrew text then reads "though Israel be *not* gathered" (AV), where "gather" means "take away, gather to your fathers", that is, a euphemism for "die" (*eg* Isa. 57:1; 2 Kings 22:20): so that Israel might not die but be glorified in the eyes of the Lord. Others emend the text as RSV, reading *lo*, "to him", instead of *lo*, "not" (the two words are pronounced the same but written slightly differently).

But such an inward-looking mission is too easy (v. 6)! This is an amazing statement when you think of how the prophets suffered at the hands of their own people: *eg* "O Jerusalem, Jerusalem, killing the prophets and stoning those who are sent to you!" (Luke 13:34; see also Isa. 6:9ff.; Ezek. 2:3–4). "Raise up" (v. 6) implies that the tribes of Jacob have fallen (Pss. 145:14; 146:8) or been reduced to abject poverty (1 Sam. 2:8; Ps. 113:7); and "restore" refers to both spiritual renewal or repentance (*eg* Jer. 23:22, "turned them"; 31:18), and physical return from exile to Jerusalem. "The preserved of Israel" (v. 6) sounds odd in this context, and although the verb appears again in verse 8 ("kept", RSV), a minor change in the Hebrew text would give the genealogical term *branches*, that is, "offspring of Israel", a good parallel to "tribes of Jacob".

"A light to the nations" was discussed at 42:6: in both contexts the phrase is closely associated with the servant and his saving significance for the world. "My salvation" (*yeshu'ah*), one of the commonest Isaianic terms, means an act of divine intervention on behalf of justice and peace (see comments on 43:3).

A DAY OF SALVATION

Isaiah 49:7–13

> [7]Thus says the Lord,
>   the Redeemer of Israel and his Holy One,
>   to one deeply despised, abhorred by the nations,
>   the servant of rulers:
> "Kings shall see and arise;
>   princes, and they shall prostrate themselves;
>   because of the Lord, who is faithful,
>   the Holy One of Israel, who has chosen you."
>
> [8]Thus says the Lord:
> "In a time of favour I have answered you,
>   in a day of salvation I have helped you;
>   I have kept you and given you
>   as a covenant to the people,
>   to establish the land,
>   to apportion the desolate heritages;
> [9]saying to the prisoners, 'Come forth,'
>   to those who are in darkness, 'Appear.'
>   They shall feed along the ways,
>   on all bare heights shall be their pasture;
> [10]they shall not hunger or thirst,
>   neither scorching wind nor sun shall smite them,
>   for he who has pity on them will lead them,
>   and by springs of water will guide them.
> [11]And I will make all my mountains a way,
>   and my highways shall be raised up.
> [12]Lo, these shall come from afar,
>   and lo, these from the north and from the west,
>   and these from the land of Syene."
> [13]Sing for joy, O heavens, and exult, O earth;

break forth, O mountains, into singing!
For the Lord has comforted his people,
and will have compassion on his afflicted.

Two prophecies of salvation, each introduced by the usual formula, "Thus says the Lord" (vv. 7 and 8), are now addressed to
the servant, who has just been given a challenging mission to the
world. The *first* of these, which consists of one verse only (v. 7),
picks out the word "servant" (or "slave") from the preceding
passage, and uses it to contrast Israel's present subservient plight
(a "slave of tyrants", NEB) with the future dominion of the
liberated "servant", chosen by the Holy One of Israel. "Deeply
despised, abhorred" (RSV) recalls the language of Lamentations
in which the ruin of humiliated Jerusalem is mourned, while the
picture of kings and princes prostrating themselves is but a fore-
taste of the scenes depicted later in the chapter (vv. 23, 26). In
these, a weak and threatened victim bitterly imagines a day when
his oppressors will pay the penalty for their cruelty. Only the
great Isaianic motifs—"Redeemer . . . Holy One of Israel . . .
faithful . . . who has chosen you", familiar to us from many other
passages (*eg* 43:3)—can raise such prophecies above the level of
hate and vengefulness to a plane where God treats us as we
deserve; a plane where the extremes of good and evil, heaven and
hell, are realities.

The *second* prophecy of salvation, addressed to "my servant,
Israel" (v. 3), is longer and infinitely more beautiful (vv. 8–13). It
embroiders a rich tapestry of ideas and images, many of them
familiar to us already. "A time of favour", like "the acceptable
year of the Lord" (61:2, AV; 58:5), echoes the word translated
"delights" in 42:1 and "well pleased" in Matthew 3:17. It means
in God's good time: our salvation depends on his will not ours.

The rest of the prophecy is clearly concerned with the salvation
of God's people, although what happens in Israel or on Mount
Zion gives light to the whole world (v. 6). "Kept" (v. 8) goes back
to "the preserved of Israel" in verse 6. We discussed the words
"covenant to the people" in the context of 42:6, but here they are
explained in terms of hope for "the land" and the "desolate

heritages"—of Israel, that is, not of the nations of the world. In verses 9–11 two images are chosen to describe the salvation of God's people. *First* it will be like a general amnesty. Prisoners will be released and come out into the light of day after long, dark imprisonment. The *second* is familiar to us from Psalm 23 and Isaiah 40:11: God will care for them like a good shepherd, feeding them, protecting them from danger, leading them by springs of water. The "scorching wind" (v. 10), or *sirocco*, can be so unbearable in the Middle East that schools and other institutions often close early when it blows. Verse 11 refers specifically to the land of Israel in the new age, where all the hills are God's mountains and all the roads God's highways: so that there will be nothing to fear.

"Lo" (v. 12) heralds the astonishing return of the exiles to their native land, which becomes the main theme of the rest of the chapter. In verse 12 we are to think of exiles coming from Mesopotamia in the north and Egypt in the west. Syene seems to allude to the well-established Jewish settlement on the island of Elephantine on the Nile, situated opposite Syene (modern Aswan). A quantity of Aramaic documents discovered there in 1903 shed light on life in that community of Jewish exiles in the fifth century B.C. By that time both Egypt and Babylon were the centres of thriving Jewish communities. So successful and well-established were they, in fact, that prophecies like the present were not fulfilled until modern times, when virtually all Egyptian and Iraqi Jews emigrated to the modern state of Israel. The Hebrew text actually reads "land of Sinim", which apparently means "land of the Chinese". While a reference to the far east would make excellent sense today, and no doubt did so at the time when an imaginative scribe wrote in this word, it can hardly be original since China was unknown in the west before the Christian era. In any case, the Isaiah Scroll from Qumran, dated first century B.C., has "Syene".

The prophecy concludes with a one-verse hymn of praise (v. 13), like those in 42:10–13, 45:8 and elsewhere. Heaven and earth are invited to join in the singing. The mountains are summoned separately in view of verse 11 and perhaps also in the light of the love for the mountains of Judah obvious throughout the book (2:2; 11:9; 25:6; 40:9; 52:7; 66:20). "Comfort" (v. 13) recalls 40:1 and other passages, and effectively sums up the content of verses 1-13. Prophecies concerning the poor and afflicted, like 1:17; 58:6-7 and 61:1-2, come home in our own day with the realization that most of the world's population is poor, and that to be true to her Biblical roots, the Church should have a special concern for the poverty-stricken in all she does.

DOUBTING ZION

Isaiah 49:14-26

¹⁴But Zion said, "The Lord has forsaken me,
    my Lord has forgotten me."
¹⁵"Can a woman forget her sucking child,
    that she should have no compassion on the son of her womb?
Even these may forget,
    yet I will not forget you.
¹⁶Behold, I have graven you on the palms of my hands;
    your walls are continually before me.
¹⁷Your builders outstrip your destroyers,
    and those who laid you waste go forth from you.
¹⁸Lift up your eyes round about and see;
    they all gather, they come to you.
As I live, says the Lord,
    you shall put them all on as an ornament,
    you shall bind them on as a bride does.

¹⁹"Surely your waste and your desolate places
    and your devastated land—
surely now you will be too narrow for your inhabitants,
    and those who swallowed you up will be far away.
²⁰The children born in the time of your bereavement
    will yet say in your ears:
'The place is too narrow for me;
    make room for me to dwell in.'
²¹Then you will say in your heart:
'Who has borne me these?

I was bereaved and barren,
  exiled and put away,
  but who has brought up these?
Behold, I was left alone;
  whence then have these come?' "

²²Thus says the Lord God:
"Behold, I will lift up my hand to the nations,
  and raise my signal to the peoples;
and they shall bring your sons in their bosom,
  and your daughters shall be carried on their shoulders.
²³Kings shall be your foster fathers,
  and their queens your nursing mothers.
With their faces to the ground they shall bow down to you,
  and lick the dust of your feet.
Then you will know that I am the Lord;
  those who wait for me shall not be put to shame."

²⁴Can the prey be taken from the mighty,
  or the captives of a tyrant be rescued?
²⁵Surely, thus says the Lord:
"Even the captives of the mighty shall be taken,
  and the prey of the tyrant be rescued,
for I will contend with those who contend with you,
  and I will save your children.
²⁶I will make your oppressors eat their own flesh,
  and they shall be drunk with their own blood as with wine.
Then all flesh shall know
  that I am the Lord your Saviour,
  and your Redeemer, the Mighty One of Jacob."

The rest of this exciting chapter deals with three questions raised by doubting Zion (vv. 14, 21, 24). Each is answered by a salvation oracle (15–20; 22–23; 25–26). It is most important to realize that in the original Hebrew, "Zion" (like all other city-names) is feminine, and so all three oracles are addressed as though to a forlorn mother afraid she will never see her children again, and they are all the more moving and effective for that.

Her *first* reaction to the news that "the Lord has comforted his people" (v. 13) is disbelief: as far as she can see, she has been abandoned by her husband (50:1) and has no cause whatever to "sing for joy" (v. 13). To someone plunged into grief and despair, there is nothing more devastating than a smiling evangelist glibly telling her to believe in God and all will be well. The prophet is sensitive to the reality of doubt and handles it sympathetically and imaginatively. Initially, he uses the image of a mother's compassion ("love" might have been simpler: NEB) for her child. The word translated "compassion" is the same as the one used in verse 13, and is closely associated with the word for "womb" in Hebrew. God's love for Zion is more enduring even than that supreme example of human love, so she may be comforted after all, and at peace like a child in its mother's arms (Ps. 131:2, RSV).

The next image may be that of an architect planning a new city, drawing innumerable sketches and diagrams (v. 16), like Ezekiel (4:1), watching the builders getting on with their work (v. 17), and finally seeing the new houses and streets brought to life, graced with the colour and excitement of busy crowds, just as a bride is adorned for her wedding (v. 18). The whole land will be filled once again with people, to such an extent that paradoxically they will complain about the lack of space in their homeland (vv. 19–20).

Verse 16 has been given another meaning by Christian writers, which would lead the whole oracle in a different direction. In the only other Biblical text about marks being imprinted on the palms of the hand, it is Christ who speaks and the "stigmata", the marks of the nails on his hands, are symbols of his love. In that context doubting Thomas takes the place of Zion (John 20:24–28). In verse 17 of Isaiah 49, the Hebrew text actually has "sons", not "builders" (RSV, NEB), and obviously intends us to think more of a mother's self-giving love for her children (vv. 15, 20) than of architects and builders. The passage ends with a marvellous hyperbole: children complaining to their mother that they do not have enough room. What better way to convince Zion that "the Lord will have compassion on his afflicted" (v. 13)?

Zion's *second* question, however, implies continuing disbelief: where have all these children come from (v. 21)? She had thought that all her children had been lost, and that she could not herself have any more, being exiled, put away, abandoned, barren. The salvation oracle that follows takes up the familiar theme of God as Lord of history: he gives the signal, just as he whistled "for the fly which is at the sources of the streams of Egypt" (7:18), and the nations of the world join forces to bring her sons and daughters home safely. Both this oracle and the next one then go on to castigate the nations that had oppressed God's people (Egypt, Assyria, Babylon) in appalling language. In verse 23, the kings and queens of the world are represented as caring for Zion's children; feeding them, washing them, changing their nappies, as it were. That is humiliating enough, but then comes one of the most offensive verses in the Old Testament:

> With their faces to the ground they shall bow down to you,
>   and lick the dust of your feet.

On the one hand, we can only try to understand, without condoning them, the bitterness and anguish that prompted such ideas and images. On the other hand, we must also remember that, as they stand, in canonical scripture, they are not directed against any actual people and must never be. They are rather aimed at the principalities and powers of evil, illustrated by historical examples, such as Babylon, Egypt and Assyria, but now totally divorced from them. Their purpose is to balance the colourful and moving images of salvation such as those in verses 8–13 above.

The *third* objection of doubting Zion (v. 24) is that, when a victory is total, there is no hope for the vanquished. The Hebrew text says nothing of tyranny: "tyrant" (RSV; "ruthless", NEB) is an emendation based on the Isaiah Scroll from Qumran and the parallel in verse 25. The Hebrew text as it stands has "righteous man", or better, "victor" (see comments on 41:2), suggesting it is even less likely that anyone will take the spoils of battle from him or rescue his captives.

The corresponding salvation oracle contains a rich concentration of familiar words and images of salvation: "contend" (cf. 50:8), "save", "Saviour" (43:3; 45:15), "Redeemer" (41:14; 43:14), "Mighty One of Jacob" (1:24; Ps. 132:5), "all flesh shall know..." (40:5–6). But the tone of the oracle, like that of the previous one, turns to violence and brutality. The "victor" (or "righteous one") of verse 24 becomes the "tyrant" in verse 25; the captives are identified as Zion's "children"; "those who contend with you" in verse 25 become "your oppressors" in verse 26, and are made to eat their own flesh and get drunk on their own blood. Once again our instant reaction to such language is one of revulsion. But there is another interpretation which is worth considering. This concerns the self-destructive effects of war. Those who develop sophisticated weapons of war are heading for disaster and will be responsible for the death of their own "flesh and blood". It ill becomes twentieth century commentators to condemn this language as primitive or barbaric when the superpowers of our day seem to be prepared to countenance just such a course of self-destructive madness, leading to the annihilation of the whole human race, not just the wicked parts of it.

I HID NOT MY FACE FROM SHAME AND SPITTING

Isaiah 50:1–11

¹Thus says the Lord:
  "Where is your mother's bill of divorce,
    with which I put her away?
  Or which of my creditors is it
    to whom I have sold you?
  Behold, for your iniquities you were sold,
    and for your transgressions your mother was put away.
²Why, when I came, was there no man?
    When I called, was there no one to answer?
  Is my hand shortened, that it cannot redeem?
    Or have I no power to deliver?
  Behold, by my rebuke I dry up the sea,
    I make the rivers a desert;
  their fish stink for lack of water,
    and die of thirst.
³I clothe the heavens with blackness,
    and make sackcloth their covering."

⁴The Lord God has given me
    the tongue of those who are taught,

that I may know how to sustain with a word
    him that is weary.
Morning by morning he wakens,
    he wakens my ear
    to hear as those who are taught.
⁵The Lord God has opened my ear,
    and I was not rebellious,
    I turned not backward.
⁶I gave my back to the smiters,
    and my cheeks to those who pulled out the beard;
    I hid not my face
    from shame and spitting.

⁷For the Lord God helps me;
    therefore I have not been confounded;
    therefore I have set my face like a flint,
    and I know that I shall not be put to shame;
⁸ he who vindicates me is near.
Who will contend with me?
    Let us stand up together.
Who is my adversary?
    Let him come near to me.
⁹Behold, the Lord God helps me;
    who will declare me guilty?
Behold, all of them will wear out like a garment;
    the moth will eat them up.

¹⁰Who among you fears the Lord
    and obeys the voice of his servant,
who walks in darkness
    and has no light,
yet trusts in the name of the Lord
    and relies upon his God?
¹¹Behold, all you who kindle a fire,
    who set brands alight!
Walk by the light of your fire,
    and by the brands which you have kindled!
This shall you have from my hand:
    you shall lie down in torment.

In chapter 50 the order of the dialogue is reversed: *first* comes the salvation oracle introduced by "Thus says the Lord" (vv. 1–3), and *second* the prophet's response on behalf of his suffering people (vv. 4–11). This rather personal or autobiographical poem is the third of the so-called "Servant Songs", discussed in connection with 42:1–4 (see further at 52:13).

The oracle is addressed this time to Zion's children, rather than Zion herself as in the previous chapter, and introduces two more images. *First*, God is Zion's husband, but he had never divorced Zion: no irrevocable "bill of divorce" had been drawn up (Deut. 24:1–4; Mark 10:2–4); separation was only temporary. *Second*, God had never sold them into slavery, like some desperate debtor. The final step in a man's downfall was when he had to sell his children to pay off a debt (2 Kings 4:1; Neh. 5:1–5). But God has no debts, no need to borrow, no creditors. So neither of these two irrevocable steps towards breaking the relationship between God and his people had been taken. Their sufferings were temporary, and, what is more, a deliberate part of God's plan to punish them, to discipline them for their "iniquities" and their "transgressions" (v. 1). They were proof that he cared for them in the same way as a father who must sometimes discipline his son (Deut. 8:5).

Verse 2 rebukes the disbelievers for their lack of faith: when he "comes with might" (*eg* 40:9–10), can they not recognize him? When he calls to them (*eg* 40:3–5), can they not respond? Then comes another brilliant progression of images, piled one on top of the other, from general language about God's saving power ("Is my hand shortened?" 50:2) to gratuitous details from the Exodus story, such as the dead fish on the dry land where the Red Sea had been parted (Exod. 14:22–29; 7:21), and (v. 3) the blackened sky that finally forced the Pharaoh to let God's people go (Exod. 10:21; 19:16; 20:21). "Redeem" (v. 2) is the word translated "ransom" in 43:3. We must remember also that in ancient myth, "sea" and "rivers" were personified as monsters whose spectacular defeat by *Yahweh* was celebrated in the Psalms (*eg* 89:9–10; 93) and in some Isaianic passages (*eg* 27:1; 44:27; 51:9–10).

The poem that follows is written in the form of a psalm of trust, moving from lamentation to confidence, like Psalm 11, Jeremiah 11:18–20 and 17:7–13. It is placed here as a comment on the preceding passage (49:14–50:3), where Zion's doubts and fears were answered with a word from God. The prophet now tells us that he has been called to do this for his people: "sustain with a word him that is weary" (v. 4). It has not been an easy role to play: he has suffered pain and indignity at the hand of incredulous and unreceptive listeners (v. 6). But he has not shrunk from his duty (v. 5), confident in the truth of his message and the power of God to help (vv. 7–9). The theme is a familiar one going back to Isaiah's vision in chapter 6, and paralleled in the stories of Moses, Elijah, Jeremiah, and the prophets in general (see my comments on 49:1–6 and 52:13–53:12). The language may have been influenced by a Babylonian ceremony in which the king was ritually beaten and humiliated, his beard pulled and his garments torn, before being triumphantly exalted (Zech. 3:1–5 may be another Biblical allusion to this). But the context rules out any royal connection here: the poem is about a prophet's lonely struggle to survive and preserve his integrity in a hostile world.

It also contains a rare glimpse into prophetic consciousness: the prophet Isaiah is "taught" by God (v. 4), awakened (inspired?) and addressed by him as his disciple, "morning by morning", like Ezekiel (Ezek. 12:8). God has "opened [his] ear", that is to say, given him an extra sensitivity to what only God's servants, like Isaiah and Paul (2 Cor. 12:4), can hear: "things that cannot be told, which man may not utter."

The protestation of innocence in verses 5–6 is a conventional part of this type of poem, as can be seen from other examples like Jeremiah 11:19 and 20:7–10.

Verses 7–9 draw on law-court jargon to express the prophet's confidence that God is on his side. Terms like "vindicate", "contend", "adversary" and "declare . . . guilty" recall trial scenes from earlier chapters (*eg* 41:21–24; 43:8–13), but here it is the lonely prophet who is the accused, and God his advocate. Two similes beautifully express the contrast between the falsely accused and his adversaries: he is as unbreakable as flint (50:7),

they are as insecure as pieces of old clothing infested with moths
(v. 9).

A similar contrast is drawn in verses 10–11 between those who
listen to the voice of the prophet and those who rage against it.
The former are characterized by faith and trust even in dark and
troubled times, described in true Isaianic terms (*eg* 9:2; 30:15);
the latter, by rejecting the prophet and plotting his destruction,
will only destroy themselves, like the oppressors in 49:26. Wilful
disobedience and arrogance are self-destructive too. In the words
of another psalm of trust (Ps. 57:6):

> They set a net for my steps;
>   my soul was bowed down.
> They dug a pit in my way,
>   but they have fallen into it themselves.

The chapter ends with one of the Old Testament texts cited in
Christian representations of Hell; 66:24 is another, as is Ecclesiasticus (*Sirach*) 7:17:

> For the punishment of the ungodly is fire and worms.

The bitter and vindictive ending to the poem, like the ending of
chapters 49, 51 and Psalm 137, is understandable (though not of
course excusable), both as a response to extreme suffering, and as
a comment on the reality of evil in the world.

LOOK TO THE ROCK FROM WHICH YOU WERE HEWN

Isaiah 51:1–8

> [1]"Hearken to me, you who pursue deliverance,
>   you who seek the Lord;
>   look to the rock from which you were hewn,
>   and to the quarry from which you were digged.
> [2]Look to Abraham your father
>   and to Sarah who bore you;
>   for when he was but one I called him,
>   and I blessed him and made him many.
> [3]For the Lord will comfort Zion;

>   he will comfort all her waste places,
>   and will make her wilderness like Eden,
>   her desert like the garden of the Lord;
>   joy and gladness will be found in her,
>   thanksgiving and the voice of song.

>   ⁴"Listen to me, my people,
>   and give ear to me, my nation;
>   for a law will go forth from me,
>   and my justice for a light to the peoples.
>   ⁵My deliverance draws near speedily,
>   my salvation has gone forth,
>   and my arms will rule the peoples;
>   the coastlands wait for me,
>   and for my arm they hope.
>   ⁶Lift up your eyes to the heavens,
>   and look at the earth beneath;
>   for the heavens will vanish like smoke,
>   the earth will wear out like a garment,
>   and they who dwell in it will die like gnats;
>   but my salvation will be for ever,
>   and my deliverance will never be ended.

>   ⁷"Hearken to me, you who know righteousness,
>   the people in whose heart is my law;
>   fear not the reproach of men,
>   and be not dismayed at their revilings.
>   ⁸For the moth will eat them up like a garment,
>   and the worm will eat them like wool;
>   but my deliverance will be for ever,
>   and my salvation to all generations."

This and the following chapter (to v. 12) comprise a rich sequence of prophetic utterances moving towards a climax in which God is proclaimed king in Jerusalem (52:7–10), and the exiles begin their dignified *Exodus* from Babylon (52:11–12). Verses 1–8 of this chapter are made up of three short prophecies, all beginning "Hearken" or "Listen", and all hinging on the word *tsedeq* or *tsedakah* (see vv. 1, 5–8); translated variously as "deliverance" (vv. 1, 5–6, 8), and "righteousness" (v. 7). In verse 1, where "pursuing *tsedek*" is parallel to "seeking the Lord" (Amos 5), it may have a more devotional or ethical meaning represented in the translations "righteousness" (AV) or "the right" (NEB). Certainly verses 1–2 together point unmistakeably to the less Temple-centred Judaism of exilic and post-exilic times, when "seeking the Lord" came close to studying the *Torah* (v. 2). The exigencies of translation must not be allowed to obscure the fact that the same Hebrew word occurs five times in eight verses, and neatly describes the recipients of the prophetic word, both as those who know what right religion is and as those who will recognize the acts of divine intervention shortly to be realized.

The *first* of the three prophecies summons those who "seek the Lord" to remember their origins: they are descended from Abraham and Sarah, and therefore inheritors of the promises to Abraham and his seed for ever (Gen. 12:1–3; 15:18; 17:3–8). Verse 1 could also refer to the "Rock that bore you" (Deut. 32:18; see footnote) and the beautiful idea that God is mother and father of us all (see Isaiah 17:10; 26:4; 30:29; 42:14), but verse 2 applies the image to the patriarchs.

In the short 'salvation hymn' in verse 3 (cf. 42:10–13; 44:23), "comfort", repeated twice as in 40:1, links the patriarchal blessing of verse 2 with the rebuilding and replanting imagery (also reminiscent of ch. 40) that follows. It is another picture of the desert blossoming like a garden, and general jubilation throughout the land.

The *second* of the three prophecies addressed to "my people ... my nation" (v. 4) declares that salvation will be universal and eternal, picking up the theme from chapters 2, 42, 49 and elsewhere. What happens in Jerusalem affects the whole world, in this case bringing justice and hope to the peoples of the world. There is a new note of urgency or immediacy in verse 5: the word translated "speedily" is a rare and striking word, and heightens the dramatic effect of these two climactic chapters. Finally verse 6 breaks out of normal prophetic ways of thinking, and imagines heaven and earth vanishing like smoke; the earth wearing out like old clothes and the human race dying like "gnats" (RSV) or "maggots" (NEB)—whereas "salvation" (*yeshu'ah*) and "deliverance" (*tsedakah*) will be for ever.

The *third* and last of the three short prophecies is addressed to those who have the *Torah* (law) within their hearts; an idea well known from Deuteronomy (*eg* 30:14), Jeremiah (31:31–34), Ezekiel (36:26–27), Paul (2 Cor 3:1–6) and others. Isaiah 8:16 is probably another example (see vol. 1, p. 94). With such inner strength, you have nothing to fear from enemies or persecutors: they will perish like a moth-eaten garment. "But my deliverance . . .": the refrain from verse 6 is repeated with the two key words reversed.

ARM OF THE LORD, AWAKE!

Isaiah 51:9–52:12

⁹Awake, awake, put on strength,
    O arm of the Lord;
awake, as in days of old,
    the generations of long ago.
Was it not thou that didst cut Rahab in pieces,
    that didst pierce the dragon?
¹⁰Was it not thou that didst dry up the sea,
    the waters of the great deep;
that didst make the depths of the sea a way
    for the redeemed to pass over?
¹¹And the ransomed of the Lord shall return,
    and come to Zion with singing;
everlasting joy shall be upon their heads;
    they shall obtain joy and gladness,
    and sorrow and sighing shall flee away.

¹²"I, I am he that comforts you;
    who are you that you are afraid of man who dies,
    of the son of man who is made like grass,
¹³and have forgotten the Lord, your Maker,
    who stretched out the heavens
    and laid the foundations of the earth,
and fear continually all the day
    because of the fury of the oppressor,
when he sets himself to destroy?

And where is the fury of the oppressor?
¹⁴He who is bowed down shall speedily be released;
    he shall not die and go down to the Pit,
    neither shall his bread fail.
¹⁵For I am the Lord your God,
    who stirs up the sea so that its waves roar—
    the Lord of hosts is his name.
¹⁶And I have put my words in your mouth,
    and hid you in the shadow of my hand,
stretching out the heavens
    and laying the foundations of the earth,
    and saying to Zion, 'You are my people.'"

¹⁷Rouse yourself, rouse yourself,
    stand up, O Jerusalem,
you who have drunk at the hand of the Lord
    the cup of his wrath,
who have drunk to the dregs
    the bowl of staggering.
¹⁸There is none to guide her
    among all the sons she has borne;
there is none to take her by the hand
    among all the sons she has brought up.
¹⁹These two things have befallen you—
    who will condole with you?—
devastation and destruction, famine and sword;
    who will comfort you?
²⁰Your sons have fainted,
    they lie at the head of every street
    like an antelope in a net;
they are full of the wrath of the Lord,
    the rebuke of your God.

²¹Therefore hear this, you who are afflicted,
    who are drunk, but not with wine:
²²Thus says your Lord, the Lord,
    your God who pleads the cause of his people:
"Behold, I have taken from your hand
    the cup of staggering;
the bowl of my wrath
    you shall drink no more;

²³and I will put it into the hand of your tormentors,
  who have said to you,
  'Bow down, that we may pass over';
and you have made your back like the ground
  and like the street for them to pass over.''

¹Awake, awake,
  put on your strength, O Zion;
put on your beautiful garments,
  O Jerusalem, the holy city;
for there shall no more come into you
  the uncircumcised and the unclean.
²Shake yourself from the dust, arise,
  O captive Jerusalem;
loose the bonds from your neck,
  O captive daughter of Zion.

³For thus says the Lord: "You were sold for nothing, and you shall be redeemed without money. ⁴For thus says the Lord God: My people went down at the first into Egypt to sojourn there, and the Assyrian oppressed them for nothing. ⁵Now therefore what have I here, says the Lord, seeing that my people are taken away for nothing? Their rulers wail, says the Lord, and continually all the day my name is despised. ⁶Therefore my people shall know my name; therefore in that day they shall know that it is I who speak; here am I."

⁷How beautiful upon the mountains
  are the feet of him who brings good tidings,
who publishes peace, who brings good tidings of good,
  who publishes salvation,
  who says to Zion, "Your God reigns."
⁸Hark, your watchmen lift up their voice,
  together they sing for joy;
for eye to eye they see
  the return of the Lord to Zion.
⁹Break forth together into singing,
  you waste places of Jerusalem;
for the Lord has comforted his people,
  he has redeemed Jerusalem.
¹⁰The Lord has bared his holy arm
  before the eyes of all the nations;

and all the ends of the earth shall see
   the salvation of our God.

¹¹Depart, depart, go out thence,
   touch no unclean thing;
 go out from the midst of her, purify yourselves,
   you who bear the vessels of the Lord.
¹²For you shall not go out in haste,
   and you shall not go in flight,
 for the Lord will go before you,
   and the God of Israel will be your rear guard.

After the opening exhortation (vv. 1–8), the next section is made
up of three units, each beginning with feminine singular imperatives (like 54:1; 60:1), and concluding with a salvation oracle (vv.
9–16; 17–23; 52:1–6).

The *first* is a cry for help characteristic of the community
lament, as Psalms 44:23 and 74:22 illustrate. In times of trouble
appeal is made to God's mighty deeds in the past: the history of
how he rescued the people of Israel from their enemies (*eg* Pss.
44; 80), or the story of creation (*eg* Ps. 74), or, as here, both
ingeniously woven together. The timeless myth of God's victory
over Rahab and the waters of the great deep is "actualized" in the
events of the Exodus, so that the cutting up of the sea-monster is
identified with the parting of the Red Sea, and the creation
mythology applied (v. 13) to the creation of Israel (cf. Exod.
15:1–18; Ps. 89:5–18; Isa. 43:1). Rahab may be identified with
Egypt, as in Isaiah 30:7. Later commentators went so far as to
identify Rahab's counterpart, Leviathan, with Assyria, and "the
dragon" with Rome (see commentary on 27:1; vol. 1, p. 224),
because these colourful myths are expressions of faith in God's
power to defeat all the powers of darkness, not just the darkness
of primeval chaos (Gen. 1:2). "The great deep" (v. 10) also
appears in Gen. 1:2, and re-emerges in the flood story (Gen.
7:11). It too symbolizes a recurring threat to the peaceful order of
human lives. In modern times, the Nazi Holocaust can be thought
of as the bursting forth of "the fountains of the great deep" (Gen.
7:11). Nevertheless, the arm of the Lord slew the dragon and
dried up the waters of that "great deep", to make a way through

the depths of the sea for the "redeemed" to pass over and the "ransomed" to come to Zion "with singing" (vv. 10–11). (For comments on verse 11, see at 35:10 where it appears in almost identical form.)

The salvation oracle in verses 12–16, whose function is to communicate God's word of comfort and encouragement to the frightened community (*eg* 41:8–10), contrasts the power of God, creator of heaven and earth—and creator of his people Israel (vv. 13 and 16)—with the futile fury of the oppressor. The word for "oppressor" is an unusual word suggesting all manner of restrictions on Israel's freedom. In Roman times, Jewish commentators noticed how similar this word (in Hebrew, *metsiq*) is to the Latin *missicius*, a term for discharged soldiers who were given Jewish land and who were inevitably associated with foreign domination.

"Bowed down" (v. 14) adds another effective detail to the picture of suffering. It is the word applied to the war-weary stranger at the gates of the city in 63:1. Even death and starvation are included here (v. 14). Yet in all these things, says the prophet, we are more than conquerors, since our God is the Lord of hosts who created heaven and earth, but who treats Zion as his own. Notice the connection between the beginning and the end of the couplet in verses 15–16: "I am the Lord your God . . . You are my people"—a fundamental doctrine of Biblical theology (see also Jer. 31:33; Hos. 2:23).

ARISE, O CAPTIVE JERUSALEM

Isaiah 51:9–52:12 (*cont'd*)

The *second* unit in this long section also begins with the language of a lament (like Lam. 1–2), enumerating the ills that have befallen the city (vv. 17–20), and concludes with another salvation oracle (vv. 21–23). "The cup of wrath" (v. 17) and its antidote, "the cup of salvation" (*eg* Ps. 116:13), are powerful images possibly derived from primitive divination rituals (like Joseph's: Gen. 44:5), although Isaiah 12:3 suggests a different picture: "with joy you shall draw water from the wells of salvation". John 4 is another illuminating passage.

Verses 19–20 are subtler and more poignant in Hebrew than the RSV suggests. "These two things" refer to two alliterative word-pairs, translated "devastation/destruction", referring to the fate of the land, and "famine/sword" referring to the fate of its inhabitants. "Condole" (v. 19, RSV) is a rather cold translation for a powerful expression of sympathy: "console" (NEB) is perhaps better.

The image of a swift and graceful antelope falling exhausted after vainly struggling to free itself from the hunters' net, marvellously expresses the frustrations and shattered hopes of Zion's children, captured by Nebuchadnezzar's armies at "the rebuke of your God" (v. 20).

The vengeful tone of verse 23 is to be understood, like the ending of the previous two chapters and Psalm 137, against the background of a frightened community fighting for its identity. The whole gamut of human nature, its strengths and its weaknesses, is displayed within the diversity of Old Testament tradition, and the gospel in such passages is that God redeems even such people from the hands of their oppressors, whether they deserve it or not.

The *third* unit, 52:1–6, follows the same pattern as the previous two units: a call to Zion to wake up and rise from the dust (vv. 1–2), and a salvation oracle (vv. 3–6). The ritual purity of the New Jerusalem, such a major theme in Ezekiel's vision (Ezek. 40–48), does not loom large in Isaianic tradition, but it appears here, and again later, in the present chapter (v. 11). See commentary on 66:1–4. "Captive" in verse 2 comes from an emended text: the Hebrew has "sit down", possibly in the sense of "relax! free at last from the dust and fetters of captivity".

The salvation oracle presents critical problems which are hard to solve. It is addressed to "you" (masculine plural) instead of Jerusalem (feminine singular) as in the previous verses. It is not in metrical form, so far as we can judge (RSV). The reference to Assyria (v. 4) is unique in these chapters, and the statement that Assyrian oppression was not deserved contradicts Isaiah 10:5 and the whole tenor of the early chapters of the book, not to mention the opening of chapter 40. Perhaps the Hebrew text is corrupt here, deliberately or accidentally changed to whitewash Israel: a minor emendation would change "for nothing" (v. 5) into "in my anger", or else the sentence might be understood, "At the beginning my people went down into Egypt . . . and at the end it was the Assyrians who oppressed them" (NEB). The ancient Greek version has "for their crimes", which would be more consistent with Isaianic theology. Verse 6 is entirely apt, however, and has the effect of linking this enigmatic oracle with the lament that precedes it. It contains or alludes to several typical prophetic motifs: the phrase "my people" (40:1; 51:16); "in that day"; "I am He" (41:4; 43:13; 46:4); and an idiom for "says the Lord" which occurs only in Haggai and here (twice in verse 5).

The sequence of prophetic utterances in chapters 51 and 52 is rounded off by a hymn and a call to action. The hymn in verses 7–10 is reminiscent of the Enthronement psalms (*eg* Ps. 93; 95–99) which celebrate the victory of *Yahweh* over the powers of chaos. It also gathers together in a beautiful form some of the great themes from earlier chapters: the hills (40:9; 49:11); the bringer of good news (40:9), whose approaching footsteps sound like music to the ears of waiting Jerusalem (v. 7); victory (RSV "salvation"); the heightened awareness (v. 8) of the "watchmen" (40:9–10; 49:18; 66:14; Ps. 126:1); comfort (v. 9; 40:1; 49:13); and (v. 10) the revelation of God's power to all the nations (42:6; 49:6).

The royal imagery of verses 7–10 is then supplemented with a call to the cultic leaders of the community to form up in a dignified procession leading out of their place of captivity (vv. 11–12). The theme of the Temple vessels, taken up from chapter 39, confirms that iniquity is pardoned and warfare ended (40:2). The other theme alluded to here explicitly is that of the Exodus: the rare word "in haste" (v. 12) occurs only in connection with the Exodus (Exod. 12:11; Deut. 16:3, AV). The New Exodus will be more dignified and secure than the old, with God himself as both vanguard and rearguard: no uncleanness, no fear, no indecent haste. The implied call to forget the "former things" (43:18) because something totally new is about to happen, provides a perfect lead into the most original prophecy in the whole book.

THE SUFFERING SERVANT—I

Isaiah 52:13–53:12

¹³Behold, my servant shall prosper,
　　he shall be exalted and lifted up,
　　and shall be very high.
¹⁴As many were astonished at him—
　　his appearance was so marred, beyond human semblance,
　　and his form beyond that of the sons of men—
¹⁵so shall he startle many nations;
　　kings shall shut their mouths because of him;
　for that which has not been told them they shall see,
　　and that which they have not heard they shall understand.

¹Who has believed what we have heard?
　　And to whom has the arm of the Lord been revealed?
²For he grew up before him like a young plant,
　　and like a root out of dry ground;
　he had no form or comeliness that we should look at him,
　　and no beauty that we should desire him.
³He was despised and rejected by men;
　　a man of sorrows and acquainted with grief;
　and as one from whom men hide their faces
　　he was despised, and we esteemed him not.

⁴Surely he has borne our griefs
　　and carried our sorrows;
　yet we esteemed him stricken,
　　smitten by God, and afflicted.
⁵But he was wounded for our transgressions,
　　he was bruised for our iniquities;
　upon him was the chastisement that made us whole,
　　and with his stripes we are healed.
⁶All we like sheep have gone astray;
　　we have turned every one to his own way;
　and the Lord has laid on him
　　the iniquity of us all.

⁷He was oppressed, and he was afflicted,
　　yet he opened not his mouth;
　like a lamb that is led to the slaughter,

and like a sheep that before its shearers is dumb,
   so he opened not his mouth.
8By oppression and judgment he was taken away;
   and as for his generation, who considered
that he was cut off out of the land of the living,
   stricken for the transgression of my people?
9And they made his grave with the wicked
   and with a rich man in his death,
although he had done no violence,
   and there was no deceit in his mouth.

10Yet it was the will of the Lord to bruise him;
   he has put him to grief;
when he makes himself an offering for sin,
   he shall see his offspring, he shall prolong his days;
the will of the Lord shall prosper in his hand;
11   he shall see the fruit of the travail of his soul and be satisfied;
   by his knowledge shall the righteous one, my servant,
      make many to be accounted righteous;
      and he shall bear their iniquities.
12Therefore I will divide him a portion with the great,
   and he shall divide the spoil with the strong;
because he poured out his soul to death,
   and was numbered with the transgressors;
yet he bore the sin of many,
   and made intercession for the transgressors.

This famous passage was, until recently, almost universally regarded by scholars as the fourth in a series of independent 'servant-songs', telling the story of a special individual figure known as the "Servant of the Lord" (*Eved Yahweh*), and discussed with little regard to their present context. The other three servant-songs are 42:1–4, 49:1–6 and 50:3–9. Discussion then hinged on the identity of the servant: is he Cyrus or Zerubbabel or Jeremiah or the prophet himself? Or does it refer to an ideal figure such as Moses or a Davidic Messiah? Is it even a prophecy about Jesus?

The situation has changed however. Commentators nowadays emphasize the continuity of the passage with what has gone before, and address themselves to the question of what it says about the servant rather than who he is. In the first place, the idea that one who was despised and rejected should come to be exalted and victorious (52:13) has been a regular theme in earlier chapters: *eg* "Fear not, you worm Jacob . . . I will make of you a threshing sledge, new, sharp, and having teeth" (41:14–15; cf. 40:27–31). The belief that what happens in Israel affects "kings" and "many nations" (52:15) is another basic element in the theology of previous chapters (*eg* 49:1, 6), and indeed of the whole book (*eg* 2:2–4). Ritual expressions like "sprinkle" (52:15; RSV has "startle"; cf. Lev. 14:7), "esteemed" (53:3–4; cf. Lev. 7:18, where RSV has "credited"), and "offering for sin" (53:10; cf. Lev. 7:1–5, where RSV has "guilt offering") follow on naturally from the community laments, salvation oracles and ritual instructions of the preceding passage just discussed (51:1–52:12).

Finally, the term "servant" itself has previously been used eleven times, all but one of them explicitly applied to Israel or Jacob; that is to say, the people of God, defeated and humiliated, but chosen and soon to be redeemed by God (41:8–9; 42:19; 43:10; 44:1–2, 21; 45:4; 49:3, 6). Two of these ten instances are in a so-called servant-song (49:3, 6), as is the eleventh (42:1), where the reference seems to be to Cyrus (see the commentary). It should be noted too that the term "his servant" occurs in 50:10, where it refers to the prophet himself, which makes it likely that the third servant-song (50:4–9) is to some extent autobiographical. These are the passages which supply the primary context for understanding this great poem, and all of them are relevant.

There is thus something of Israel in this best-known of all the Isaianic "servants". But there is also something of the messenger of 52:7, and of the prophet-servant of 50:4–9, who, like him, are not named. It does not require much imagination to see that, just as the author, whose mission was to comfort his people and bring them good tidings in exile, identified himself with the messenger and prophet of these chapters, so the agony and the ecstasy in this passage in some way reflect the prophet's own experience. The passage is about the possibility of justice after oppression, forgiveness through suffering, and exaltation after humiliation, and this revelation applies as much to the author as to listening Israel; as much to the one as to the many. In this sense Christians who see in the poem a prototype of Jesus and their own salvation are not stretching it beyond what it will bear.

Verses 13–15 introduce the subject by describing the exaltation of the servant in language taken almost directly from chapter 6. In the prophet's vision "in the year that King Uzziah died" it was God himself who was "high and lifted up" (6:1); here it is his servant who shall be "exalted and lifted up, and shall be very high" (v. 13). This is a remarkable example of the continuity of Isaianic tradition from chapter 6 to chapter 52; the same phrase appears again in 57:15 (RSV this time has "high and lofty One"). But it also clearly indicates that this new revelation is something which transcends all that has gone before: the glory that is to appear through the life, suffering and exaltation of the servant is compared to the glory of God. Such a way of thinking follows on from the victory and enthronement of God in 52:7–10 and the New Exodus in 52:11–12, which will transcend human imaginings.

Verses 14–15 similarly stress the novelty of what is to happen, like the famous words of 43:18–19: "Remember not the former things... Behold, I am doing a new thing." "He shall startle" (RSV) is an ingenious suggestion, widely accepted by modern commentators and fitting well into the context, but the word is quite common in Hebrew and normally means "he shall sprinkle", as in the leprosy ritual (Lev. 14:7), for example. Similar words are used in more spiritual passages, such as a prayer for forgiveness (Ps. 51:7), and a prophecy of hope for a new start in the life of Israel (Ezek. 36:25). This would make the ritual imagery seem all the more appropriate here.

The beginning of the poem is written in the first person singular (52:13–15), because here God is introducing his servant as he does in 42:1. But 53:1–6 are written in the first person plural as though spoken by a chorus, who see in the events they describe the story of their own salvation. The section is in two parts. The *first* describes a situation of suffering and misunderstanding (vv. 1–3); the *second* is about healing and forgiveness (vv. 4–6). The suffering is primarily physical: the servant is disfigured, so ugly that he is hardly recognizable as a human being (vv. 2–3;

cf. 52:14). His afflictions are described as *pains* and *sicknesses*, like the diseases of Job (*eg* Job 2:7–8; 16:6–17; 19:17–22). Of course his suffering symbolically includes all types of suffering, "sorrows" and "grief" (RSV) as well as physical pain, but the picture of a man wracked with disease, disfigured by sores and deformities of some kind—unidentified like the sufferer himself—is poignant enough as it stands without any further interpretation. The normal meaning of the words in verse 3, repeated in verse 4, is "pain" and "sickness".

The servant's suffering is also social: he is an outcast, again like Job (*eg* Job 30). The word for "men" in verse 3 is unusual and implies men of high status. He was ritually unclean too, like a leper, if the word "esteem" has a technical sense here as it has in Leviticus 7:18 (RSV "credited").

The healing and forgiveness in the *second* part of this section (vv. 4–6) do not yet apply to the servant himself: his reward is to come later (vv. 10ff). They apply to the community: "with his stripes we are healed . . . the Lord has laid on him the iniquities of us all" (vv. 5–6). Two ideas are interwoven here: the prophet suffering for his people as Moses did (Deut. 3:26) or was prepared to do (Exod. 32:32); and the scapegoat on the Day of Atonement bringing forgiveness to the community by bearing "all their iniquities upon him to a solitary land" (Lev. 16:22). It is no use asking how is this possible or how does it work: the community is speaking, the people of God, and they are simply describing their experience of vicarious suffering in their midst.

THE SUFFERING SERVANT—II

Isaiah 52:13–53:12 (*cont'd*)

The next section of the poem (vv. 7–12) is closely parallel to the previous one, and is also in two parts, the *first* of which describes the servant's suffering. This time it is depicted in terms of oppression and injustice: he was falsely accused and put to death as a common criminal (vv. 7–9). His innocence is emphasized (v. 9), and again the ritual language is continued, both in the image of a lamb led to the slaughter (cf. Jer. 11:19) and, in the *second* part, in the interpretation of his life as an "offering for sin" (v. 10). The suffering was all part of God's plan: "the will of the Lord shall prosper in his hand" (v. 10).

Verses 8 and 9 seem to say that the servant is put to death and buried. But in the Psalms, death, Sheol, the Pit, and similar expressions are not always to be taken literally: they can also refer to extremes of danger or suffering (*eg* Ps. 18:4–5; Isa. 38:17). The expression "with a rich man in his death" (v. 9), however, seems to add a circumstantial detail to the account as though to make it clear that he really does die. Some scholars have found the reference to "a rich man" unexpected here and substitute "tyrant" or the like. But the parallel "wicked/rich man" is by no means impossible, especially when we remember the aristocratic overtones of the "men" who despise and reject him in verse 3.

However that may be, the extreme suffering of the servant— even unto death—is interpreted here, by a leap of faith, as God's will. This is a theme familiar to us from the very beginning of the book, except that in chapter 1 (vv. 4–6) and elsewhere (*eg* 10:5–6; 40:1–2) the suffering is deserved, whereas here it is undeserved. The prophet is entering new territory for an Old Testament writer, but what in essence he is saying is that somehow or other the community experiences healing, forgiveness and righteousness, as on the Day of Atonement (Lev. 16:22). Divine intervention has done what they could not do themselves: it has removed their sins and transformed suffering into a source of hope and healing. Psalm 51:10–17 offers a rough parallel, but there is no other Old Testament passage where such a way of thinking is developed. So unexpected is it that even Matthew quotes verse 4 in a totally different context (Matt. 8:17). Not until 1 Peter 2:24 is the full meaning of the passage appreciated. And Paul discovers the truth about the death of Christ without reference to Isaiah 53: *ie* "For as by one man's disobedience many were made sinners, so by one man's obedience many will be made righteous" (Rom. 5:19).

Verse 11 of Isaiah 53 expresses more than any other verse in this unique poem the transition from suffering to exaltation, from travail to a life of vision and fulfilment. It reads literally "out of [or following] the travail of his soul he will see and be satisfied". The Hebrew is clear as it stands, and reminiscent of a verse from Psalm 17 (see v. 15):

> As for me *I shall behold* thy face in righteousness;
>   when I awake, *I shall be satisfied* with beholding thy form.

In verse 11, there is no necessity to paraphrase as the RSV does, or to introduce an object for "see", although a Qumran Isaiah scroll has "light" and is followed by the New English and Jerusalem Bibles. Nor need we get into a discussion about whether the death and resurrection implied are to be taken literally or not. This is the one passage in the Old Testament in which vicarious suffering is explicit, and for that reason alone, we are justified in expecting other unparalleled ideas and images.

The unique blend of prophetic, cultic, liturgical and theological ways of thinking in this poem, its climactic position in the Babylonian chapters of Isaiah, and yet, at the same time, its continuity with what goes before, make it hard to summarize. But if we think of a prophet like Moses to lead a New Exodus (52:11–12), one who is willing to suffer for his people (Exod. 32:32), and of a priest to establish purity for the procession back to Zion (52:11), and above all of a passionate belief in the power of God to bring salvation out of suffering—all typical exilic themes as we have seen—then the author's intention perhaps becomes clearer.

Two political events, very much "in the news" around the middle of the sixth century B.C., may have helped to form this leap of faith in his mind. The *first*, the release of the captive king Jehoiachin in 760 B.C., was of great theological importance, as we can see from the references to it at the end of 2 Kings and Jeremiah. The *second*, the appearance of Cyrus on the scene as the first real challenge to Babylonian supremacy around 547 B.C., also gave new hope to the exiles, as we saw in our discussion of 44:28 and 45:1. But the prime mover behind the salvation oracles and hymns of praise in these chapters, including this profoundest of all the Isaianic poems, must be the Isaianic tradition itself from which they grew. Nurtured within Israel's prophetic movement from the eighth century B.C. down to the Babylonian exile in the sixth, and beyond, the faith of Isaiah has left its mark upon Biblical tradition. Faith in God's power in spite of the evidence, not because of it, is a theme we have traced back to the image of Jerusalem "the faithful city" in chapter 1, alone in a desolate world, and the Immanuel prophecy ("If you will not believe, surely you shall not be established") in chapter 7—products of an age of constant crisis, defeat and humiliation. The same theme is here triumphantly expressed in a period of exile: God's servant is exalted and his sufferings transformed into a source of healing and forgiveness.

The story of how Jews and Christians down the centuries have responded to the poem about the Suffering Servant is long and complex. In a remarkable ancient Jewish version, for example, the servant is, in the very first verse (52:13), identified as "the Messiah"; but the sufferings in 53:3, 5, 7–9 are transferred from him to the community. So the servant rescues his people from their plight in more conventional ways. It may well be that this change came after the split between Judaism and Christianity, when Christians monopolized the passage. At any event, it is significant that of the many passages from the Book of Isaiah that are prescribed to be recited regularly in the synagogue, this is not one; whereas for Christians this, of all Old Testament passages, came to be cited as a major scriptural authority for their belief in the saving life, death and resurrection of Jesus Christ. For them the servant is Jesus, despised and rejected by men, silent before his accusers, condemned unjustly to death, buried in the tomb of the rich Joseph of Arimathea. The poem speaks also of the redeeming power of his suffering and death, and indeed of his resurrection and exaltation to the right hand of God. As we saw, too, the opening verse almost implies that this servant of the Lord is divine. Like the Isaianic verses which have been taken to refer to the nativity (1:3; 7:14) and the early ministry of Jesus (9:1–2), this is a poem that has been removed from its context in the life of ancient Israel and brilliantly used to enrich and interpret the response of Christians to the life, death and resurrection of Jesus Christ. Handel's *Messiah* is only one of many familiar examples of how this can be done.

THE HERITAGE OF THE LORD'S SERVANT

Isaiah 54:1–17

¹"Sing, O barren one, who did not bear;
 break forth into singing and cry aloud,
 you who have not been in travail!
 For the children of the desolate one will be more
  than the children of her that is married, says the Lord.
²Enlarge the place of your tent,
 and let the curtains of your habitations be stretched out;
 hold not back, lengthen your cords
 and strengthen your stakes.
³For you will spread abroad to the right and to the left,
 and your descendants will possess the nations
 and will people the desolate cities.

⁴"Fear not, for you will not be ashamed;
 be not confounded for you will not be put to shame;
 for you will forget the shame of your youth,
 and the reproach of your widowhood you will remember no more.
⁵For your Maker is your husband,
 the Lord of hosts is his name;
 and the Holy One of Israel is your Redeemer,
 the God of the whole earth he is called.
⁶For the Lord has called you
 like a wife forsaken and grieved in spirit,
 like a wife of youth when she is cast off,
 says your God.
⁷For a brief moment I forsook you,
 but with great compassion I will gather you.
⁸In overflowing wrath for a moment
 I hid my face from you,
 but with everlasting love I will have compassion on you,
 says the Lord, your Redeemer.

⁹"For this is like the days of Noah to me:
 as I swore that the waters of Noah
 should no more go over the earth,
 so I have sworn that I will not be angry with you
 and will not rebuke you.

¹⁰For the mountains may depart
  and the hills be removed,
 but my steadfast love shall not depart from you;
  and my covenant of peace shall not be removed,
  says the Lord, who has compassion on you.

¹¹"O afflicted one, storm-tossed, and not comforted,
  behold, I will set your stones in antimony,
  and lay your foundations with sapphires.
¹²I will make your pinnacles of agate, your gates of carbuncles,
  and all your wall of precious stones.
¹³All your sons shall be taught by the Lord,
  and great shall be the prosperity of your sons.
¹⁴In righteousness you shall be established;
  you shall be far from oppression, for you shall not fear;
  and from terror, for it shall not come near you.
¹⁵If any one stirs up strife,
  it is not from me;
 whoever stirs up strife with you
  shall fall because of you.
¹⁶Behold I have created the smith
  who blows the fire of coals,
  and produces a weapon for its purpose.
 I have also created the ravager to destroy;
¹⁷ no weapon that is fashioned against you shall prosper,
  and you shall confute every tongue that rises against you in
   judgment.
 This is the heritage of the servants of the Lord
  and their vindication from me, says the Lord."

After the servant's final victory over suffering and death (ch. 53), there remain two appendices, as it were, before the Babylonian vision is complete. The one spells out the details of his heritage, the return from exile (54:1–10) and a new Jerusalem (vv. 11–17); the other is an invitation to share in the fruits of the new age (ch. 55). Like a number of earlier passages, chapter 54 is written in the second person singular feminine, as though addressed to an abandoned wife, "forsaken and grieved in spirit" (v. 6). The effect, less obvious in English than in Hebrew, is to give the whole passage a tender beauty as when one who is friendless and vulnerable is given hope by the one with power to give it. Jerusalem is the abandoned wife, and God the powerful, loving husband.

In a miracle, like the birth of Isaac when Sarah was past childbearing age (Gen. 11:30; 17:15–21; 21:1–7), she will have more children than anyone else. There will not be room in Jerusalem for them all (v. 2), and they will settle all over the world, leading the nations and reviving the desolate cities (v. 3). If verse 1 alludes to Sarah, as "the quarry from which you were digged" (51:1), verse 2 perhaps refers to the tent where she lived and where Isaac was born (Gen. 13:18; 18:1). She will have to enlarge it greatly if it is to have room for all her descendants. Certainly verse 3 recalls God's promise to Abraham (Gen. 22:15–18) and its fulfilment in the days of Isaac; see Gen. 26:1–5, 12–16, and especially verse 22:

> So he called its name Rehoboth, saying, "For now the Lord has made room for us, and we shall be fruitful in the land".

Is it a coincidence that these reminiscences of the patriarchal promise appear immediately after a poem about the self-sacrifice of the Lord's servant, just as in Genesis the promise is renewed immediately after the story of the binding of Isaac (Gen. 22:15–18)?

Verses 4–10 are further expressions of God's love for Zion. Her husband will return and prove to her that he never stopped loving her; her shame, her loneliness and grief will be forgotten for ever. Her husband is the Lord of hosts, creator of Israel, and his love for her is described as, on the one hand, "great compassion" (vv. 7–8, 10), a warm, intimate word in Hebrew; and, on the other hand, "everlasting love" (Hebrew *hesed*), a morally stronger term associated with "loyalty" (vv. 8, 10), "covenant" (v. 10) and "Redeemer" (vv. 5, 8).

That tragic interlude of separation and grief is now reduced in retrospect to "a brief moment" (vv. 7–8) when God, as it were, lost his temper: "overflowing wrath" is a memorable, strident phrase (*shetseph ketseph* in Hebrew), but it is also compared to the cataclysm of Noah's flood (vv. 9–10). Both were unbearable while they lasted, but both were eventually over and a new covenant was made (Gen. 9:8–17) that would not be broken. "Covenant" in such contexts means "promise" rather than any other kind of agreement. Just as in the days of Noah, God swore never again to "destroy all flesh" (Gen. 9:15), so now he has sworn never again to lose his temper. The new age about to dawn will be characterized by God's "steadfast love" (*hesed*), "peace" (*shalom*, that is, health, security, wholeness), and "compassion" (v. 10). Turning a familiar Zion image upside down, mountains that can never be moved (*eg* Ps. 46:2; 93:1; 96:10) will "depart and the hills be removed" (v. 10) before that promise will be broken.

The other part of the servant's heritage is to be a new, rebuilt Jerusalem (vv. 11–17). Zion is again addressed herself, this time as "afflicted . . . not comforted" (cf. 49:13), and, to continue the flood image from verse 9, "storm-tossed". Her new foundations, pinnacles, gates and outer wall (NEB has "boundary-stones" here, v. 12) will be, as in the vision of John of Patmos (Rev. 21:18–21), made of precious stones; a scene of breathtaking beauty. As in Revelation too, there is no temple and no need for priests since the citizens will be taught by the Lord himself (v. 13; Rev 21:22). There will be no oppression or terror or strife (vv. 14–15). It will be a "city of righteousness" again (1:27), as in an earlier vision (28:16–17). On the attitude of the Book of Isaiah to the Temple, see the commentary on 1:10–17 (vol. 1, pp. 14ff.), 44:28 and 66:1–4.

The smith, maker of deadly instruments of destruction and often blamed (like arms dealers in our own day) for the spread or escalation of war, is here (v. 16) cut down to size. He was created by God and so entirely under his control. The same applies to the "ravager", a term used most memorably in the story of the Passover where it is applied to the "exterminating angel" that slew the Egyptian first born (Exod. 12:23—"destroyer", RSV). No sophisticated military weapon, no destructive force can ever break through Zion's defences (v. 17).

The mention of the "tongue that rises against you" (v. 17) clearly suggests legal imagery again: the New English Bible has "you shall rebut every charge brought against you". But in view of the military language that precedes it, perhaps we are also intended to recognize an allusion to the Assyrian crisis and the way language was used to terrify Jerusalem then (36:11–13; see also 28:11–13).

"Heritage" or "inheritance" is an emotive word, recalling the allocation of land to the tribes of Israel (*eg* Josh. 11:23), but far more than that too (see Ps. 119:111; cf. Ps. 16:6; Isa. 49:8):

> Thy testimonies are my heritage for ever;
>   yea, they are the joy of my heart.

"Vindication" (RSV, v. 17) is yet another translation for *tsedakah*. The Authorized Version has "righteousness", but perhaps "their due reward" gets the sense best in the present context.

COME TO ME, ALL YOU WHO THIRST

Isaiah 55:1–13

> [1]"Ho, every one who thirsts,
>   come to the waters;
>   and he who has no money,
>   come, buy and eat!
>   Come, buy wine and milk
>   without money and without price.
> [2]Why do you spend your money for that which is not bread,
>   and your labour for that which does not satisfy?
>   Hearken diligently to me, and eat what is good,
>   and delight yourself in fatness.
> [3]Incline your ear, and come to me;
>   hear, that your soul may live;
>   and I will make with you an everlasting covenant,
>   my steadfast, sure love for David.
> [4]Behold, I made him a witness to the peoples,
>   a leader and commander for the peoples.
> [5]Behold, you shall call nations that you know not,
>   and nations that knew you not shall run to you,
>   because of the Lord your God, and of the Holy One of Israel,
>   for he has glorified you.

6"Seek the Lord while he may be found,
    call upon him while he is near;
7let the wicked forsake his way,
    and the unrighteous man his thoughts;
let him return to the Lord, that he may have mercy on him,
    and to our God, for he will abundantly pardon.
8For my thoughts are not your thoughts,
    neither are your ways my ways, says the Lord.
9For as the heavens are higher than the earth,
    so are my ways higher than your ways
    and my thoughts than your thoughts.

10"For as the rain and the snow come down from heaven,
    and return not thither but water the earth,
making it bring forth and sprout,
    giving seed to the sower and bread to the eater,
11so shall my word be that goes forth from my mouth;
    it shall not return to me empty,
but it shall accomplish that which I purpose,
    and prosper in the thing for which I sent it.

12"For you shall go out in joy,
    and be led forth in peace;
the mountains and the hills before you
    shall break forth into singing,
    and all the trees of the field shall clap their hands.
13Instead of the thorn shall come up the cypress;
    instead of the brier shall come up the myrtle;
and it shall be to the Lord for a memorial,
    for an everlasting sign which shall not be cut off."

Chapter 55 is an invitation to share in the fruits of the new age, described so magnificently in the preceding chapters. They are free and offered to everyone, rich and poor, Jew and Gentile alike (vv. 1–5). The new age is of God, not man (vv. 6–9), foretold by the prophets and therefore inevitable (vv. 10–11); it is also everlasting (vv. 3, 12–13). This is a chapter where God's love for all people and the dependability of his word are celebrated as nowhere else in the Old Testament.

The invitation to the poor (v. 1, "he who has no money") to eat and drink what is good, strikes to the heart of Biblical theology.

The water, the wine, the milk, the bread and the "fatness" (v. 2) offered here are not of this world; this is a feast like the one in chapter 25 where everyone will be satisfied. For some this is the same invitation as that in Proverbs chapters 8 and 9, where the Lady Wisdom invites us into her House of Seven Pillars to study and to learn what it is to be God's people:

> "Come, eat of my bread
>> and drink of the wine I have mixed.
> Leave simpleness and live,
>> and walk in the way of insight."

(Prov. 9:5–6)

> "For he who finds me finds life
>> and obtains favour from the Lord."

(Prov. 8:35)

Others see here an invitation to share in the body and blood of Christ. Either way the clue to its meaning is to be found in chapter 12 (see v. 3):

> With joy you will draw water from the wells of salvation.

The theme of living water flows through the Bible from the Psalmist longing for God "as a hart longs for flowing streams" (Ps. 42:1) to the "spring of water welling up to eternal life" in the fourth Gospel (John 4:14) and the "fountain of the water of life" which is "without price" in the Apocalypse (Rev. 21:6; 22:17).

Verse 3 comes very near the words of Christ: "This cup is the new covenant in my blood" (1 Cor. 11:25). To those who accept the invitation, God will extend his everlasting covenant with David. This is a reference to the royal protocol of such texts as Psalm 89, Nathan's prophecy (2 Sam. 7) and David's last words (2 Sam. 23), where God establishes an everlasting covenant with his *Messiah* or "anointed one". God guarantees his "steadfast love" (*hesed*) for, and his "faithfulness" to (translated "sure love" in RSV), David and his descendants for ever. "Steadfast love" is plural in Hebrew, and implies repeated acts of divine intervention in which God reveals his love: "to love you faithfully as I loved David" (NEB). Just as David stands out as a successful leader (v. 4), prototype of the Messiah, bearing witness to the justice and love of God, so now Israel will bring that justice and love to the notice of the nations of the world (v. 5).

The next stanza of this great hymn (vv. 6–9) is a call for repentance: "Seek the Lord . . . call upon him . . . [forsake wickedness] . . . return to the Lord". The need for renewal is a recurring theme in Isaiah (*eg* 43:18–19); nothing short of a new creation is needed (65:17–18) and the destruction of the world as we know it (ch. 24). The "faithful city" poem in chapter 1 tells the same story. To enter the new age means leaving behind our earthly thoughts and ways, and grasping instead heavenly ideals and realities; or in Paul's terms, crucifying the flesh and living by the Spirit (Gal. 5:24–5). That is the difference between the "present Jerusalem" and the "Jerusalem above", between slavery and freedom (Gal. 4:25–6).

Verses 10–11 take up again the theme with which the Babylonian chapters began: "the word of our God will stand for ever" (40:8). The extended simile is beautiful and effective: just as rain and snow cannot help watering the earth and making things grow once they fall from the clouds, so God's word from heaven, once spoken by the mouth of his prophet, cannot fail to be fulfilled. God's purpose cannot be thwarted by evil or doubt or despair. In verse 11 the "word" almost takes on its own personality as it does in the Wisdom of Solomon in the Apocrypha (Wisdom 18: 14–16):

> For while gentle silence enveloped all things,
> and night in its swift course was now half gone,
> thy all-powerful word leaped from heaven, from the royal throne,
> into the midst of the land that was doomed,
> a stern warrior carrying the sharp sword of thy authentic command,
> and stood and filled all things with death,
> and touched heaven while standing on the earth.

From such passages it is but a short step to the prologue of the fourth Gospel where "the Word became flesh and dwelt among us, full of grace and truth" (John 1:14).

Finally (vv. 12–13) we return to the familiar themes of a New

Exodus (*eg* 48:20–21; 52:11–12) and the jubilant participation of all nature in the event (*eg* 35:1–2; 41:17–20; 44:23). But more; just as the Pillar of Salt was a permanent reminder of the destruction of Sodom and Gomorrah (Gen. 19:24–28; Luke 17:32), so the miraculous forests of cypress and myrtle in the wilderness will be a permanent memorial of this mighty act of God, exquisite evidence of the joy and peace of the New Age.

A HOUSE OF PRAYER FOR ALL NATIONS

Isaiah 56:1–8

¹Thus says the Lord:
　"Keep justice, and do righteousness,
　for soon my salvation will come,
　　and my deliverance be revealed.
²Blessed is the man who does this,
　　and the son of man who holds it fast,
　who keeps the sabbath, not profaning it,
　　and keeps his hand from doing any evil."

³Let not the foreigner who has joined himself to the Lord say,
　　"The Lord will surely separate me from his people";
　and let not the eunuch say,
　　"Behold, I am a dry tree."
⁴For thus says the Lord:
　"To the eunuchs who keep my sabbaths,
　　who choose the things that please me
　　and hold fast my covenant,
⁵I will give in my house and within my walls
　　a monument and a name
　　better than sons and daughters;
　I will give them an everlasting name
　　which shall not be cut off.

⁶"And the foreigners who join themselves to the Lord,
　　to minister to him, to love the name of the Lord,
　　and to be his servants,
　every one who keeps the sabbath, and does not profane it,
　　and holds fast my covenant—

⁷these I will bring to my holy mountain,
   and make them joyful in my house of prayer;
their burnt offerings and their sacrifices
   will be accepted on my altar;
for my house shall be called a house of prayer
   for all peoples.
⁸Thus says the Lord God,
   who gathers the outcasts of Israel,
I will gather yet others to him
   besides those already gathered."

In the last few chapters (*ie* 51–55) it was almost as though the long line of Isaianic tradition that began with the eighth century B.C. prophet had reached its climax: what more could be said about the Creator and Redeemer of Israel? Yet in chapter 56 we immediately break new ground: so much so that scholars for about a century have assumed that a new author takes over at this point: "Trito-Isaiah", a third Isaiah, a contemporary of Haggai and Zechariah about 530–520 B.C. It is most unlikely that chapters 56–66 were written by the same author; just as improbable as the assumption that chapters 1–39 were all by a single person known as "Proto-Isaiah". But certainly many passages in these chapters are elucidated by such early post-exilic books as Haggai, Zechariah, Malachi, Jonah and Chronicles in a context of rebuilding and restoration in Judah. Some of the high hopes expressed in chapters 40–55 have not been fulfilled. The mass return of exiles from Babylon never materialized. There was opposition to the rebuilding of the Temple at Jerusalem, both from the Samaritans in the north (*eg* Neh. ch. 4) and from within the Jewish community itself (Isa. 66:1–4). Relations between Jews and Gentiles in the Persian Empire raised new problems: strict legislation on foreign marriages (Neh. 13:23–27) and food laws (Lev. 11; Dan. 1:8–16) represent one reaction; our first passage here, Isaiah 56:1–8, represents another.

Verse 1 brings together the familiar Isaianic themes of "justice" and "righteousness" (first heard in chapter 1) with the proclamation, so wonderfully developed in chapters 40–55, that "salvation" is near. It will be remembered that in Hebrew, one word means both "righteousness" and "deliverance" (or 'victory', 'triumph'); it is this word (*tsedakah*) that is repeated here in both its senses. No longer is the appeal for justice sanctioned by warnings of doom and judgment as in the eighth century B.C. prophecy: it is now seen as a symptom of the new age. Happiness consists of keeping the Sabbath day and doing no wrong (v. 2), which is another way of saying that joy and innocence will abound.

There follows a remarkable commentary on verse 2, explaining that the terms "man" and "son of man" (NEB, "mortal") include all members of the human race, not just Jews. Just as Jesus interpreted the commandment "Love your neighbour" (Lev. 19:18) with the Parable of the Good Samaritan, so verses 3ff. here tell us that in effect verses 1–2 are addressed to foreigners and eunuchs. Justice and righteousness are universal virtues; the exquisite joy of sabbath rest is open to all mankind. Even the Temple is no longer barred to non-Jews (vv. 6–8). In the new age, laws like Deuteronomy 23:1–6 will be repealed and the people of God increased by proselytes. There has been universalism in earlier Isaianic prophecies (*eg* 2:1–4; 11:1–9; 45:22–23) but nowhere is it so developed as here. Two factors are probably involved: *first* the shift away from a Temple-centred religion and from the preoccupation with ritual purity to more universal virtues; and *second* a new realization that the people of God are strengthened and enriched by the influx of new blood, and not necessarily adulterated.

Verse 3 contains the kind of lament that prompted the salvation oracles of, for example, 41:8–10 and 14–16: the foreigners have been afraid of *apartheid*, and the eunuchs afraid of ritual impurity which prevents them from entering the Temple area (Deut. 23:1) and of childlessness (the "dry tree" in v. 3 is a barren "family tree"). Then the formula, "Thus says the Lord" introduces three salvation oracles. In the *first* (vv. 4–5), the eunuchs—and with them we are no doubt intended to include women, lepers and other outcasts—are told that membership of Israel depends not on physical or ritual matters, but on obedience:

> He is a Jew who is one inwardly, and real circumcision is a matter of the heart, spiritual and not literal (Rom. 2:29; cf. Deut. 30:6).

The phrase *Yad vaShem*, "a monument and a name" (v. 5), has been applied to the Holocaust Memorial in Jerusalem where the six million victims of Nazi persecution, not all of them Jews but including gypsies, homosexuals and other outcasts, are remembered. The new converts will be given a name above every name, as citizens of the new Jerusalem and inheritors of the promises to Abraham and his descendants.

The *second* oracle (vv. 6–7) concerns foreigners who wish to adopt the Jewish way of life, and to "love the name of the Lord, and to be his servants". They are told that they will be welcomed into full membership of the people of God: their presence in the Temple, their prayers, their sacrifices will be acceptable to God. In the new age, the criteria for admission into the Temple will be moral and spiritual criteria, not social or political or racial. The Temple is open to all (v. 7). In Paul's famous words (Gal. 3:28–29):

> There is neither Jew nor Greek, there is neither slave nor free, there is neither male nor female; for you are all one in Christ Jesus. And if you are Christ's, then you are Abraham's offspring, heirs according to promise.

The *third* oracle (v. 8) sums up the new teaching. The new Israel, gathered from the ends of the earth, will be greater than the old Israel, because it will embrace Gentiles and the "wealth of the nations" (61:6; 66:12) as well. This is an unusually clear appeal to the Church to cut through barriers of tradition and convention and open its doors to outcasts.

AN ATTACK ON CORRUPTION IN HIGH PLACES

Isaiah 56:9–57:13

> ⁹All you beasts of the field, come to devour—
>   all you beasts in the forest.
> ¹⁰His watchmen are blind,
>   they are all without knowledge;
>   they are all dumb dogs,
>   they cannot bark;
>   dreaming, lying down,
>   loving to slumber.

¹¹The dogs have a mighty appetite;
  they never have enough.
The shepherds also have no understanding;
  they have all turned to their own way,
  each to his own gain, one and all.
¹²"Come," they say, "let us get wine,
  let us fill ourselves with strong drink;
and tomorrow will be like this day,
  great beyond measure."

¹The righteous man perishes,
  and no one lays it to heart;
devout men are taken away,
  while no one understands.
For the righteous man is taken away from calamity,
² he enters into peace;
they rest in their beds
  who walk in their uprightness.
³But you, draw near hither,
  sons of the sorceress,
  offspring of the adulterer and the harlot.
⁴Of whom are you making sport?
  Against whom do you open your mouth wide
  and put out your tongue?
Are you not children of transgression,
  the offspring of deceit,
⁵you who burn with lust among the oaks,
  under every green tree;
who slay your children in the valleys,
  under the clefts of the rocks?
⁶Among the smooth stones of the valley is your portion;
  they, they, are your lot;
to them you have poured out a drink offering,
  you have brought a cereal offering.
  Shall I be appeased for these things?
⁷Upon a high and lofty mountain
  you have set your bed,
  and thither you went up to offer sacrifice.
⁸Behind the door and the doorpost
  you have set up your symbol;
for, deserting me, you have uncovered your bed,

you have gone up to it,
  you have made it wide;
and you have made a bargain for yourself with them,
  you have loved their bed,
  you have looked on nakedness.
⁹You journeyed to Molech with oil
  and multiplied your perfumes;
you sent your envoys far off,
  and sent down even to Sheol.
¹⁰You were wearied with the length of your way,
  but you did not say, "It is hopeless";
you found new life for your strength,
  and so you were not faint.

¹¹Whom did you dread and fear,
  so that you lied,
and did not remember me,
  did not give me a thought?
Have I not held my peace, even for a long time,
  and so you do not fear me?
¹²I will tell of your righteousness and your doings,
  but they will not help you.
¹³When you cry out, let your collection of idols deliver you!
  The wind will carry them off,
  a breath will take them away.
But he who takes refuge in me shall possess the land,
  and shall inherit my holy mountain.

Following the exceptionally generous attitude towards foreigners expressed in verses 1–8, the next prophecy is a bitter attack on corruption within Israel. It concerns Israel's leaders, "his watchmen" (v. 10) and "the shepherds" (v. 11), who are condemned in language we have not met since chapters 28–31. Either this passage was prompted by specific events or conditions under Sheshbazzar or Zerubbabel (*eg* Ezra chs. 1–4; Hag. ch. 1) about which we know virtually nothing, or else it dates, like much of Jeremiah (*eg* ch. 6), Ezekiel (*eg* ch. 34) and the early chapters of Isaiah, from pre-exilic times. Whatever its date, this out and out rejection of the 'Establishment' has the very moving effect of highlighting the prophet's recurring discrimination in favour of the poor, the foreigners and the outcasts.

With heavy sarcasm, wild beasts are invited to come and feast on defenceless Israel (v. 9). The "watchmen", that is, Israel's leaders (Jer. 6:17), are as useless as guard-dogs that cannot bark (v. 10), having overeaten and drunk too much. The indolence, self-indulgence, greed, and crass stupidity of these Israelites are contrasted with the foreigners' virtues extolled in verses 1–8. Verse 12 sounds like part of a drinking song. Compare it with Amos 4:1–3 or Wisdom of Solomon chapter 2:

"Come therefore, let us enjoy the good things that exist.
and make use of the creation to the full as in youth.
Let us take our fill of costly wine and perfumes...
Let us oppress the righteous poor man;
let us not spare the widow...".

(Wisdom 2:6–7, 10)

Chapter 57 begins, exactly as does Wisdom chapter 3, with a comment on the fate of the righteous victims of these thoughtless revellers:

But the souls of the righteous are in the hand of God,
and no torment will ever touch them.
In the eyes of the foolish they seemed to have died,
and their departure was thought to be an affliction...
but they are at peace.

(Wisdom 3:1–3)

The notion that death is a merciful release from suffering occurs in Job (3:13–19). It is an elaboration of the cry of Elijah (1 Kings 19:4) or Jonah (Jon. 4:3, 8) or Jeremiah (20:15–17):

"Cursed be the man who brought the news to my father,
'A son is born to you,' making him very glad.
Let that man be like the cities
which the Lord overthrew without pity...
because he did not kill me in the womb;
so my mother would have been my grave,
and her womb forever great".

More relevant here, however, may be the tradition that the good King Josiah's untimely death was to protect him from the unbearable sight of Jerusalem destroyed (see 2 Kings 22:20):

> Therefore, behold, I will gather you to your fathers, and you shall be gathered to your grave in peace, and your eyes shall not see all the evil which I will bring upon this place.

Others argue that "beds" in verse 2 should be taken literally, thinking perhaps of didactic passages like Psalms 127:2. But surely in the present context, where injustice and violence prevail, the thought is that "peace" will not come to the righteous until after death, as in the passages from Wisdom and 2 Kings just quoted.

Verses 3–13 of chapter 57 may be understood as another trial scene like 41:1–7 or 43:8–13. The accused are summoned (v. 3), their crimes relentlessly enumerated (vv. 4–11) and their sentence passed (vv. 12–13). Sexual expressions dominate the scene, as so often in prophetic attacks on Israel's disobedience, not necessarily because sacred prostitution and other orgiastic rites were actually practised "on every high hill and under every green tree" (Deut. 12:2; 2 Kings 17:10) at the time, but because such scenes, more than any other image, conjure up the right picture of jealousies, disloyalty, fatal fascination and broken hearts. Such is the destructive and disturbing power of *all* alternatives to the love of God, not just that of a primitive Canaanite fertility cult. It was the literal interpretations of such passages as this which led to brutal witch-hunts (authorized by Exod. 22:18) only a couple of centuries ago, and to some odd views about sex that are still with us today.

"Sorceress" (57:3) is the term used in legislation about "witches" (cf. Exod. 22:18); "adulterer" strictly refers only to a man who has sex with someone else's wife (Exod. 20:14); while "harlots" were often foreign women (Prov. 2:16; 7:10–27), and social outcasts without family or friends in the community. The two latter terms are associated with transgression and deceit, and savagely contrasted with the behaviour of normal parents (v. 4). The pictures in verse 5 of priapic orgies and bloody child-sacrifice are especially vivid, and again references to Ahab (or *Ahaz* in 2 Kings 16:3–4), Manasseh (2 Kings 21:3–9), and others, only furnish us with more examples of the same, but without evidence that such things actually went on in Jerusalem. They are spine-chilling symbols of temptation and disobedience, not accounts of what happened or of what the prophet is attacking: he certainly has in mind far more than any specific Canaanite rituals.

The rest of the accusation (vv. 6–11) is written in the second person feminine singular, as though addressed to the evil sorceress or harlot herself; that is, to Israel, God's unfaithful wife. In 49:14, 50:1 and Hosea (chs. 1–3), God takes her back; here she gets no help from him (vv. 12–13). The "smooth stones" in verse 6 suggest some kind of idol-worship. Others translate the word "creatures" (NEB) and find a reference to snake-worship. There is irony in the mention of "portion . . . lot", since both are emotive words for Israel's true inheritance, here related to pagan cult-objects. The same applies to the words (v. 8) "door . . . doorpost" (*mezuzah*), which are so important in Jewish tradition (Deut. 6:9; 11:20).

The details of verses 7–10 are difficult perhaps because of the taboo nature of the subject. The last phrase in verse 8, for example, appears to mean "you have gazed on an erection" (RSV has the euphemism "nakedness", while NEB ingeniously emends to "in the heat of your lust"). Molech (v. 9) is usually thought to be a pagan deity, but may in fact be a term for a particular kind of sacrifice. The general cumulative effect of the passage, however, is clear: it is intended to imply that Israel enjoyed the harlot's profession and devoted much expense and endless effort to plying it well. The application of the image to fallen Jerusalem is obvious (1:21):

How the faithful city has become a harlot!

Verse 11 reminds us that the whole passage is metaphorical. It concerns the strained relationship between God and his people. He has been patient, but they have pushed his patience to its limit. To continue the love imagery, God's jealousy has become unbearable to him, and he is going to turn on them. "I will tell of your righteousness" (v. 12) misses the point; "I will denounce" (NEB) is better. No good deeds can help them. Without love, to paraphrase Paul (1 Cor. 13:3), righteousness "profiteth nothing" (AV). When they cry out for help, as they have done so often in the past (*eg* Judg. 6:7), he will not answer; and their idols, insubstantial creations of their own hands, will be blown away like leaves in the wind. "A breath" (v. 13) is the word translated "vanity [of vanities]" in Ecclesiastes (NEB "utter emptiness"), and "idols" in Jonah 2:8.

Notice how the author (in the second half of v. 13) concludes the section with the blessing of the righteous. More often in the Bible, especially in the Wisdom literature (*eg* Prov. chs. 1–9), including the Sermon on the Mount (Matt. 7:24–27), the teacher ends on a cautionary note with the fate of the wicked. Here there is no doubt where the prophet's bias lies, and then verse 13 leads naturally into the next section.

GOD'S LOVE FOR ALL HIS CREATURES

Isaiah 57:14–21

14And it shall be said,
"Build up, build up, prepare the way,
remove every obstruction from my people's way."
15For thus says the high and lofty One
who inhabits eternity, whose name is Holy:
"I dwell in the high and holy place,
and also with him who is of a contrite and humble spirit,
to revive the spirit of the humble,
and to revive the heart of the contrite.
16For I will not contend for ever,
nor will I always be angry;
for from me proceeds the spirit,
and I have made the breath of life.
17Because of the iniquity of his covetousness I was angry,
I smote him, I hid my face and was angry;
but he went on backsliding in the way of his own heart.
18I have seen his ways, but I will heal him;
I will lead him and requite him with comfort,
creating for his mourners the fruit of the lips.
19Peace, peace, to the far and to the near, says the Lord;
and I will heal him.
20But the wicked are like the tossing sea;

for it cannot rest,
        and its waters toss up mire and dirt.
²¹There is no peace, says my God, for the wicked."

After the obscenities of verses 3-13, verses 14-15 look back
thoughtfully to earlier visions. The mysterious "it shall be said" in
verse 14 recalls the angelic voices in chapter 40, speaking tenderly
to Jerusalem. The "[high]way" through the wilderness for "my
people" links together this verse, 40:3, 52:12 and 35:8-10. Verse
15 contains verbal allusions to chapter 6 where the prophet actually saw the One who "inhabits eternity", "sitting upon a throne,
high and lifted up" (6:1). In that vision Isaiah discovered that
God not only dwells in "the high and holy place", but also with
him who "is of a contrite and humble spirit".

The verb translated "inhabit" and "dwell" (v. 15) here (it is the
same verb) has special theological nuances. From it is derived the
word *mishkan* or "tabernacle" (Exod. 25: 8-9; Rev. 21:3), and
also the later Jewish term *shekinah*, "divine presence". Just as
"the Word became flesh and *dwelt* among us" (John 1:14), so
here God *dwells* among the humble and the broken-hearted: his
presence is with them. In a way this passage is a spiritual interpretation of chapter 40: the people in need (40: 1, 7) are the
"poor in spirit" (Matt. 5:3), spiritual exiles; and the way through
the wilderness is a spiritual pilgrimage. Chapter 58: 6-7 applies
similar language to the salvation of the poor (Luke 6:20).

Verse 16 of chapter 57 is God's ultimate answer to Isaiah's
"How long, O Lord?" (6:11). Justice—"contend" is a legal term
(*eg* 41:21, "your case"; 50:8)—and anger should by rights continue unabated for ever, but the Creator loves his creatures: he
gave them life (Gen. 2:7), he gave them individuality. "The
breath of life" (v. 16) in Hebrew is a plural word, translated
"living creatures" (NEB), and in later Jewish tradition, "souls".
The apocryphal Wisdom of Solomon takes this line of thought a
stage further: "For thou lovest all things that exist . . . lovest the
living" (Wisdom 11:24-26).

Israel's tragic history is summed up in verse 17: Amos 4:6-12
spells it out in lurid detail, as do the speeches of Samuel (1 Sam.
12:6-25), Jeremiah (7:21-34) and others. The implication here

seems to be that even the destruction of Jerusalem and the Babylonian exile have not cured them: they go on "backsliding in the way of [their] own heart[s]". This being so, their only hope is for God to heal them, not because they repent or in any other way seek to deserve forgiveness, but because he chooses to. The gospel of unmerited grace or justification by faith alone, not good works, is then spelt out in verse 18: "while [they are] yet sinners" (Rom. 5:8), he will "heal" them, "lead" them and "comfort" them. He will rescue them in spite of their character and their actions, not because of them. Others, with different theological presuppositions, argue that "his way" refers to the suffering of the people of Israel or even to their repentance, and that God's forgiveness is conditional on that. But there is nothing in the text that suggests this, and verses 15–16 surely imply that God's motives for healing their wounds were very different. The expression "requite him with comfort" (v. 18) also suggests a departure from strict principles of justice, and "mourners" are not the same as penitent sinners.

Verse 19 in Hebrew begins with a striking phrase, "creator of the fruit of the lips", which can be taken either with verse 18 in the sense of speaking words of comfort to the mourners (so RSV, moving the phrase back to that verse), or as a description of the quaint but memorable saying that follows: "peace, peace, to the far and to the near". Either way it would perfectly describe a prophetic saying as an act of divine creativity like the birth of Israel (43:1, 15) or the spiritual rebuilding of a sinner (Ps. 51:10). "To the far and to the near" means to all people, far and near, thinking perhaps again of 56:1–8. "Peace" (*shalom*) covers more than rest from tribulation (57:2) and freedom from war; in particular it includes health (53:5; see AV), and here perhaps also peace of mind.

Finally "the wicked" are defined as those who will never know that "peace" (vv. 20–21). They are like the "tossing sea" (RSV) or "troubled sea" (NEB), polluted by the flotsam and jetsam of their past deeds. The image is a powerful one, recalling on the one hand, the mythical sea-monsters, Rahab and Leviathan, symbols

of evil (*eg* 27:1; 51:9–10; Rev. 21:1); and on the other, by
contrast, some of the exquisite Isaianic descriptions of peace and
faith (see 32:17–18; cf. 30:15):

> And the effect of righteousness will be peace,
>   and the result of righteousness quietness and trust for ever.
> My people will abide in a peaceful habitation,
>   in secure dwellings and in quiet resting places.

The epigram in 57:21, which occurs also, for editorial reasons, at
the end of chapter 48, has a chilling finality about it in this context
too: the stormy sea of wickedness and guilt cannot be stilled. But
the next chapter envisages a means of forgiveness, as on the fast
of the Day of Atonement.

TRUE PENITENCE

Isaiah 58:1–14

> ¹"Cry aloud, spare not,
>   lift up your voice like a trumpet;
> declare to my people their transgression,
>   to the house of Jacob their sins.
> ²Yet they seek me daily,
>   and delight to know my ways,
> as if they were a nation that did righteousness
>   and did not forsake the ordinance of their God;
> they ask of me righteous judgments,
>   they delight to draw near to God.
> ³'Why have we fasted, and thou seest it not?
>   Why have we humbled ourselves, and thou takest no knowledge
>   of it?'
> Behold, in the day of your fast you seek your own pleasure,
>   and oppress all your workers.
> ⁴Behold, you fast only to quarrel and to fight
>   and to hit with wicked fist.
> Fasting like yours this day
>   will not make your voice to be heard on high.
> ⁵Is such the fast that I choose,
>   a day for a man to humble himself?

Is it to bow down his head like a rush,
    and to spread sackcloth and ashes under him?
Will you call this a fast,
    and a day acceptable to the Lord?

⁶"Is not this the fast that I choose:
    to loose the bonds of wickedness,
    to undo the thongs of the yoke,
to let the oppressed go free,
    and to break every yoke?
⁷Is it not to share your bread with the hungry,
    and bring the homeless poor into your house;
when you see the naked, to cover him,
    and not to hide yourself from your own flesh?
⁸Then shall your light break forth like the dawn,
    and your healing shall spring up speedily;
your righteousness shall go before you,
    the glory of the Lord shall be your rear guard.
⁹Then you shall call, and the Lord will answer;
    you shall cry, and he will say, Here I am.

"If you take away from the midst of you the yoke,
    the pointing of the finger, and speaking wickedness,
¹⁰if you pour yourself out for the hungry
    and satisfy the desire of the afflicted,
then shall your light rise in the darkness
    and your gloom be as the noon-day.
¹¹And the Lord will guide you continually,
    and satisfy your desire with good things,
    and make your bones strong;
and you shall be like a watered garden,
    like a spring of water,
    whose waters fail not.
¹²And your ancient ruins shall be rebuilt;
    you shall raise up the foundations of many generations;
you shall be called the repairer of the breach,
    the restorer of streets to dwell in.

¹³"If you turn back your foot from the sabbath,
    from doing your pleasure on my holy day,
and call the sabbath a delight
    and the holy day of the Lord honourable;

if you honour it, not going your own ways,
  or seeking your own pleasure, or talking idly;
¹⁴then you shall take delight in the Lord,
  and I will make you ride upon the heights of the earth;
I will feed you with the heritage of Jacob your father,
  for the mouth of the Lord has spoken."

Chapter 58 is in two parts: the *first* is a stern appeal for justice and generosity (vv. 1–7); the *second* is a beautiful account of the happiness that awaits those who heed it (vv. 8–14). The prophet's starting-point, as in the more familiar chapter 61, is the Day of Atonement, the fast when, to the sound of the trumpet, liberty is proclaimed "throughout the land to all its inhabitants" (Lev. 25:9–10). The day "acceptable to the Lord" mentioned in verse 5 is the day on which the 'acceptable year of the Lord' (61:2), the 'jubilee year' of Leviticus chapter 25, is proclaimed. The only true way to observe the fast is by liberating the oppressed, and sharing your bread with the hungry, and your home with the homeless (vv. 6–7). A self-indulgent display of sackcloth and ashes is not enough. This is a remarkable development of the familiar prophetic teaching on "the blood of bulls . . . new moons and appointed feasts" (1:11–15). It should be compared with chapter 56 which deals with the sabbath, another day which should be marked by justice and generosity (Deut. 5:12–15).

In verse 1 the fast is proclaimed throughout the land in the prescribed manner (Lev. 25:9), but the trumpet-call reveals their guilt: oppression, hunger and poverty in the land are exposed. Verses 2–5 sarcastically describe how people try to observe the fast: daily worship and study (v. 2); fasting and self-denial (vv. 3, 5, where "humbling oneself" refers to Lev. 16:29–31); bowing the head, and sackcloth and ashes (v. 5). Without "righteousness" and "justice" (RSV "ordinance", v. 2), outward observances—the formalities of organized religion—are not acceptable to God (vv. 4–5). Without a generous spirit, fasting can easily lead to selfishness (v. 3), irritability (v. 4) and the suffering of the underprivileged members of society.

Verses 6 and 7, contrasted with the pathetic excuses in verse 3, recall the judgment on the sheep and the goats in Matthew

25:31ff. Only by removing injustice and oppression, and by helping the hungry, the homeless and the naked, can the acceptable day of the Lord be properly observed (vv. 8–9, 14). Then, and then only, a new age will dawn for the righteous (v. 8). The description contains many familiar Isaianic themes: light (9:2; 42:6; 49:6; 60:1–3); "righteousness" (*eg* 41:2, 10; 51:5–6, 8); the Lord as rearguard (52:12). "Healing" refers literally to the new skin that grows over a wound, and so recalls 1:5–6 and 53:2–6. More examples of cruelty are listed in verses 9–10, but they too can be removed, and with them the darkness and gloom of sin and guilt.

More and more images accumulate for the new age (vv. 11–12). The people will never again be lost, without a leader. In the "shimmering heat" (v. 11, NEB; RSV has "with good things") they will be protected and refreshed, their thirst quenched, their weary limbs strengthened. They will be like a well-watered garden or a fountain that never dries up. It will be as though the walls of Jerusalem were rebuilt (v. 12), and the "city of righteousness, the faithful city" (1:26) restored to its former glory. The meaning of the whole passage is neatly summed up in the second half of verse 12: if you liberate the oppressed, feed the hungry and clothe the naked, the ruins will be rebuilt—it depends on you. You are the "rebuilders", you are the "restorers". The New Jerusalem will be founded on justice and righteousness.

Verses 13 and 14, looking back to chapter 56, declare that the same applies to the sabbath. Abused as it was by self-indulgence, hypocrisy and the exploitation of the poor, sabbath observance could be condemned by Isaiah (*eg* 1:13):

New moon and sabbath and the calling of assemblies—
  I cannot endure iniquity and solemn assembly.

But properly observed, it brings delight to God's people. The imagery in verse 14 is military. In battle, to capture the high ground is synonymous with being victorious; victory means recovering the land that is rightfully yours and enjoying the fruits of the heritage of your fathers. The picture occurs in a number of passages (*eg* Ps. 18:33; Hab. 3:19):

He made him ride on the high places of the earth,
　　and he ate the produce of the field;
and he made him suck honey out of the rock,
　　and oil out of the flinty rock.
Curds from the herd, and milk from the flock....

(Deut. 32:13–14)

Legislation for "a sabbath of solemn rest for the land" in Leviticus 25:4 links this last vision with the jubilee call in verse 1.

ESTRANGEMENT FROM GOD

Isaiah 59:1–21

¹Behold, the Lord's hand is not shortened, that it cannot save,
　　or his ear dull, that it cannot hear;
²but your iniquities have made a separation
　　between you and your God,
　and your sins have hid his face from you
　　so that he does not hear.
³For your hands are defiled with blood
　　and your fingers with iniquity;
　your lips have spoken lies,
　　your tongue mutters wickedness.
⁴No one enters suit justly;
　　no one goes to law honestly;
　they rely on empty pleas, they speak lies,
　　they conceive mischief and bring forth iniquity.
⁵They hatch adders' eggs,
　　they weave the spider's web;
　he who eats their eggs dies,
　　and from one which is crushed a viper is hatched.
⁶Their webs will not serve as clothing;
　　men will not cover themselves with what they make.
　Their works are works of iniquity,
　　and deeds of violence are in their hands.
⁷Their feet run to evil,
　　and they make haste to shed innocent blood;
　their thoughts are thoughts of iniquity,
　　desolation and destruction are in their highways.

⁸The way of peace they know not,
    and there is no justice in their paths;
they have made their roads crooked,
    no one who goes in them knows peace.
⁹Therefore justice is far from us,
    and righteousness does not overtake us;
we look for light, and behold, darkness,
    and for brightness, but we walk in gloom.
¹⁰We grope for the wall like the blind,
    we grope like those who have no eyes;
we stumble at noon as in the twilight,
    among those in full vigour we are like dead men.
¹¹We all growl like bears,
    we moan and moan like doves;
we look for justice, but there is none;
    for salvation, but it is far from us.
¹²For our transgressions are multiplied before thee,
    and our sins testify against us;
for our transgressions are with us,
    and we know our iniquities:
¹³transgressing, and denying the Lord,
    and turning away from following our God,
speaking oppression and revolt,
    conceiving and uttering from the heart lying words.
¹⁴Justice is turned back,
    and righteousness stands afar off;
for truth has fallen in the public squares,
    and uprightness cannot enter.
¹⁵Truth is lacking,
    and he who departs from evil makes himself a prey.

The Lord saw it, and it displeased him
    that there was no justice.
¹⁶He saw that there was no man,
    and wondered that there was no one to intervene;
then his own arm brought him victory,
    and his righteousness upheld him.
¹⁷He put on righteousness as a breastplate,
    and a helmet of salvation upon his head;
he put on garments of vengeance for clothing,
    and wrapped himself in fury as a mantle.

¹⁸According to their deeds, so will he repay,
  wrath to his adversaries, requital to his enemies;
to the coastlands he will render requital.
¹⁹So they shall fear the name of the Lord from the west,
  and his glory from the rising of the sun;
for he will come like a rushing stream,
  which the wind of the Lord drives.

²⁰"And he will come to Zion as Redeemer,
  to those in Jacob who turn from transgression, says the Lord.
²¹"And as for me, this is my covenant with them, says the Lord. My spirit which is upon you, and my words which I have put in your mouth, shall not depart out of your mouth, or out of the mouth of your children, or out of the mouth of your children's children, says the Lord, from this time forth and for evermore."

In a brief introduction the prophet tells the people that present suffering is due to their own sin, and not to any impotence on God's part (vv. 1–3). The passage is quite general and could refer to many different situations. But probably, as with other passages in chapters 56–66, we should think of the period immediately following the fall of Babylon, when prophecies and expectations, such as those brilliantly expressed in chapters 40–55, were not fulfilled (see Hag.1). The chapter is nonetheless Isaianic for all that. The "dull ears" in verse 1 hark back to 6:10, and the bloodstained hands in verse 3 to 1:15. Notice also how the repetition of "you" and "your" (nine times in vv. 2–3) makes it clear where the blame lies.

Verses 4–8 consist of an extended discourse, in the manner of some of the Psalms (*eg* Ps. 55:9–11; Ps. 58:3–5; see also Paul's use of such psalms and of the present passage in Rom. 3:10–18), on injustice, dishonesty and violence. The law courts are riddled with injustice (v. 4). The word translated "empty pleas" occurs in Genesis 1:2 ("without form"), and "lies" is the term used in the ninth commandment (Exod. 20:16; Deut. 5:20): "you shall not bear false witness". Such actions breed ("conceive ... bring forth") nothing but trouble for their perpetrators and others. "Mischief" (RSV, NEB) is a weak translation: the word is translated "travail" in 53:11 and "trouble" in the famous epigram: "Man is born to trouble as the sparks fly upward" (Job 5:7). Similarly the last word in verse 4 is a more sinister term for "evil" than either "iniquity" (RSV) or "trouble" (NEB) suggest.

Snakes and spiders' webs (v. 5) are universally used as symbols of any type of deadly threat to the structure of society (cf. 11:8). "Evil" would again be better in verses 6–7 than "iniquity". Verse 7 is strongly reminiscent of part of the opening discourse in Proverbs: its first words are close to Proverb 1:16; and a concentration of words for "way", "road", "path", *etc*, in the sense of "way of life, course of action" is characteristic of many passages in that book (*eg* Provs. 1:15, 19; 2:8–9, 12–13, 15, 18–20). The passage ends (v. 8), like chapters 48 and 57, with a firm statement that the "way of peace" is out of reach of the wicked.

The rest of the chapter has a liturgical form, comprising a lament in which the people admit their guilt and their helplessness (vv. 9–15*a*), and a salvation oracle (see commentary on 41:8–16) promising action on the part of God their Redeemer (vv. 15*b*–21). Their plight is initially described in terms of darkness (vv. 9–10); the light of justice and righteousness is now so far away from them that they cannot see it in the gloom. Amos' famous description of the longed-for "day of the Lord" was perhaps in our author's mind (Amos 5:18–19):

> It is darkness, and not light;
> > as if a man fled from a lion,
> > and a bear met him;
> or went into the house and leaned with his hand against the wall,
> > and a serpent bit him.

The meaning of the last words of verse 10 is not agreed: "like dead men in the ghostly underworld" (NEB) is one suggestion; "among those in full vigour we are like dead men" (RSV) is another more traditional one.

The similes in verse 11 seem to suggest a change of tone from growling (angrily? resentfully?) like bears (referring to vv. 9–10), to moaning (sadly? timidly?) like doves in the subsequent confession (vv. 12–13). Notice how "righteousness" alternates with "salvation" in this passage (vv. 9, 11, 14, 16–17), as in chapter 51, Psalm 132 (vv. 9 and 16) and elsewhere.

Of the various Hebrew terms for "sin", the one translated here "transgression" denotes rebellion, and it is significant that it is the one repeated three times in the confession (vv. 12–13). Their crimes are against God: "as you did it to one of the least of these my brethren, you did it to me" (Matt. 25:40). There is a proverb on the same theme (Prov. 17:5):

He who mocks the poor insults his Maker.

In a most effective scene (v. 14), justice, righteousness, truth and honesty are personified as noble men and women rebuffed, tripped up in the public square or kept out of the city altogether; while people like Job, who "depart from evil" (Job 1:1; 28:28), are at the mercy of thugs and murderers (RSV v. 15, "makes himself a prey"), or "thought [to be] a madman" (NEB).

The salvation oracle (vv. 15b–21) comes as the divine response to Israel's lament. Strictly only verse 21 is an oracle; that is, God's own words. The rest of the passage uniquely describes in narrative form how God intervened in this situation of injustice and evil, and took the law into his own hands. Like the unjust judge in the parable (Luke 18:1–8) he acted because he was angry, not because his importunate people deserved it (v. 15b). Verses 15–16 suggest that, like the weary, bloodstained stranger in chapter 63, God is a reluctant warrior, intervening only when he saw there was no other way, but perhaps all the more ferociously for that. His breastplate and helmet are the same as Paul's (Eph. 6:14–16). Garments of vengeance and "fury" (or "zeal" 9:7; 37:32), however, in place of Paul's shield of faith and the sword of the spirit and the equipment of the gospel of peace, remind us that God's ways are not our ways, his battle not our battle—"lest Israel vaunt themselves . . . saying, 'My own hand has delivered me'" (Judg. 7:2). This battle is God's final cosmic engagement with evil, involving the whole world (vv. 18–19), before he comes to Zion as Redeemer (v. 20).

The image of God's glory in verse 19, coming "like a shining river, the spirit of the Lord hovering over it" (NEB) or "like a

rushing stream, which the wind of the Lord drives" (RSV), is
difficult, not only because several of the words used are rare, but
also because the same Hebrew word can mean either "wind" or
"spirit" (as in Gen. 1:2). Another possibility, based on the old
creation myth (*eg* Ps. 74:13–15; see commentary on 51:9–10),
would be; when the enemy comes like a river (or flood), the spirit
of the Lord puts him to flight.

"Those in Jacob who turn from transgression" (v. 20) alludes to
another Zion hymn (1:27) earlier in the book.

Finally verse 21 places the seal of divine authority on the
prophet's words: God's spirit is upon him (61:1; 2 Sam. 23:2); his
prophecies were placed on his lips by God, and will never be
forgotten. The covenant with, or "promise" to, (*eg* 55:3) the new
Jerusalem is everlasting.

ARISE, SHINE; FOR YOUR LIGHT HAS COME

Isaiah 60:1–14

> ¹Arise, shine; for your light has come,
> and the glory of the Lord has risen upon you.
> ²For behold, darkness shall cover the earth,
> and thick darkness the peoples;
> but the Lord will arise upon you,
> and his glory will be seen upon you.
> ³And nations shall come to your light,
> and kings to the brightness of your rising.
>
> ⁴Lift up your eyes round about, and see;
> they all gather together, they come to you;
> your sons shall come from far,
> and your daughters shall be carried in the arms.
> ⁵Then you shall see and be radiant,
> your heart shall thrill and rejoice;
> because the abundance of the sea shall be turned to you,
> the wealth of the nations shall come to you.
> ⁶A multitude of camels shall cover you,
> the young camels of Midian and Ephah;
> all those from Sheba shall come.

They shall bring gold and frankincense,
    and shall proclaim the praise of the Lord.
7All the flocks of Kedar shall be gathered to you,
    the rams of Neba-ioth shall minister to you;
they shall come up with acceptance on my altar,
    and I will glorify my glorious house.

8Who are these that fly like a cloud,
    and like doves to their windows?
9For the coastlands shall wait for me,
    the ships of Tarshish first,
to bring your sons from far,
    their silver and gold with them,
for the name of the Lord your God,
    and for the Holy One of Israel,
    because he has glorified you.

10Foreigners shall build up your walls,
    and their kings shall minister to you;
for in my wrath I smote you,
    but in my favour I have had mercy on you.
11Your gates shall be open continually;
    day and night they shall not be shut;
that men may bring to you the wealth of the nations,
    with their kings led in procession.
12For the nation and kingdom
    that will not serve you shall perish;
    those nations shall be utterly laid waste.
13The glory of Lebanon shall come to you,
    the cypress, the plane, and the pine,
to beautify the place of my sanctuary;
    and I will make the place of my feet glorious.
14The sons of those who oppressed you
    shall come bending low to you;
and all who despised you
    shall bow down at your feet;
they shall call you the City of the Lord,
    the Zion of the Holy One of Israel.

Chapters 60–62 comprise, for the most part, one long prophecy of
salvation, addressed like earlier passages (*eg* 40:9; 49:14–26;
51:17–23; 52:1–2; 57:6–12) to Jerusalem herself, still in ruins,

still a city "forsaken" (cf. 62:4). The section develops many Isaianic themes already familiar to us, and includes some of the most frequently quoted texts in the Old Testament.

The imagery in verses 1–3 is exceedingly effective although its familiarity may obscure this. There are two words for "arise". "Arise, shine" in verse 1 means "Stand up and let us see you in all your radiant glory". The long night of suffering is over, a new day had dawned for her, a day when she can get up out of the dust where she has lain for so long, forsaken and dejected. The other word for "rise" is usually used of the sun, but here it is twice used of the rising of the glory of the Lord (vv. 1–2); that is to say, "the sun of righteousness... with healing in its wings" (Mal. 4:2). Finally the author brilliantly combines the two when he describes the revival of Jerusalem in verse 3 as the appearance in the blackness of the morning star, proclaiming to the nations that dawn is near. The word for "brightness" came to be used as the name for the planet Venus, the morning star. The idea looks back to 9:1–2 (also 58:8; 59:9), and on to the start of three out of the four Gospels (Matt. 2:2; 4:15–16; Luke 1:78–9; John 1:4–5).

Verses 4–9 of Isaiah 60 describe what it is that will make Jerusalem radiant (v. 5). *First* (v. 4), her sons and daughters will return from exile. "Carried in the arms" (RSV) is awkward and no doubt based on the picture in 49:22. The Hebrew probably means "beside them and supported by them" (NEB is similar); a touching scene of brothers helping their sisters to cover the last part of their long journey home. *Second*, the wealth of nations will begin to flow into Jerusalem to beautify and enrich the new Temple (vv. 7, 13). The notion that the Temple at Jerusalem had such wealth and international status goes back to legends about Solomon (1 Kings ch. 10), but it was also fostered by the fact that at times it certainly was the centre of a mammoth commercial enterprise. When, for instance, Jerusalem was destroyed by the Romans in A.D. 70, it is said that the price of gold fell dramatically as the wealth of the Temple was released on to the imperial markets.

"The abundance of the sea" (v. 5) means rich imports either from over the sea (from Tarshish, Cyprus or the like), or from maritime nations such as Tyre and Lebanon. The picture of camel caravans (v. 6) streaming into Jerusalem, laden with colourful and exotic merchandise, needs no comment. Midian and Ephah refer to the region in north-western Arabia, east of the Gulf of Aqaba, which for centuries controlled the trade routes to South Arabia, East Africa and the East. Sheba includes both South West Arabia and Somalia in East Africa, both famous for the production of incense. The semi-legendary source of gold, Ophir (1 Kings 10:11; Job 28:16), may have been in East Africa too. Midian, Ephah and Sheba were all sons of Abraham's wife, Keturah, (whose name incidentally means "incense") (Gen. 25:1–4), while Kedar and Nebaioth (v. 7) are nomadic peoples descended from Ishmael (Gen. 25:13); whose "hand [was] against every man and every man's hand against him" (Gen. 16:12).

Verses 8–9 turn next to the arrival of "ships of Tarshish" from Spain in the West. The description of their white sails like fleeting clouds or doves flying swiftly home to their dovecots, recalls the prophet's impression of the arrival of the Ethiopian ambassadors in chapter 18. The precious cargo of these exotic vessels includes more of Zion's sons returning home, bringing back gold and silver to replace that which had been removed from the Temple (2 Kings 25:15).

Rebuilding will be carried out by foreign workmen, and servants will be found for Zion among their kings. We have met this arrogant attitude towards Israel's defeated enemies before (*eg* 49:22–23, 26; 51:22–23; see the commentary on these passages for a full discussion). The second half of verse 10 is a theological comment on the subject and suggests that belief in God's love implies also belief in his wrath, in his dealings both with Israel and the nations.

The open gates in verse 11 not only facilitate the movement of the nations' treasures into the city, but also symbolize peace and security. See Revelation 21:25.

Verse 12 sounds a threatening, judgmental note, rather out of tune with the rest of the passage. It is written in a different metre and may well be an independent comment reflecting a situation in which Jerusalem was once again under threat, perhaps from the Samaritans or the Ammonites (Neh. 4). A parallel in the apocryphal book of Ecclesiasticus (*Sirach*) confirms this (and in equally nasty language):

> With two nations my soul is vexed,
>   and the third is no nation:
> Those who live on Mount Seir, and the Philistines,
>   and the foolish people that dwell in Shechem.

> (50:25–26)

The arrival of timber for the Temple is described (60:13) including cedars of Lebanon, and cypress (1 Kings 6:9–10). It is revealing to see how the forests of cedar, plane and pine that heralded the miracle of the New Exodus in 41:19, are here cut down for timber to be used in the rebuilding of the Temple. There will always be tension between the natural beauty of the world about us and man-made institutions, however exquisitely built and for however great a cause.

Justice is relentlessly meted out to Israel's enemies (v. 14), and the New Jerusalem will then be known as "the City of the Lord", and the "Zion of the Holy One of Israel". A small change of vowel in the Hebrew word for "Zion" would give the translation "a monument to the Holy One of Israel". Either way the link between God and his city is secure; the glory of God and the glory of the New Jerusalem are synonymous (vv. 7, 9, 13).

YOUR SUN SHALL SET NO MORE

Isaiah 60:15–22

> 15Whereas you have been forsaken and hated,
>   with no one passing through,
> I will make you majestic for ever,
>   a joy from age to age.
> 16You shall suck the milk of nations,
>   you shall suck the breast of kings;
> and you shall know that I, the Lord, am your Saviour
>   and your Redeemer, the Mighty One of Jacob.

¹⁷Instead of bronze I will bring gold,
  and instead of iron I will bring silver;
instead of wood, bronze,
  instead of stones, iron.
I will make your overseers peace
  and your taskmasters righteousness.
¹⁸Violence shall no more be heard in your land,
  devastation or destruction within your borders;
you shall call your walls Salvation,
  and your gates Praise.

¹⁹The sun shall be no more
  your light by day,
nor for brightness shall the moon
  give light to you by night;
but the Lord will be your everlasting light,
  and your God will be your glory.
²⁰Your sun shall no more go down,
  nor your moon withdraw itself;
for the Lord will be your everlasting light,
  and your days of mourning shall be ended.
²¹Your people shall all be righteous;
  they shall possess the land for ever,
the shoot of my planting, the work of my hands,
  that I might be glorified.
²²The least one shall become a clan,
  and the smallest one a mighty nation;
I am the Lord;
  in its time I will hasten it.

The second part of this chapter is rich in emotive theological vocabulary: peace, righteousness, salvation, glory, everlasting light, the land. It envisages a time when present grief (v. 15), violence (v. 18), mourning (v. 20) and vulnerability (v. 22) will give way to the delights and strengths of the new age. The main part of the prophecy is in the form "instead of X there will be Y" (vv. 15, 17–18), or "X will become Y" (vv. 19, 21–22).

Zion is again addressed as a woman "forsaken and hated", and without a friend to visit her (v. 15). If we drop the metaphor, then "passing through" would refer to the coming and going of the merchants and caravans, referred to in the first half of the chapter. In the new age she will become the centre of attraction again, beautiful to behold and the darling of every generation. Nourished by the nations, cradled in the arms of kings (cf. 49:23), she will recognize her Lord and Saviour, her Redeemer, "the Mighty One of Jacob" (v. 16). The last words appear at the end of chapter 49 as well.

The progression upwards from wood to bronze to gold, and from stone to iron to silver (v. 17), contrasts the decadence of the present age with the glory of the future, worthlessness with immense value, drabness with shining beauty. Instead of the rigours and bitterness with which the people were afflicted under hard taskmasters in Egypt (Exod. 1:11–13), "peace" (*shalom*) and "righteousness" (*tsedakah*) will reign again in Jerusalem. The allusion to the Exodus story is obvious. Never again (v. 18) will the cries of the victims of crime and violence be heard in the land, or the crash of falling masonry as enemies breach the city wall, because the new walls will be called "salvation" (*yeshu'ah*), a word synonymous with divine protection (eg 26:1; 37:35); and the new gates, permanently open (v. 11) and used only for peacetime processions and festivities, will be called "Praise", a name related to Hebrew words for "Psalm" and "Hallelujah".

In verses 19–20 the prophet's imagination breaks out of conventional categories and anticipates the dazzling vision of the New Jerusalem in the apocalypse of St John:

> And the city has no need of sun or moon to shine upon it, for the glory of God is its light, and its lamp is the Lamb. By its light shall the nations walk; and the kings of the earth shall bring glory into it, and its gates shall never be shut by day—and there shall be no night there; they shall bring into it the glory and the honour of the nations.
>
> (Rev. 21:23–26)

Yet it is not far from the more conventional picture of blazing light with which the chapter began, or the vision of the Lord of hosts reigning on Mount Zion in 24:23. The "sun of righteousness" that shines in Zion is a sun that never sets (v. 20)—an image which is then spelt out in plain language: "your days of mourning shall be ended". Death will be no more; in the words of the "Isaiah Apocalypse": "He will swallow up death for ever, and the Lord God will wipe away tears from all faces" (25:8). Surely this is not just about the end of the Babylonian Exile in the sixth century B.C. It speaks to us also of eternal life in the city of God.

We are the "righteous" people (v. 21); "righteous" in the saving sense of both "innocent" and "victorious" (eg 41:2; 51:1). We are to possess the land for ever, planted there by God like a forest of young trees. We who were once a mere remnant—if the Lord of hosts had not left us a few survivors, we should have been like Sodom, and become like Gomorrah (1:9)—are now a mighty nation (v. 22). From a human standpoint it may look as though we are small and weak and forsaken, but in God's eyes we are strong and secure. Remember Gideon (Judg. 6:15; 7:2), David (1 Sam. 17:14, 33, 42), and, in Isaianic tradition, Jerusalem herself (37:22). Here again perhaps traditions, preserved in the annual celebration of the Passover, are alluded to:

"A wandering Aramean was my father; and he went down into Egypt and sojourned there, few in number; and there he became a nation, great, mighty, and populous."

(Deut. 26:5; cf. Exod. 1:1–14)

In God's time the worm is transformed into a "threshing sledge, new, sharp, having teeth" (41:14–15); and a grain of mustard seed, the smallest of all seeds, becomes the greatest of shrubs, "so that the birds of the air come and make their nests in its branches" (Matt. 13:31–32).

LIBERTY TO THE CAPTIVES

Isaiah 61:1–11

[1]The Spirit of the Lord God is upon me,
    because the Lord has anointed me
to bring good tidings to the afflicted;
    he has sent me to bind up the brokenhearted,
to proclaim liberty to the captives,
    and the opening of the prison to those who are bound;

²to proclaim the year of the Lord's favour,
    and the day of vengeance of our God;
    to comfort all who mourn;
³to grant to those who mourn in Zion—
    to give them a garland instead of ashes,
  the oil of gladness instead of mourning,
    the mantle of praise instead of a faint spirit;
  that they may be called oaks of righteousness,
    the planting of the Lord, that he may be glorified.
⁴They shall build up the ancient ruins,
    they shall raise up the former devastations;
  they shall repair the ruined cities,
    the devastations of many generations.

⁵Aliens shall stand and feed your flocks,
    foreigners shall be your ploughmen and vinedressers;
⁶but you shall be called the priests of the Lord
    men shall speak of you as the ministers of our God;
  you shall eat the wealth of the nations,
    and in their riches you shall glory.
⁷Instead of your shame you shall have a double portion,
    instead of dishonour you shall rejoice in your lot;
  therefore in your land you shall possess a double portion;
    yours shall be everlasting joy.

⁸For I the Lord love justice,
    I hate robbery and wrong;
 I will faithfully give them their recompense,
    and I will make an everlasting covenant with them.
⁹Their descendants shall be known among the nations,
    and their offspring in the midst of the peoples;
  all who see them shall acknowledge them,
    that they are a people whom the Lord has blessed.

¹⁰I will greatly rejoice in the Lord,
    my soul shall exult in my God;
  for he has clothed me with the garments of salvation,
    he has covered me with the robe of righteousness,
  as a bridegroom decks himself with a garland,
    and as a bride adorns herself with her jewels.
¹¹For as the earth brings forth its shoots,
    and as a garden causes what is sown in it to spring up,

so the Lord God will cause righteousness and praise
to spring forth before all the nations.

As a context for this famous chapter we are to think first, as in the
case of chapter 58, of the Day of Atonement, a day of fasting and
spiritual renewal, and the day on which the jubilee year was to be
proclaimed. The chapter is in a sense a sermon on Leviticus 25: a
sermon on planting (v. 3), rebuilding (v. 4) and new growth (v.
11), on the one hand; and a sermon on freedom (v. 1) and justice
(v. 8) on the other. Jesus preached a sermon on the same text in a
Nazareth synagogue (Luke 4:16–30). Today the chapter has been
an inspiration and a challenge to Christians living under dictator-
ships in Latin America and elsewhere, and is a fundamental text
in Liberation Theology.

The prophet first gives his credentials: he is no false prophet
(Jer. 23:16–22; Amos 7:14). The spirit is upon him as it was upon
Moses (Num. 11:25) and the servant of the Lord (42:1–4). He has
been anointed like a priest (Exod. 29:1–9), clothed in garments of
salvation and a robe of righteousness (v. 10), again like a priest
(Ps. 132:9, 16), and called to minister to those in trouble (vv.
1–3). Nowhere is there a prophet's ordination "after the order of
Melchizedek" better described. Both in early Christianity and in
the Qumran sect, liberty is proclaimed by one like Melchizedek,
who is both priest and king (Gen. 14:18); the embodiment of
Israel's hopes: "and this is the moment of the Year of Grace for
Melchizedek; and he will by his strength, judge the holy ones of
God, executing judgment . . ." (G. Vermes, *Dead Sea Scrolls in
English* (1975), pp. 266–7). Hebrews chapter 7 is a Christian
discourse on the same theme.

The four categories of people to whom the prophet is called to
bring news (v. 1) are paired in an interesting way, seemingly to
emphasize the need to include victims of both material and spiritual distress. This is certainly true of the *first* pair: the poor or
"afflicted" (RSV) are paired with the "brokenhearted". In the
second, "captives" are to be physically released from their captivity, while "the opening of the eyes" (in Hebrew) of those who
are bound suggests again perhaps release from spiritual bondage.

The word "liberty" belongs to the legal practicalities of Leviticus chapter 25. The word translated "opening of the eyes" occurs only here but is exactly in line with 9:2, 53:11 and 66:14.

Verse 2 refers at the same time to the jubilee year in Leviticus, and to the Day of the Lord: *eg* "In that day the branch of the Lord shall be beautiful and glorious . . . (Isa. 4:2); and "In that day the Lord with his hard and great and strong sword will punish Leviathan . . ." (27:1). The fulfilment of such prophecies marks the dawn of a new age (cf. Luke 4:21).

Comfort for the bereaved is chosen as the theme for the next verse (v. 3): the mourners are pictured putting away their funeral garb (2 Sam. 13:19; Jer. 6:26) and dressing instead for a banquet. In a powerful image their change of heart is symbolized by new names, "oaks of righteousness" (or "victory" as in 41:2) and the "planting of the Lord"; names which remind us that the jubilee year was "a sabbath of solemn rest for the land" (Lev. 25:5). Ancient ruins will be rebuilt and cities repaired (v. 4). New shepherds, ploughmen and vinedressers will appear to care for the land (v. 5). God's people (v. 6) will be set apart from common tasks: "a kingdom of priests and a holy nation" (Exod. 19:6). Like Aaron and his sons, the priests, they will be given rich gifts (Exod. chs. 28–29): the "wealth of the nations" will be theirs (60:6). Their new found joy will be double their previous shame (v. 7).

Verse 8 takes us back to chapter 1 and the eternal principle on which Isaianic "holiness" is founded (1:17; 5:7; 32:1; 42:1). "Robbery and wrong" (RSV) involves a textual emendation based on ancient versions: the Hebrew text actually reads "robbery with a burnt offering" (RSV footnote), which although grammatically rather odd, makes good sense. This would then be another comment on ritualism and hypocrisy like 1:11 or Amos 5:21–22:

> I hate, I despise your feasts,
>> and I take no delight in your solemn assemblies.
> Even though you offer me your burnt offerings and cereal offerings,
>> I will not accept them.

Not for the first time would Isaianic prophecy be condemning the hypocrisy of immoral worshippers. To be true to his covenant God must punish them; but this time the verse ends with an apparent allusion to his promise to Abraham and his seed for ever, and a "recompense" that eventually brings them happiness and hope (v. 9).

Finally (vv. 10–11) the prophet sings a hymn of thanksgiving on behalf of his people (like Ps. 138). The New Jerusalem will be adorned like a bride or a bridegroom for their wedding (Rev. 21:2; cf. also 52:1–2), clothed in garments of salvation and right-eousness like the priests in Psalm 132 (vv. 9, 16). The hymn ends where we began with a vision of the land celebrating its jubilee year (Lev. 25), showing the world what true "righteousness" (or "triumph") and praise really mean.

FOR ZION'S SAKE I WILL NOT KEEP SILENT

Isaiah 62:1–12

¹For Zion's sake I will not keep silent,
 and for Jerusalem's sake I will not rest,
until her vindication goes forth as brightness,
 and her salvation as a burning torch.
²The nations shall see your vindication,
 and all the kings your glory;
and you shall be called by a new name
 which the mouth of the Lord will give.
³You shall be a crown of beauty in the hand of the Lord,
 and a royal diadem in the hand of your God.
⁴You shall no more be termed Forsaken,
 and your land shall no more be termed Desolate;
but you shall be called My delight is in her,
 and your land Married;
for the Lord delights in you,
 and your land shall be married.
⁵For as a young man marries a virgin,
 so shall your sons marry you,
and as the bridegroom rejoices over the bride,
 so shall your God rejoice over you.

⁶Upon your walls, O Jerusalem,
   I have set watchmen;
 all the day and all the night
   they shall never be silent.
 You who put the Lord in remembrance,
   take no rest,
⁷and give him no rest
   until he establishes Jerusalem
   and makes it a praise in the earth.
⁸The Lord has sworn by his right hand
   and by his mighty arm:
 "I will not again give your grain
   to be food for your enemies,
 and foreigners shall not drink your wine
   for which you have laboured;
⁹but those who garner it shall eat it
   and praise the Lord
 and those who gather it shall drink it
   in the courts of my sanctuary."

¹⁰Go through, go through the gates,
   prepare the way for the people;
 build up, build up the highway,
   clear it of stones,
   lift up an ensign over the peoples.
¹¹Behold, the Lord has proclaimed
   to the end of the earth:
 Say to the daughter of Zion,
   "Behold, your salvation comes;
 behold, his reward is with him,
   and his recompense before him."
¹²And they shall be called The holy people,
   The redeemed of the Lord;
 and you shall be called Sought out,
   a city not forsaken.

Most of this chapter is addressed (like ch. 60) to demoralized
Zion, as a deserted wife, and promises her salvation. But the
prophet's impatience intrudes in verse 1 where he turns to us, as it
were, and confides that, for Zion's sake, he cannot rest. He must
do something to raise her flagging spirits; and then he proceeds to

reassure her, in another beautiful prophecy of salvation, that the Lord still loves her and has not deserted her (vv. 2–5). "Vindication" (or better "triumph", NEB; this is the word *tsedek* again; see the commentary on 41:2) is again paired with "salvation" as in the previous chapter (61:10), and the "light" theme from 60:1–3 is further developed. "Brightness" (NEB "sunrise") is the same astronomical term used in 60:3, and the new image of a blazing torch, piercing the darkness (we might say, "as on the day of Midian", Isa. 9:4; see also Judg. 7:16, 20) is added.

The prophecy proper begins with a general introduction in which Zion's future is gloriously and mysteriously summed up (v. 2). Nations and kings will see her triumph and new glory, and she will be given a new name determined by God. "Give" (NEB "pronounce") is a technical legal term meaning literally "designate", and the word-games in verse 4 can have nothing to do with the name-prophecy here in verse 2. The Apocalypse of John, as so often, gives us the key (Rev. 2:17):

> To him who conquers I will give some of the hidden manna, and I will give him a white stone, with a new name written on the stone which no one knows except him who receives it.

By naming the new "city of God", her Founder and Architect symbolizes his ultimate triumph.

Elsewhere "the hand of . . . God" (v. 3) is little more than a synonym for the power of God (59:1; Ps. 78:42: RSV "power"). But here, with typical Isaianic imagination, God is pictured as holding up the new city, like some exquisite jewelled crown, for all to gaze upon in admiration.

The two new names in verse 4 are actually quite ordinary girls' names. (Forsaken and Desolate are of course not real names.) *Hephzibah* ("My delight is in her") occurs once in the Bible (2 Kings 21:1) and is also the name of a kibbutz in modern Israel. *Beulah* ("Married") is remembered in Mae West's immortal words, "Beulah, peel me a grape!" (*I'm No Angel*, 1933). Neither name qualifies as a new name worthy to be given by God to his new city (v. 2). The author is merely exploiting the meaning of the names for his own prophetic purpose, as is done in the case of the name *Immanuel* in 7:14 (and 8:8–10), and possibly the name *Isaiah* itself in 37:2 (see commentary). A further play on words occurs in verse 5 where the verb "marry" moves nearer its sense of "possess" or "rule over" (as in 26:13; 1 Chron. 4:22): as a young man takes a virgin in hand, so shall Zion's strong sons take their mother in hand to guide her and protect her. Jerusalem is moreover, like God's bride (as in 61:10; Rev. 21:2), loved, cherished and enjoyed by him. The Song of Solomon has traditionally been interpreted as containing some of the love-songs which God and Israel/Jerusalem sing to one another.

It is most unlikely that verses 6–7 refer to anything the prophet himself has done, such as placing watchmen on the city walls or instructing his disciples in any way. Surely God is the speaker, as in 40:1, deploying members of his heavenly court—"watchmen", "recorders" (the word translated "you who put the Lord in remembrance" is actually the technical term used in 37:2 of a royal official)—to ensure that Zion's case is given top priority. The Lord's solemn oath in verses 8–9 continues the same royal court imagery. He guarantees that never again will enemy invaders, like the Assyrians (chs. 36–37) or Babylonians (ch. 39), or possibly, in a post-exilic context, Persian tax-collectors, confiscate the produce of the land. God's people will be free to bring their gifts of grain and wine to the Temple at Jerusalem, where they can participate in jubilant communion feasts (Deut. 12:17–18). The "courts", originally perhaps a non-technical term, later referred to the specially fenced off areas in the Second Temple, designed to keep apart gentiles, women, "Israel" and the priests (*eg* 1 Chron. 28:12; Ps. 65:4).

Finally in words derived from earlier passages (*eg* 40:3; 49:22), the prophet calls upon his people to enter the holy city (vv. 10–12). Earlier the call was to return from exile; now it is to enter the New Jerusalem. "The highway" (v. 10) is the great ramp running along the city wall up to each gate, like Bethlehem Road leading up to Jaffa Gate on the west side of the Old City of Jerusalem today. An "ensign" (or "signal", NEB) is to be raised as a rallying point for Israel and the nations (5:26; 11:12; 49:22). The whole earth (v. 11) will hear about the "salvation" or "victory" (52:10) of Zion, and the Lord's marvellous "reward" or "recompense" (40:10).

The four names given to the New Israel in verse 12 are once more grouped in two pairs. "The holy people" goes back to the creation of Israel at Sinai (Exod. 19:5–6; 22:31), but strikes a familiar Isaianic chord too (*eg* 6:3; 11:9; 48:2; 52:1). It is paired with "Sought out" (RSV), a weak translation obscuring the religious overtones of the word which is used for "consulting an oracle" (Judg. 1:1) and "seeking the Lord" (Isa. 55:6; Amos. 5:6, 14). "The holy people" will be sought out, consulted as a source of wisdom, justice and truth (2:2–4; 55:5). "Redeemed" (v. 12) is another Isaianic term referring literally to what a kinsman does in exactly the situation implied by the last term, "forsaken", used of a deserted wife (cf. v. 4). God's people will be established again in Jerusalem, their confidence restored; "a light to the nations" (42:6; 49:6).

THE GRAPES OF WRATH

Isaiah 63:1–6

> [1]Who is this that comes from Edom,
>   in crimsoned garments from Bozrah,
> he that is glorious in his apparel,
>   marching in the greatness of his strength?
>
> "It is I, announcing vindication,
>   mighty to save."
>
> [2]Why is thy apparel red,
>   and thy garments like his that treads in the wine press?
>
> [3]"I have trodden the wine press alone,
>   and from the peoples no one was with me;
> I trod them in my anger
>   and trampled them in my wrath;
> their lifeblood is sprinkled upon my garments,
>   and I have stained all my raiment.
> [4]For the day of vengeance was in my heart,
>   and my year of redemption has come.

⁵I looked, but there was no one to help;
　I was appalled, but there was no one to uphold;
so my own arm brought me victory,
　and my wrath upheld me.
⁶I trod down the peoples in my anger,
　I made them drunk in my wrath,
　and I poured out their lifeblood on the earth."

The next scene is one of the most vivid and awe-inspiring in the whole of the Prophetic literature. It has left a deep impression on the Church's heritage both in the Bible (Rev. 14:17–20; 19:15) and in the hymn-book:

Mine eyes have seen the glory of the coming of the Lord;
He hath trampled out the vintage where the grapes of wrath are stored.

Before we recoil in disgust, however, from these images of blood and vengeance, there are two important points to be taken into account. *First,* the context was established by chapter 61: the jubilee year, the year of release, is inseparable from "the day of vengeance" (61:2; 63:4). The "day of vengeance" is when a just regime takes over from an evil and oppressive one, and that very often means a bloodbath. Long before the advent of Liberation Theology, it was obvious that to "bring good tidings to the afflicted" and "proclaim liberty to the captives" (61:1) may involve violence: gentle political persuasion may not be enough. These chapters are about justice (*eg* 61:8); human rights as laid down in the laws of Leviticus (25:10). There is plenty in the Old Testament about God's love and compassion: indeed the very next passage (vv. 7ff.) is one of the loveliest examples. But chapters 60–62 are about the year of redemption, and that involves the brutal fact that evil has to be destroyed. It is in this context that we must interpret 63:1–6.

The *second* easily overlooked consideration about this passage is that far from dwelling crudely on the gory details of the slaughter itself, as in less subtle passages (*eg* ch. 34), and gloating over the fate of the victims (*eg* 49:26; 51:22–23), the prophet uses metaphorical language throughout, and what is more, chooses to describe a scene many miles from the battleground itself, and some time after the dreadful deed is over. One can even detect a note of weariness in the description (*eg* vv. 1, 5). It is almost as though the Day of Judgment is too cruel, too painful to contemplate, and the exhausted, bloodstained victor is thankful it is all over.

The dialogue at the gate of the city between a watchman on guard-duty and the mysterious stranger, brilliantly picks up the note of expectancy from 62:6–7, and prepares us for the news of victory, carried, not as before by a messenger (52:7–10) or the prophet (61:1–3), but by God himself. The first question is an elaboration of the conventional formal challenge, "Halt! Who goes there?" Edom, and Bozrah—Edom's greatest city (34:6)—in the first place merely denote the direction from which the stranger approaches, namely, from the south. But it was from the south, from Edom, that Yahweh in the old days had marched forth when the "earth trembled . . . and the mountains quaked" (Judg. 5:4–5; Deut. 33:2; cf. Hab. 3:3). "Edom" in Hebrew also suggests "red" (v. 2); and "Bozrah" suggests gathering grapes (Lev. 25:5, 11). So both names in the question are clues to the answer. In view of this there is really no point in arguing about why the Edomites should have been selected for this special treatment, here or in chapter 34: both "Edom" and "Bozrah" are elaborate symbols.

The mighty stranger's tired and bedraggled appearance is described in some detail (v. 1). His garments are stained red; he looks swollen (NEB "his muscles stand out"). The traditional translation "glorious" (RSV, AV) is by no means certain. He is "stooping" (NEB): again "marching" (RSV) is not what the text actually has. Above all he is apparently unrecognizable: bloodstained, disfigured, stooping, alone.

His answers explain what had happened. He has had to fight alone with no-one to help him (59:16). He was "appalled" at the enormity of his gruesome task (v. 5): the word is used in this sense in Psalm 143:4 and Daniel 8:27. He was supported, or as we might say, spurred on by his wrath (v. 5). But this is all over now. He has come to Jerusalem to bring good tidings (61:1), to publish salvation (52:7), to announce that "my year of redemption has come" (v. 4).

The first answer "It is I . . ." (v. 1) beautifully recalls those great moments of divine self-revelation in chapters 41–45 and 48, and also the "I am" sayings of Christ in the fourth Gospel. It is worth pausing to consider the paradox that here, as in the New Testament, God appears as a weary, bloodstained warrior, commanding our sympathy and respect, rather than our fear. The application of this passage to Christ's struggle, and in particular the association between the bloodshed in battle and the wine drunk in the remembrance of his death, is inevitable:

And he said to them, "This is my blood of the new covenant, which is poured out for many. Truly, I say to you, I shall not drink again of the fruit of the vine until that day when I drink it new in the kingdom of God".

(Mark 14:24–25)

The wine produced in this wine-press, however, out of the grapes of wrath, is the blood of the wicked, while the wine of the sacrament is made from the "true vine" because it is the blood of Jesus Christ (John 15:1–6).

OUR FATHER IN HEAVEN—I

Isaiah 63:7–64:12

7I will recount the steadfast love of the Lord,
    the praises of the Lord,
  according to all that the Lord has granted us,
    and the great goodness to the house of Israel
  which he has granted them according to his mercy,
    according to the abundance of his steadfast love.
8For he said, Surely they are my people,
    sons who will not deal falsely;
    and he became their Saviour.
9In all their affliction he was afflicted,
    and the angel of his presence saved them;
  in his love and in his pity he redeemed them;
    he lifted them up and carried them all the days of old.

¹⁰But they rebelled
    and grieved his holy Spirit;
  therefore he turned to be their enemy,
    and himself fought against them.
¹¹Then he remembered the days of old,
    of Moses his servant.
  Where is he who brought up out of the sea
    the shepherds of his flock?
  Where is he who put in the midst of them
    his holy Spirit,
¹²who caused his glorious arm
    to go at the right hand of Moses,
  who divided the waters before them
    to make for himself an everlasting name,
¹³ who led them through the depths?
  Like a horse in the desert,
    they did not stumble.
¹⁴Like cattle that go down into the valley,
    the Spirit of the Lord gave them rest.
  So thou didst lead thy people,
    to make for thyself a glorious name.

¹⁵Look down from heaven and see,
    from thy holy and glorious habitation.
  Where are thy zeal and thy might?
    The yearning of thy heart and thy compassion
    are withheld from me.
¹⁶For thou art our Father,
    though Abraham does not know us
    and Israel does not acknowledge us;
  thou, O Lord, art our Father,
    our Redeemer from of old is thy name.
¹⁷O Lord, why dost thou make us err from thy ways
    and harden our heart, so that we fear thee not?
  Return for the sake of thy servants,
    the tribes of thy heritage.
¹⁸Thy holy people possessed thy sanctuary a little while;
    our adversaries have trodden it down.
¹⁹We have become like those over whom thou hast never ruled,
    like those who are not called by thy name.

¹O that thou wouldst rend the heavens and come down,
    that the mountains might quake at thy presence—
²as when fire kindles brushwood
    and the fire causes water to boil—
to make thy name known to thy adversaries,
    and that the nations might tremble at thy presence!
³When thou didst terrible things which we looked not for,
    thou camest down, the mountains quaked at thy presence.
⁴From of old no one has heard
    or perceived by the ear,
no eye has seen a God besides thee,
    who works for those who wait for him.

⁵Thou meetest him that joyfully works righteousness,
    those that remember thee in thy ways.
Behold, thou wast angry, and we sinned;
    in our sins we have been a long time, and shall we be saved?
⁶We have all become like one who is unclean,
    and all our righteous deeds are like a polluted garment.
We all fade like a leaf,
    and our iniquities, like the wind, take us away.
⁷There is no one that calls upon thy name,
    that bestirs himself to take hold of thee;
for thou hast hid thy face from us,
    and hast delivered us into the hand of our iniquities.

⁸Yet, O Lord, thou art our Father;
    we are the clay, and thou art our potter;
    we are all the work of thy hand.
⁹Be not exceedingly angry, O Lord,
    and remember not iniquity for ever.
    Behold, consider, we are all thy people.
¹⁰Thy holy cities have become a wilderness,
    Zion has become a wilderness,
    Jerusalem a desolation.
¹¹Our holy and beautiful house,
    where our fathers praised thee,
has been burned by fire,
    and all our pleasant places have become ruins.
¹²Wilt thou restrain thyself at these things, O Lord?
    Wilt thou keep silent, and afflict us sorely?

The long prayer that takes up the rest of chapter 63 and the whole of 64 is what is technically described as a "community lament", like Psalm 44 and Lamentations chapter 5. It contains various elements, beginning with an account of God's mighty acts on behalf of his people (vv. 7–14). A lament over the ruins of the Temple follows (vv. 15–19), then a prayer for help and forgiveness (ch. 64). A penitent note is discernible throughout, and the emphasis is exclusively on the divine initiative. God is their saviour, not because of anything they have done to deserve it, but because he loves them as a father loves his child (63:16; 64:8).

Verses 7–14 then are rather like a confession of faith: we believe in God who abundantly blessed us . . . named us as his people . . . suffered with us . . . lifted us up and carried us "all the days of old" (63:9). "Steadfast love" (RSV) in verse 7 is plural (as in 55:3; Ps. 89:49; Lam. 3:22, *etc*) and concrete, not abstract: hence "acts of unfailing love" (NEB). "Mercy" (also v. 7) is always associated with warmth and "tenderness" (NEB). Verse 8 touchingly presents God as a father turning a blind eye to the evil propensities of his sons. "Salvation" mercifully does not depend on our good deeds.

Verse 9 as it stands (there are variant readings) says that God suffers with his people, "afflicted in their affliction". The idea of a remote Creator unmoved by the sufferings of his creatures is unbiblical, and supremely rejected by the centurion at the cross (see Mark 15:39):

> And when the centurion, who stood facing him, saw that he thus breathed his last, he said, "Truly this man was the Son of God!"

An ancient Greek rendering of the Bible marvellously picks this up in its rendering of verse 9:

> In their afflictions no messenger, no angel saved them, but the Lord himself through his love and compassion for them.

God himself lifted them up like a shepherd (40:11) and carried them like a mother (46:3).

After a single verse on how the people's disobedience turned God into their enemy (63:10), there comes a brief but allusive recital of the Exodus story, in the form of a question: where is the God of the Exodus now (vv. 11–14)? The "days of old" (v. 11) include both the age of patriarchal promise (Gen. 15) and the age of Moses in the wilderness (Hos. 2:14–15). The phrase translated "Moses his servant" (RSV, v. 11) is difficult: it actually means "Moses, and his people" (AV), or he "who drew out his people" (NEB), since the name *Moses* is traditionally derived from a word meaning "to draw water from a well" (Exod. 2:10). "The shepherds" (RSV) are Moses and Aaron, Israel's leaders in the wilderness. The belief that God dwells in the midst of his holy people goes back to the building of the Tabernacle in the wilderness (*eg* Exod. 25:8; 29:46) and reappears in the vision of the New Jerusalem (Rev. 21:3) and the Prologue to the fourth Gospel (John 1:14). The phrase "*his* holy Spirit" (v. 10) occurs only here in the Old Testament and is one of several expressions, like "the Name", "the Glory", the *Shekinah* (or "presence"), often used in Jewish theology in place of the name of God itself.

The words for "waters" and "depths" (vv. 12–13) have important mythological associations as we saw at 51:9–10 and elsewhere (*eg* 44:27), but here the role of Moses (v. 12) and the animal similes in verses 13–14 keep the passage in touch with the events of the Exodus story itself. Strong and sure-footed as horses, the people traversed the wilderness in safety; like cattle on the familiar track homewards, they made their way finally to the rest and peace of the Promised Land.

OUR FATHER IN HEAVEN—II

Isaiah 63:7–64:12 (*cont'd*)

The lament in 63:15–19 makes up the core of the prayer in chapters 63 and 64, pleading with God to return to his people, to be once more their Father and their Redeemer. "Look down from heaven and see [our suffering]" is a frequent cry in lamentations like this (*eg* Lam. 1:11; 3:63; 5:1; see also Ps. 80:14). Solomon's great prayer in the newly dedicated Temple uses similar language (1 Kings 8:30):

"And hearken thou to the supplication of thy servant and of thy people Israel, when they pray toward this place; yea, hear thou in heaven thy dwelling place; and when thou hearest, forgive."

"Zeal" and "might" (63:15) denote the special energy God devotes to caring for his people: see the commentary on 9:7 (vol. 1, p. 100–101) and 37:32. "The yearning of thy heart and thy compassion" are further evidence of God's deep emotional involvement with the affairs of this world. He is no abstraction; no distant source of all being.

Verse 16, together with 64:8, show how prayers beginning "Our Father..." (*Paternoster*) were already a familiar part of Jewish tradition before New Testament times. As we have seen, images of God as Father and Mother are there in the Old Testament. The verse as a whole means that, if we are cut off from our people or our land, as Jews in all ages have been, and the promise to Abraham seems far removed from us, then we must turn directly to God our Father in heaven and "our Redeemer from of old".

Underlying verse 17 is the paradox that all we do is governed by God but at the same time we feel guilt when we do wrong. But so also is the belief that a change of heart, activated by God, is a possibility (Jer. 31:31–34; Heb. 8:8–12). This is a prayer for the ability to repent, like that of the Psalmist (51:10):

Create in me a clean heart, O God,
  and put a new and right spirit within me.

Finally (vv. 18–19) the actual state of affairs in Israel is described although not in sufficient detail to enable us to identify any historical situation. The Temple has been desecrated, the land taken over by some evil power, and the people frightened into doubting whether they are God's holy people, his "own possession" (Exod. 19:5–6) after all. "Return" (v. 17) means "Come back to us", but also "Think again; do not be angry with us for ever!"

The next part of the prayer begins with an agonizingly wistful *cri de coeur*, corresponding to the "How long, O Lord?" of other prayers (*eg* Pss. 79:5; 90:13; Isa. 6:11). There are several examples of this cry in the Psalms (*eg* 14:7; 55:6), and Job 14:13 is another:

Oh that thou wouldest hide me in Sheol,
  that thou wouldest conceal me until thy wrath is past,
  that thou wouldest appoint me a set time, and remember me!

Here a sense of guilt (vv. 5–7) seems to have convinced the speaker that his prayer is unlikely to be answered. But what he longs for, hoping against hope, is a theophany like Elijah's (1 Kings 19), or like the ones described in Psalm 18:7–15 and elsewhere (*eg* Exod. 19:16–25; Deut. 33:2; Judg. 5:4–5), where God's mysterious power is revealed in fire, earthquake, wind and storm, to encourage his people and terrify his enemies. Verses 4 and 5 of chapter 64 go beyond the spectacular trappings of a confrontation between man and God, and comment on the experience itself. See Paul's paraphrase of Isaiah 64:4 (in 1 Cor. 2:9–11):

"What no eye has seen, nor ear heard,
  nor the heart of man conceived,
  what God has prepared for those who love him,"
God has revealed to us through the Spirit.

The apocalyptic experiences of Moses (Exod. 3), Elijah (1 Kings 19), Isaiah (ch. 6), Daniel (chs. 8–12) and others are what this prayer is about: evidence that God is not far off, but near to all who call upon him in spirit and in truth (55:6). Verse 5*a* of Isaiah 64 sums it up beautifully:

Thou meetest him that joyfully works righteousness.

God encounters those who remember him in his ways. The very act of reciting the story of their redemption brings God's people into his presence with thanksgiving (Ps. 48:9–11).

Inveterate sinfulness and uncleanness, however, have kept God and his people apart. The encounter they long for is impossible while God is angry (v. 5*b*). Even the good they try to do is polluted, their feeble efforts overwhelmed by sin, like leaves blown away in the wind (v. 6). They are morally unfit to approach

God, just as a leper, or anyone else polluted by physical uncleanness is unfit to approach the Temple (Lev. chs. 13–15). Verse 7 describes a spiritual wilderness where no-one can pray to God or grasp his helping hand in time of need, because they are convinced that he has abandoned them in the toils of their sin. The Hebrew word translated "delivered" (NEB "abandoned") usually means "melted"; which would not be impossible here: God has melted them; *ie* broken their spirit, shattered their faith (as in Ezek. 21:15) beneath the enormity of their guilt.

The last stanza of the prayer (vv. 8–12) is slightly more hopeful in its plea for forgiveness. "Yet" (or "but now") in verse 8 usually marks a change of key. The emotive title "our Father" is quoted from 63:16, and the statement that we are clay in God's hands can be used to condemn (Jer. ch. 18), but also to comfort. The sinner's only hope is to put himself totally into God's hands in penitence and faith: maybe God will "create in [him] a clean heart ... [and] rebuild the walls of Jerusalem" (Ps. 51:10, 18). The causal connection between the sins of the people and the scenes of desolation and ruin in Judah, has been a theme from the beginning (1:2–9; 40:1–2). The prophet, like the author of Psalm 51, sees forgiveness in terms of rebuilding and restoration.

He longs to get back to the days when the Temple still stood in all its glory, and his forefathers sang psalms there (the word for "praise", v. 11, is closely related to the Hebrew title of the Book of Psalms) innocently and securely. Such longings for the restoration of the Temple are exceptional in Isaianic tradition, and we would probably be justified in arguing that (as in Ps. 51) the emphasis is more on forgiveness and spiritual renewal than on the actual physical rebuilding of the Temple. So vehement are the attacks on hypocrisy and ritualism throughout the book (1:12–17; 58:6–7; 66:1–4), and references to a new temple so rare and insignificant in comparison, that it would be safe to say that faith, justice and salvation are much more central to the Isaianic vision than institutionalized worship. The very next chapter begins with an attack on ritual (65:1–7). A New Jerusalem without a temple is a possibility (65:17–25), and indeed, in some visions, an ideal (Rev. 21:22).

THE SHEEP AND THE GOATS

Isaiah 65:1–16

[1]I was ready to be sought by those who did not ask for me;
  I was ready to be found by those who did not seek me.
 I said, "Here am I, here am I,"
  to a nation that did not call on my name.
[2]I spread out my hands all the day
  to a rebellious people,
 who walk in a way that is not good,
  following their own devices;
[3]a people who provoke me
  to my face continually,
 sacrificing in gardens
  and burning incense upon bricks;
[4]who sit in tombs,
  and spend the night in secret places;
 who eat swine's flesh,
  and broth of abominable things is in their vessels;
[5]who say, "Keep to yourself,
  do not come near me, for I am set apart from you."
 These are a smoke in my nostrils,
  a fire that burns all the day.
[6]Behold, it is written before me:
  "I will not keep silent, but I will repay,
 yea, I will repay into their bosom
[7] their iniquities and their fathers' iniquities together,
                                                    says the Lord;
 because they burned incense upon the mountains
  and reviled me upon the hills,
 I will measure into their bosom
  payment for their former doings."

[8]Thus says the Lord:
 "As the wine is found in the cluster,
  and they say, 'Do not destroy it,
  for there is a blessing in it,'
 so I will do for my servants' sake,
  and not destroy them all.

⁹I will bring forth descendants from Jacob,
    and from Judah inheritors of my mountains;
  my chosen shall inherit it,
    and my servants shall dwell there.
¹⁰Sharon shall become a pasture for flocks,
    and the Valley of Achor a place for herds to lie down,
    for my people who have sought me.
¹¹But you who forsake the Lord,
    who forget my holy mountain,
  who set a table for Fortune
    and fill cups of mixed wine for Destiny;
¹²I will destine you to the sword,
    and all of you shall bow down to the slaughter;
  because, when I called, you did not answer,
    when I spoke, you did not listen,
  but you did what was evil in my eyes,
    and chose what I did not delight in."

¹³Therefore thus says the Lord God:
  "Behold, my servants shall eat,
    but you shall be hungry;
  behold, my servants shall drink,
    but you shall be thirsty;
  behold, my servants shall rejoice,
    but you shall be put to shame;
¹⁴behold, my servants shall sing for gladness of heart,
    but you shall cry out for pain of heart,
    and shall wail for anguish of spirit.
¹⁵You shall leave your name to my chosen for a curse,
    and the Lord God will slay you;
    but his servants he will call by a different name.
¹⁶So that he who blesses himself in the land
    shall bless himself by the God of truth,
  and he who takes an oath in the land
    shall swear by the God of truth;
  because the former troubles are forgotten
    and are hid from my eyes."

The oracles in chapters 65 and 66 are intended as answers to the prayer in 63:7–64:12. Indeed 65:6 explicitly answers the plaintive question at the end of 64: "I will not keep silent . . .". But another element is introduced into the final scenario of the Book of Isaiah: the division of God's people into the sheep and the goats (Matt. 25), those "who have sought me" (65:10) and "you who forsake the Lord" (v. 11). Elsewhere the division is between Israel and the nations, or between Jerusalem and her enemies. Here a new realism appears, influenced no doubt by the situation in some reborn Jewish community after the exile, perhaps in Judah itself, but equally true of every human institution. Just think of the sorry tale of Judah's kings and the Temple at Jerusalem, as recounted in Samuel and Kings, and, nearer home, of the State of Israel and the Christian Church.

The *first* oracle (vv. 1–7) begins appropriately with a statement about God's readiness to answer prayers; even unspoken prayers, even before they are uttered. The meaning of "seek" was discussed in connection with 55:6: "Seek the Lord while he may be found . . .". "Here am I, here am I" (v. 1) beautifully epitomizes that encounter between God and man described in 64:5, as does the picture in verse 2 of God standing with hands outstretched to welcome his prodigal son home (Luke 15:20). All the more biting is the attack in the same verse on those who continue to "walk in a way that is not good, following their own devices".

Verses 3–7 are another catalogue of forbidden cultic practices and superstitions, like the list in 57:1–13. They include sacrificing "in gardens" (1:29; 17:10; 66:17), presumably to pagan deities, when all sacrifice was banned except at the Temple in Jerusalem. Burning incense "upon bricks" (RSV) or "on brick altars" (NEB) implies another breach of Mosaic law (*eg* Deut. 27:6). Verse 4 refers to forbidden rituals for raising the dead, as in the Witch of Endor story (1 Sam. ch. 28), and consulting oracles, as perhaps in the story of Jacob's dream at Bethel (Gen. 28:10–22); both practices forbidden on pain of death (*eg* Deut. 18:9–14). Unclean meat ("abominable things") includes not only swine's flesh, but also meat not slaughtered or prepared according to the strict kosher laws (*eg* Lev. ch. 11; Deut. 12:15–16; 14:1–21). The "broth" referred to may be an infringement of the law forbidding the boiling of meat in milk (Exod. 23:19; 34:26; Deut. 14:21), which became a major element in Jewish food law: meat and dairy produce of any kind can never be served at the same meal.

Verse 5 is a comment on the hardening attitudes of the idolaters towards God, and of God, enraged by their abominations (of which he keeps a record, v. 6), towards them. His answer to the plea in 64:12 is that he is going to punish them in full for their crimes as well as for those of their ancestors. The individualism of Jeremiah (*eg* Jer. 31:30) and Ezekiel (*eg* Ezek. ch. 18) is less important for the author here than the frightening solidarity of the Gadarene swine (Matt. 8:28–34).

The *second* oracle (vv. 8–12) is built round a traditional vintage song (like the ones referred to in 16:10), in which the words, "Do not destroy it, for there is a blessing in it", are applied to the people of God. For the sake of the few righteous ones, his servants, God will not destroy his people totally. First, he will reward his servants by separating them from the rest of Judah and settling them on his mountains (Hermon, Tabor, Carmel, Zion and the rest), in lovely Sharon (33:9; 35:2; and see also Song 2:1), and in the Valley of Achor, the "door of hope" (Hos. 2:15). So much for "my people" who have "sought God" and responded to his intervention (v. 1).

For the sour grapes in the bunch, those who worship forbidden deities like *Gad* ("Fortune") and *Meni* ("Destiny"), and never come to the Temple in Jerusalem (v. 11), there will be sword and destruction. Little is known of popular religion in Biblical times, apart from the fact that one of the tribes of Israel was called "Gad", and there is a mention in the Koran of a pre-Islamic goddess, "Manat", who may be the female equivalent of *Meni*.

A *third* oracle (vv. 13–16) is addressed to those who did not obey the Mosaic law or listen to the prophets (v. 12). It invidiously contrasts their fate with that of "my servants" (vv. 13–14). Perhaps Jesus had this passage in mind when he told the parable of the rich man and Lazarus (Luke 16:19–31). These prophets (v. 12) will become a curse on the lips of the righteous, synonymous with death, while the righteous will gain a new name (or *reputation*) as God's faithful servants. The name of the "God of Truth" will be for ever on their lips. "Truth" (*amen* in Hebrew) suggests above all, "permanence, solidarity, firmness", and is also closely related to words for "faith" and "believing" as the word-play in 7:9 illustrated. Such a God forgets our "former troubles" (v. 16) and a new beginning is possible.

THE DAWNING OF A NEW AGE

Isaiah 65:17–25

17"For behold, I create new heavens
  and a new earth;
 and the former things shall not be remembered
  or come into mind.
18But be glad and rejoice for ever
  in that which I create;
 for behold, I create Jerusalem a rejoicing,
  and her people a joy.
19I will rejoice in Jerusalem,
  and be glad in my people;
 no more shall be heard in it the sound of weeping
  and the cry of distress.
20No more shall there be in it
  an infant that lives but a few days,
  or an old man who does not fill out his days,
 for the child shall die a hundred years old,
  and the sinner a hundred years old shall be accursed.
21They shall build houses and inhabit them;
  they shall plant vineyards and eat their fruit.
22They shall not build and another inhabit;
  they shall not plant and another eat;
 for like the days of a tree shall the days of my people be,
  and my chosen shall long enjoy the work of their hands.
23They shall not labour in vain,
  or bear children for calamity;
 for they shall be the offspring of the blessed of the Lord
  and their children with them.
24Before they call I will answer,
  while they are yet speaking I will hear.

²⁵'The wolf and the lamb shall feed together,
    the lion shall eat straw like the ox;
    and dust shall be the serpent's food.
They shall not hurt or destroy
    in all my holy mountain,
                    says the Lord.''

Fourth in the final series of prophecies, this famous passage contains the most elaborate vision of the new age in a book full of such visions (*eg* 2:2–4; 4:2–6; 9:2–7; 11:1–9; 25:6–9; 32:15–20; 35:1–10; 41:17–20, *etc*). The key word, familiar to us from chapters 40–55 in particular, is "create", repeated three times in the first two verses (vv. 17–18). Just as for the author of Genesis 1, the three-fold repetition of this theological term in one verse (1:27) signified the crowning achievement of the Creator of heaven and earth, so now the same term is used to herald the climax of the Book of Isaiah. The "creation" of Israel was a relatively frequent motif in earlier chapters (*eg* 43:1, 15); but here the rebuilding of Jerusalem and the restoration of Israel are visualized in the context of the creation of a new heaven and a new earth. The scene is repeated at the end of the book (66:22–23), and again at the very end of the Bible (Rev. chs. 21–22). Earlier passages drew on the Exodus traditions to express the belief that what was about to happen was a New Exodus (*eg* 43:18–19; 48:21–22; 52:11–12). Here the author deliberately alludes to the creation story (vv. 17, 25) to make the point that what is about to happen is nothing short of a new creation.

The "former things" (43:18) in verse 17, which incidentally provide a link with the end of the preceding prophecy, will be forgotten and a new age will dawn. Notice the present tenses in verses 17–18 and the imperatives so characteristic of Isaianic tradition (*eg* 51:1, 7; 52:1, 11; 62:10): they express the author's belief that he is already living in the New Age—"the kingdom of God is at hand" (Mark 1:15; Matt. 4:17). Part of the new experience of liberation from the past is the confidence that, unlike any previous experience, this one will never end (v. 18). Weeping and crying for help will never again be heard in the streets of

Jerusalem, a theme familiar to us from 25:8 and 42:2 (see commentary).

Verses 20–25 then spell out why the New Jerusalem is to be the cause of such eternal jubilation. Much of this passage is in negative terms, as befits the account of a new world that beggars description. Just as theologians argue that all we can know of God is that he is not visible, not mortal, not fallible, not like us in any way (55:8), so we are to imagine here something totally new, totally other, conceivable only when all familiar images and analogies have been transcended.

First there will be no more untimely deaths: everyone, from the smallest babe in arms to the oldest person, will live a full life. Normal life expectancy will be a hundred years (not seventy or eighty: Ps. 90:10), and anyone who fails to reach that age will be a conspicuous and tragic exception to prove the rule (v. 20). One might add that presumably the problem of caring for the vastly increased number of elderly people will be solved somehow. "The sinner" (RSV) is out of place here, and should probably be translated "the one who falls short of a hundred" (NEB).

Next there will be peace, security and success (vv. 21–23). People will be free to live in homes they have built for themselves and to enjoy the fruit of the vines they have cultivated. That is to say, there will be no more enemy invasions or property disputes. In the words of another prophet (Mic. 4:4):

> But they shall sit every man under his vine and under his fig tree, and none shall make them afraid.

The image of an ancient tree in verse 22 is readily understandable: the oak, for example, can live for eight hundred years. Job even implies that a tree is immortal:

> For there is hope for a tree,
>   if it be cut down, that it will sprout again,
>   and that its shoots will not cease.
> Though its root grow old in the earth,
>   and its stump die in the ground,
> yet at the scent of water it will bud
>   and put forth branches like a young plant.

But man dies, and is laid low;
　　man breathes his last, and where is he?

(Job 14:7–10)

The "tree of life" in the garden of Eden is another Biblical example.

"My chosen [ones]" (v. 22) is a cautionary reference back to 65:15 and the sad fact that this is not a vision of universal salvation: "many are called, but few are chosen" (Matt. 22:14).

Verse 23 contains a further allusion to Genesis, and the promise of an antidote to the curse of the human race: man's heavy toil (Gen. 3:17–19) will always be rewarded with success, and a woman's labour pains (Gen. 3:16) will always be blessed with the birth of a perfect child. Prayer too will never be in vain: even before it is uttered, God will answer (v. 24; 65:1).

The final scene (v. 25) is inspired by the prophecy beginning "The wolf shall dwell with the lamb..." (11:6–9), but resemblances are superficial. The words for "lamb" and "snake" are different, for example; and the clause about the snake eating dust comes from Genesis 3, not Isaiah 11. The verse consists of three clauses about the eating habits of wild animals (wolf, lion, snake), and a concluding statement that "they" (presumably the wild animals) will cease from hurting and destroying "in all my holy mountain". As in chapter 11, surely this is not a vision of Evelyn Waugh's *Happier Hunting Ground* (for deceased pets), but an allegory. Greed and rapacity will give way to gentleness and generosity so that the weak (40:11) will have as much to live on as the powerful. The proud free spirit of adventure (1 Pet. 5:8) will be restrained in the interests of those who have to get on with the less glamorous jobs. Those who, although wise as serpents, use their skill to deceive and exploit, will be punished (Gen. 3:14–15). Many scholars omit the clause about the snake (see NEB): it is certainly the only judgmental note in the piece. But surely the point is obvious: antidotes will be found for the curses on men and women, but none for the serpent.

The Genesis allegory is most effectively introduced to complete the picture begun in verse 17. From the beginning (chs. 1–2, 5, *etc*), justice and the end of oppression have been central

Isaianic themes. It is no accident that they are central to this vision of a new world too.

A SACRIFICE ACCEPTABLE TO GOD

Isaiah 66:1–6

¹Thus says the Lord:
"Heaven is my throne
  and the earth is my footstool;
what is the house which you would build for me,
  and what is the place of my rest?
²All these things my hand has made,
  and so all these things are mine,
                                    says the Lord.
But this is the man to whom I will look,
  he that is humble and contrite in spirit,
  and trembles at my word.

³"He who slaughters an ox is like him who kills a man;
  he who sacrifices a lamb, like him who breaks a dog's neck;
he who presents a cereal offering, like him who offers swine's blood;
  he who makes a memorial offering of frankincense, like him who
    blesses an idol.
These have chosen their own ways,
  and their soul delights in their abominations;
⁴I also will choose affliction for them,
  and bring their fears upon them;
because, when I called, no one answered,
  when I spoke they did not listen;
but they did what was evil in my eyes,
  and chose that in which I did not delight."

⁵Hear the word of the Lord,
  you who tremble at his word:
"Your brethren who hate you
  and cast you out for my name's sake
have said, 'Let the Lord be glorified,
  that we may see your joy';
  but it is they who shall be put to shame.

6"Hark, an uproar from the city!
    A voice from the temple!
  The voice of the Lord,
    rendering recompense to his enemies!"

The Temple never looms large in Isaianic tradition, but here in
the *fifth* oracle in the final series (vv. 1–4) we find expressed
genuine opposition to the institution. God demands a humble and
contrite spirit, to which we might add, from chapter 1, justice,
rather than a stone building and elaborate rituals. The harsh tone
of this passage suggests that it reflects a period of internal argument within a Jewish community, probably in Jerusalem during
the years leading up to the rebuilding of the Temple in 515 B.C.
We know there was opposition to the Temple for other reasons at
that time (Hag. 1:1–11), and that it took the threat of capital
punishment to get it built (Ezra 6:6–12). But it seems that from an
early time, and certainly from the Exile on, there were some who
believed that God dwells among his people even when there is no
temple at Jerusalem (cf. Exod. 25:8; 29:45), and that spiritual
realities are more important than ritual (*eg* Ps. 51; 1 Sam. 15:22–
23; Jer. 31:31–34). Synagogues or something like them probably
existed in Babylon (Ezek. 14:1), and by A.D. 70, when the Second
Temple was destroyed by the Romans, Judaism had the inner
spiritual strength to survive without it. Indeed Judaism in all its
rich diversity has existed for far longer without a temple than with
one, and Jewish prayers for the rebuilding of the Temple express
more than hope for a new building on the site of the Dome of the
Rock in Jerusalem. The New Testament represents a similar shift
in emphasis—*eg*:

> For we are the temple of the living God; as God said, "I will live in
> them and move among them . . ." (2 Cor. 6:16).

In the final apocalyptic vision of the New Jerusalem, there is no
temple; "for its temple is the Lord God the Almighty and the
Lamb" (Rev. 21:22).

"Heaven" and "earth" were summoned as witnesses in chapter
1, and have been adduced as evidence of the power and glory of
their Creator more than once since then (*eg* 40:12; 42:5; 45:18;

48:13). Here they are, in his eyes, mere sticks of furniture (v. 1): how then could he require anything built by mere mortals? The language is reminiscent of Psalm 132, although the subject is quite different. "All these things" (v. 2) is usually taken to refer to heaven and earth, and "came to be" (RSV, "are mine") is an allusion to Genesis 1 (*eg* "and it was so"). But possibly the author is thinking of the stones of the Temple just mentioned, and contrasting them with the "living stones" of a spiritual house—cf:

> Come to him, to that living stone, rejected by men but in God's sight chosen and precious; and like living stones be yourselves built into a spiritual house, to be a holy priesthood, to offer spiritual sacrifices acceptable to God through Jesus Christ.
>
> (1 Pet. 2:4–5)

Psalm 51:16–19 makes the connection too.

The three virtues listed in verse 2 nicely sum up Isaianic moral teaching. Humility was demanded from the beginning in those vitriolic attacks on the arrogance of affluent Jerusalem with which the early chapters were filled (*eg* 2:12–19; 3:16; 5:11–12). The contrite spirit of those who acknowledge their failures and throw themselves on God's mercy, is similarly called for in prophecies against hardness of heart and inveterate sin (*eg* 6:9–10; 30:1–5). Appeals for receptivity and obedience to the prophet's words have taken up long sections of the Babylonian chapters (*eg* 41:1; 42:18; 44:1; 48:1; 49:1). Micah's list is different but closely related: "to do justice, and to love kindness, and to walk humbly with your God" (Mic. 6:8).

Verse 3 contains an astonishingly bitter attack on temple ritual: four normally acceptable rites (Lev. chs. 1–3) are bracketed with murder and other ritually unclean practices which are evil in God's eyes. The word "like" in each clause (RSV) is not in the Hebrew, and the New English Bible suggests that all eight acts are equally included in the summary at the end of the verse: "all these are the chosen practices of men who revel in their own loathsome rites". Verse 4 seems to mean that God plans to apply these very practices—slaughter, sacrifice, *etc*—to their perpetrators. It is certainly a very gruesome prophecy, composed by someone quite out of sympathy with the temple rituals, as the first Isaiah was (1:15–17).

The *sixth* prophecy (vv. 5–6) is in two parts. The first part is addressed to those whose virtues are recommended in verse 2, and announces judgment on "the brethren who hate you". This seems to be further evidence of internal rivalry, possibly between the pro-Temple party who seek God's glory in a new building (Hag. 1:8; 2:3, 7, 9), and an anti-Temple party who describe themselves as "humble and contrite in spirit" (v. 2). Others see here an early example of anti-Samaritan polemic since hostility between the Jews and the Samaritans, especially on the question of the Temple, is mentioned already in Nehemiah (ch. 4). Verse 6 would then be a further prophecy against the Samaritans. The form of the prophecy is reminiscent of the opening of Amos:

> The Lord roars from Zion,
> and utters his voice from Jerusalem.

> (Amos 1:2; cf. Joel 3:16)

In Hebrew the same word for "sound, voice" is repeated three times at the beginning of each clause (see NEB):

> That *roar* from the city,
> that *uproar* from the temple,
> is the *sound* of the Lord dealing retribution to his foes.

But here too, surely the prophecy could be directed at those who have chosen their own ways (v. 4), devoting their energies to ritual instead of justice and humility. Jeremiah's 'Temple Sermon' expresses this well:

> Will you steal, murder, commit adultery, swear falsely, burn incense to Baal, and go after other gods that you have not known, and then come and stand before me in this house, which is called by my name, and say, "We are delivered!"—only to go on doing all these abominations? Has this house, which is called by my name, become a den of robbers in your eyes?

> (Jer. 7:9–11; cf. Matt. 21:13)

Formal worship can lead to judgment and shame, as well as joy and glory.

REJOICE WITH JERUSALEM

Isaiah 66:7–17

⁷"Before she was in labour
   she gave birth;
before her pain came upon her
   she was delivered of a son.
⁸Who has heard such a thing?
   Who has seen such things?
Shall a land be born in one day?
   Shall a nation be brought forth in one moment?
For as soon as Zion was in labour
   she brought forth her sons.
⁹Shall I bring to the birth and not cause to bring forth?
   says the Lord;
shall I, who cause to bring forth, shut the womb?
   says your God.

¹⁰"Rejoice with Jerusalem, and be glad for her.
   all you who love her;
rejoice with her in joy,
   all you who mourn over her;
¹¹that you may suck and be satisfied with her consoling breasts;
that you may drink deeply with delight
   from the abundance of her glory."

¹²For thus says the Lord:
   "Behold, I will extend prosperity to her like a river,
      and the wealth of the nations like an overflowing stream;
   and you shall suck, you shall be carried upon her hip,
      and dandled upon her knees.
¹³As one whom his mother comforts,
   so I will comfort you;
you shall be comforted in Jerusalem.
¹⁴You shall see, and your heart shall rejoice;
   your bones shall flourish like the grass;
and it shall be known that the hand of the Lord is with his servants,
   and his indignation is against his enemies.

15"For behold, the Lord will come in fire,
  and his chariots like the storm-wind,
 to render his anger in fury,
  and his rebuke with flames of fire.
16For by fire will the Lord execute judgment,
  and by his sword, upon all flesh;
  and those slain by the Lord shall be many.

17"Those who sanctify and purify themselves to go into the gardens, following one in the midst, eating swine's flesh and the abomination and mice, shall come to an end together, says the Lord."

The little group of oracles in these verses may be taken as a *seventh* prophecy in the long series that concludes the book.

The images of a mother giving birth to a son (vv. 7–9), feeding him at her breast (vv. 10–11) and dandling him on her knee (vv. 12–14), follow on from earlier passages where they are applied to Zion (49:15–16; 54:1; 65:23) and to God as mother of Israel (42:14; 46:3; also Deut. 32:18). Here, with God's help (v. 9), Zion is the jubilant mother, and a rejuvenated nation her son. The birth is miraculous: the curse of Eve (Gen. 3:16), ameliorated in 65:23, is now removed altogether (v. 7), or at least reduced to a momentary pang (v. 8). Many would say that the rebirth of Israel in 1948, out of the ashes of the holocaust, was nothing short of a miracle. God's hand was at work in these events as in all history: what he began with the decree of Cyrus in 538 B.C. (2 Chron. 36:22–23; Isa. 44:28; 45:1–2), and continued with the United Nations resolution in 1948, he will finish one day (v. 9).

The colourful hymn of thanksgiving in verses 10–16 consists of a call to join in the celebrations (vv. 10–11) and a prophecy of salvation introduced by the formula, "For thus says the Lord..." (vv. 12–14). The initial part recalls some of the celebrated Zion-hymns like Psalms 46, 48, 122 and Isaiah 12, which express, wistfully and movingly, Israel's love of Zion. The transformation from mourning to joy is reminiscent of Psalm 126:5–6, but perhaps also of the near contemporary Zechariah (8:19):

Thus says the Lord of hosts: The fast of the fourth month, and the fast of the fifth, and the fast of the seventh, and the fast of the tenth, shall be to the house of Judah seasons of joy and gladness, and cheerful feasts; therefore love truth and peace.

Verse 11 has a moving tenderness in it, expressing delight both at the new found peace and security of the children of Zion (Ps. 131:2), and at their prosperity and exquisite contentment (*eg* ch. 12; 25:6–9). The phrase translated "abundance of her glory" (RSV, v. 11) occurs only here and perhaps should be taken as another detail of the mother imagery: NEB has "delighting in her plentiful milk".

The prophecy of salvation is in two parts, as so often, combining beautiful pictures of hope for the righteous, with bitter, vengeful images of judgment for the wicked. First, in v. 12, "prosperity" (Hebrew, *shalom*) is compared to a great, slow-moving river like the Nile or the Euphrates, and to a rushing torrent (RSV "stream"), like those that carry the melted snow of Mount Hermon headlong down the wadis. "The wealth of the nations" echoes 61:6.

At first sight the mother imagery in verses 12 and 13 seems to describe Zion's care for her children, as in verses 7–11. But there is no word for "her" ("her hip . . . her knees") in the Hebrew text of verse 12, and the following verse suggests that here again God himself is being compared to a confident, experienced mother, caring for her children. "Comfort", which occurs three times in verse 13, is of course a key word right from the start of the Babylonian chapters (40:1; 49:13).

"You shall see" (v. 14; without an object as in 53:11) means "your eyes will be opened, you will have a vision". The word for "grass" here is not the one used in 40:6–7 ("All flesh is grass"), but the word for new growth such as the first plants that appeared on the earth at creation (Gen. 1:11–12), and the green pastures of Psalm 23 (v. 2).

The tragic corollary of this fine picture of new life and growth is the destruction of the wicked. "The hand of the Lord", that is, his powerful protection, is over his servants, but his indignation is against his enemies (v. 14). This is the "wrath" of the Day of the Lord (*eg* Isa. 26:20; Ezek. 21:31; Nahum. 1:6; Zeph. 3:8). Fire,

flames, "whirlwind" (NEB), chariots, sword, corpses, all traditional elements in the description, are included (vv. 15–16), and
so is the universal dimension of divine judgment: it will be ex-
ecuted "upon all flesh" (v. 16). "Those slain by the Lord will be
many" implies that they will be in the majority on the battlefield:
only the few will be saved. The fire of God's judgment is a
recurring Isaianic theme from chapter 6, where it brings forgiveness (v. 7) as well as doom (v. 13), to the eternal Hell-fire at the
end of this final chapter (v. 24).

Verse 17 lists some of those to be slain by the Lord, and again,
as in verse 3, they include people guilty of ritual crimes, such as
taking part in pagan rites and eating unclean food, rather than
moral or social evils. "Gardens" were mentioned in 1:29, where
more details are given, and in 65:3. The enigmatic phrase "following one in the midst" is possibly elucidated by Ezek. 8:7–13:
the New English Bible has "one after another in a magic ring".

"Come to an end" is etymologically associated with the word
for "whirlwind" (NEB) in verse 15, and gives the whole prophecy
an air of spectacular finality. We are dealing here with matters of
ultimate responsibility before God.

A NEW HEAVEN AND A NEW EARTH

Isaiah 66:18–24

18"For I know their works and their thoughts, and I am coming to
gather all nations and tongues; and they shall come and shall see my
glory, 19and I will set a sign among them. And from them I will send
survivors to the nations, to Tarshish, Put, and Lud, who draw the bow,
to Tubal and Javan, to the coastlands afar off, that have not heard my
fame or seen my glory; and they shall declare my glory among the
nations. 20And they shall bring all your brethren from all the nations as
an offering to the Lord, upon horses, and in chariots, and in litters, and
upon mules, and upon dromedaries, to my holy mountain Jerusalem,
says the Lord, just as the Israelites bring their cereal offering in a clean
vessel to the house of the Lord. 21And some of them also I will take for
priests and for Levites, says the Lord.

²²"For as the new heavens and the new earth
   which I will make
 shall remain before me, says the Lord;
   so shall your descendants and your name remain.
²³From new moon to new moon,
   and from sabbath to sabbath,
 all flesh shall come to worship before me,
                                        says the Lord.

²⁴"And they shall go forth and look on the dead bodies of the men that
have rebelled against me; for their worm shall not die, their fire shall
not be quenched, and they shall be an abhorrence to all flesh."

The final prophecy begins with the characteristically Isaianic "I
am . . ." (*eg* 46:9; 51:12, 15). It also embraces the whole world,
which is another Isaianic characteristic (*eg* 11:9; ch. 24; 49:1).
But it goes farther than previous prophecies in two remarkable
respects. The "survivors" (v. 19) are explicitly commissioned to
"declare my glory among the nations"—to those "that have not
heard my fame or seen my glory"—and priests and Levites are to
be recruited from among the nations (v. 21). This must be the
final *coup de grâce* to the exclusivist ambitions of the Temple
establishment, attacked so violently and so consistently
throughout the Book of Isaiah (see commentary on 65:1–7).

The Hebrew is difficult, perhaps because of the sheer originality and unexpectedness of the passage which the minds of
scribes could not cope with. As it stands, the Hebrew text of verse
18 begins with an independent pronoun, "I" or "I am . . .", but
has no verb or predicate to go with it. "Their works and their
thoughts" (v. 18) similarly stands alone in the sentence, and
Hebrew has "it is coming" not "I am coming" (RSV). Most
English versions follow the ancient Greek tradition, inserting a
word for "know" and changing the verb to first person singular
(RSV, NEB). This is effect transmutes verse 18 into a prophecy
spoken by the Lord himself. Perhaps we should put more emphasis on that opening pronoun: four times the phrase "says the
Lord" is repeated in this short section (vv. 20–23), and the purpose of this final word of God is to establish an everlasting
covenant, like the covenant with Noah (see v. 22), or with Israel

(Deut. 5:1–21), in which God is the proposer and initiator: thus "I for my part . . ." (cf. the emphasis in Exod. 20:2).

The promised sign or "miracle" (v. 19) is not explained. It could be astronomical like Isaiah's miracle (38:7–8), or like the star in the east which led the wise men to Bethlehem (Matt. 2:1–12), or like one of the traditional phenomena that were expected to herald the coming of a New Age (*eg* 24:23; Joel 2:30–31; Mark 13:24–27). But could it not rather be the new heaven and the new earth of verse 22, which, like the rainbow in Genesis chapter 9, will be an everlasting sign of God's promise to his people?

Some of the "survivors" are to be sent out into the world like apostles (v. 19). The names of the "coastlands afar off" are not all known for certain: another indication perhaps of the constant reinterpretation and reworking of such arresting texts in the centuries after they were originally written. *Tarshish* is well known to have been a Phoenician colony in Spain (2:16). *Tubal* was on the shores of the Black Sea and *Javan* (the Hebrew form of the Greek name "Ionia") could include both mainland Greece and Greek colonies in Ionia and Asia Minor. *Put* and *Lud* "who draw the bow" were apparently in North Africa (Gen. 10:6, 13; Jer. 46:9; Ezek. 30:5). But the Hebrew text has the Assyrian name "Pul" (*ie* Tiglath Pileser; 2 Kings 15:19), not *Put*, and there is another "Lud", grouped with Assyria in Genesis 10:22. Instead of "draw the bow" some experts prefer to read "Meshek" (NEB), another region of Asia Minor, often grouped with *Javan* and *Tubal* (*eg* Ezek. 27:13). No doubt this variety reflects the desire of later generations to relate their own knowledge of the world, and their own role in it as God's people, to the text of scripture. Isaiah 49:12 has had a similar history.

The return of the exiles in verse 20 recalls 49:22, 60:4–5 and other passages. But here they are brought to Jerusalem as an "offering to the Lord" from the nations, a quite revolutionary notion of Gentile sacrifice compared without comment to Israelite sacrifice. In verses 20–21 technical cultic language is uniquely applied to Gentile activity, taking the hospitable words of 56:1–8 one stage farther. The mode of transport is also new and rather exotic: horses, chariots, and mules are familiar enough (*eg* Josh. 11:4; 2 Sam. 18:9; Ezek. 39:20); but "litters" (NEB "wagons") are mentioned only once in the Bible apart from this passage (Num. 7:3, "covered wagons"); and "dromedaries" only mentioned here alone.

Verses 22–23 read like a new covenant or promise, like the words of God to Noah (Gen. 9:12–16), or to Abraham and his descendants for ever (Gen. 15:5). "The new heavens and the new earth which I will make" will be a sign, like the rainbow in the sky after the Flood, that the promise is everlasting. The prophet adds to the patriarchal promise of descendants, the promise that their name, their reputation for justice and faith, will endure for ever as well. The climax of this new promise is that "all flesh" will come to worship at Jerusalem, and those despised festivals, sabbaths, new moons and other appointed feasts (ch. 1:11–15) will be transformed into universal expressions of humility and obedience to God (66:1–2). Only Zechariah 14:16 and perhaps Malachi 1:11 in the Old Testament go as far as this in their vision of a New Age.

But, alas, there is the last verse of Isaiah. It is so ugly and savage that it has long been the custom in synagogue worship to repeat verse 23 again after it. We have had occasion to comment on the darker side of God's justice more than once (at 49:25–26 or 51:22–23, *eg*), and here we can but repeat that the more colourful the pictures of salvation for those who are saved on the Day of Judgment, the more colourful, it seems to Old Testament thinking, must be the images of doom and destruction for those who are rejected. This is one of the few Old Testament texts in which the medieval notion of Hell-fire could find scriptural authority. It is already quoted in Mark 9:48. But already also, in 26:19 (like this verse belonging to the final stages of Isaianic tradition), we found belief in the resurrection of the dead. With that beautiful verse rather than Isaiah 66:24 in mind, and with it Ezekiel's vision of new life in the valley of dry bones (Ezek. 37:1–14) and Daniel's fully-fledged doctrine of hope beyond the grave (Dan. 12:2–3), we take our leave of Isaianic prophecy, sure in the faith that a promise which outlives "the new heavens and the new earth" will transcend death as well (26:19):

> O dwellers in the dust,
>> awake and sing for joy!
> For thy dew is a dew of light,
>> and on the land of the shades thou wilt let it fall.

FURTHER READING

P. R. Ackroyd, *Exile and Restoration* (Old Testament Library) (SCM Press and Westminster Press, 1968)

R. E. Clements, *Isaiah and the Deliverance of Jerusalem* (Journal for the Study of the Old Testament Press, Sheffield, 1980)

R. Coggins and others (editors), *Israel's Prophetic Tradition* (Cambridge University Press, 1982)

J. H. Eaton, *Festal Drama in Deutero-Isaiah* (SPCK, 1979)

D. R. Jones, "Isaiah 40–66" in *Peake's Commentary on the Bible*, Revised Edition (Nelson, 1962)

C. R. North, *The Second Isaiah* (Clarendon Press, Oxford, 1964)

G. von Rad, *Old Testament Theology*, Volume II (Oliver and Boyd, and Harper and Row, 1965)

G. Vermes, *The Dead Sea Scrolls in English* (Penguin Books, 1975)

C. Westermann, *Isaiah 40–66* (Old Testament Library) (SCM Press and Westminster Press, 1969)

R. N. Whybray, *Isaiah 40–66* (New Century Bible) (Oliphants, 1975)

(See also Further Reading, vol. 1)